D1571576

KOSODE: 16th–19th Century Textiles from the Nomura Collection

KOSODE

16th–19th Century Textiles from the Nomura Collection

Amanda Mayer Stinchecum

———————

with essays by
Monica Bethe and Margot Paul
edited by
Naomi Noble Richard and Margot Paul

Japan Society and Kodansha International

KOSODE 16th–19th Century Textiles from the Nomura Collection
is a catalogue published in conjunction with an exhibition shown at
Japan House Gallery in the spring of 1984 and organized by Japan
Society in association with the National Museum of Japanese History,
Sakura, Japan.
The exhibition and publication were made possible by grants from
the Nomura Shōjirō Memorial Fund at Japan Society, the Friends of
Japan House Gallery, and the continuing support of The Andrew W.
Mellon Foundation and Lila Acheson Wallace.

NOTE: In notes and bibliography all Japanese authors' names are
in Japanese order, surname first. In text references to twentieth-
century Japanese persons the name is given in the order preferred
by the individual.

Designed by Kiyoshi Kanai, New York, N.Y.
Printed in Japan by Dai Nippon Printing Company, Inc.
Set in Caledonia by U.S. Lithograph, New York, N.Y.
Text paper is Royal Art Coat 93.5 kg.
Manuscript processed at the Princeton University Computer Center,
Princeton, N.J.

Colorplate photographs by Nishikawa Takeshi Copyright © by
Kodansha International Ltd., except for nos. 10, 13, 18, 26, 30, 32, 33,
46, and 49, which were courtesy of the National Museum of Japanese
History.
Black-and-white photographs courtesy of the Nomura family.
Line drawings by Laura Hartman, New York, N.Y., except for the
botanical drawings.

Cover illustration: Colorplate 20 "Kosode Screen in Kanbun Style
with Waves and Fish Nets".

Hardcover edition distributed in the United States by Kodansha
International/USA Ltd., through Harper & Row, Publishers, Inc.,
10 East 53rd Street, New York, N.Y. 10022.
Softcover edition distributed by Japan Society,
333 East 47th Street, New York, N.Y. 10017.
Published by Japan Society, 333 East 47th Street, New York, N.Y.
10017 in association with Kodansha International Ltd., 12–21,
Otowa 2-chome, Bunkyo-ku, Tokyo 112 and Kodansha International/
USA Ltd., 10 East 53rd Street, New York, N.Y. 10022 and The
Hearst Building, 5 Third Street, Suite 430, San Francisco, Ca. 94103.

Library of Congress Catalogue Card Number 83–82639.
ISBN 0–87011–429–8 (hardcover)
ISBN 0–913304–18–2 (softcover)
ISBN 4–7700–0902–X (in Japan)
All rights reserved by Japan Society, Inc.

CONTENTS

FOREWORD — Rand Castile — 9

PREFACE — Margot Paul — 10

A CREATIVE CONNOISSEUR: NOMURA SHŌJIRŌ — Margot Paul — 12

KOSODE: TECHNIQUES AND DESIGNS — Amanda Mayer Stinchecum — 22

COLOR: DYES AND PIGMENTS — Monica Bethe — 58

CHRONOLOGY — 77

CATALOGUE — Amanda Mayer Stinchecum — 79

APPENDICES

    1. Lining Inscriptions — Alex Kerr — 192

    2. Weave Structures and Woven Pattern — Translated and adapted by — 196

    3. Changes in Kosode Dimensions — Amanda Mayer Stinchecum — 198

    4. Measurements and Cutting Layouts — 200

    5. Dyes and Colors — Monica Bethe — 202

FOOTNOTES — 210

GLOSSARY — 220

BIBLIOGRAPHY — 224

FOUNDERS AND FRIENDS OF JAPAN HOUSE GALLERY — 228

DIRECTORS OF JAPAN SOCIETY — 228

OFFICERS OF JAPAN SOCIETY AND ART COMMITTEES — 229

INDEX — 230

FOREWORD

Few nations have paid less attention to fashion and more to form in clothing than the Japanese. Japan has maintained a single tradition in clothing over many centuries. The kimono, modern descendant of the *kosode*, persists as the national dress. Kimono are still worn at New Year's, for tea ceremonies, and occasionally to shrines and temples. They lend their wearers an air of timeless, gracious formality. It is as if one would walk the ancient streets of Siena today and still see—on occasions other than the Palio—the sleeves, skirts, and blouses these Italians once festooned with embroidery and couched gold and silver, the whole appended by mounted jewels.

The effect of timelessness in Japanese dress is a startling acknowledgement of the persistence of ancient taste in the culture. Despite the important contributions of contemporary Japanese designers one suspects the twenty-first century will not see the disappearance of the kimono. The Japanese are loath to discard an idea once it has been perfected.

Style and fashion, individual preference and the love of novelty, have found expression far less in the cut of Japanese garments than in the patterning and decoration of their fabrics. This book and the exhibition for which it serves as catalogue present superb examples of Japanese textile design for the *kosode*. These come from Nomura Shōjirō, distinguished connoisseur, whose large collection was purchased in 1974 by Japan's Agency for Cultural Affairs and is now owned by the National Museum of Japanese History at Sakura, outside Tokyo.

Bringing the Nomura textiles before the American public has been an eight-year task. Foremost among the many people without whose cooperation neither exhibition nor book would have come to pass are Mr. and Mrs. Shizuo Morris Nomura, son-in-law and daughter of Nomura Shōjirō. We are greatly indebted to their generosity and enthusiasm, patience and tact.

I should like also to express appreciation to the Agency for Cultural Affairs for its many good offices, and to Dr. Nishikawa Kyotaro and Mr. Yamamoto Nobuyoshi for their wise counsel. Special thanks is owing the late Mr. Kurata Bunsaku, who was instrumental in obtaining the collection for the National Museum in Sakura and in introducing us to the Nomura family.

Many of the staff of the National Museum of Japanese History have given cordial aid to this project, in particular the director, Mr. Inoue Mitsusada; Professor Tanabe Saburonosuke; and the section chief, Mr. Kitazawa Katsuhiko. The help they provided was indispensable.

Margot Paul was a valued member of Japan House Gallery staff from 1971 to 1981 and was responsible during that time for many distinguished publications presented by the Gallery. We are pleased, thankful, and honored that she has continued her association with the Gallery and the Japan Society in order to see the Nomura textile project to its successful conclusion.

Maryell Semal continues to oversee all aspects of the registration of art for exhibitions in the Gallery. Hisayoshi Ota is responsible for many details of installation and book design. Alexandra Munroe, present editor of Gallery publications, has advanced the project at all stages and has been instrumental in preparing ancillary materials. Mitsuko Maekawa patiently assisted throughout.

Naomi Richard brought acumen, concentration, and devotion to the editing of this book. Her task was complicated by the technical problems of presenting a mass of material written or compiled by diverse authors. If there are editorial heavens, Mrs. Richard must have one all to herself.

The exhibition and catalogue were made possible by grants from the Nomura Shōjirō Memorial Fund at Japan Society, the Friends of Japan House Gallery, and the continuing support of the Andrew W. Mellon Foundation and Lila Acheson Wallace.

We are indebted to the Society's Nomura Fund Committee, comprised of Lily Auchincloss, Rand Castile, William Lieberman, David MacEachron, Porter McCray, Margot Paul, and John Rosenfield, for their good cooperation in this long-term program. Our Art Advisory Committee, chaired by Porter McCray, and our association of Friends, chaired by Lily Auchincloss, also contributed importantly to this exhibition and catalogue. On behalf of the Society and the Gallery I wish to thank these generous and helpful associates.

RAND CASTILE
Director
Japan House Gallery

PREFACE

In Japan the textile arts have always been regarded among the most valuable assets of the material culture. Cloth and clothing have been given and received by the imperial court as largesse and tribute of undisputed worth; they have been presented to retainers as rewards for special services, handed down as heirlooms, preserved as significant mementos of exalted personages. In the visual arts garments are rendered with the most loving attention to detail—from the diapered designs painstakingly rendered in cut gold leaf on the sculpted robes of twelfth-century Buddhist icons to the breathtaking *kosode* seen in eighteenth-century prints of beautiful women.

The attention paid to dress in Japanese literature reflects the view that the colors, designs, and materials of clothing reveal not only the taste but the sensibility and character of the wearer. This attitude is common to all periods and in all classes from the court aristocracy to the military elite to rich commoners. In the *Tale of Genji*, a fictional narrative of court life written about the year 1000, not even insignificant attendants are presented without minute descriptions of their attire:

> Six little girls . . . in attendance . . . were dressed in mantles with white scarves lined with pink; their tunics were of scarlet, worn with facings blue outside and light green within.[1]

The *Tale of the Heike*, written in the thirteenth century, deals mainly with an armed struggle for power in which the losing clan was annihilated and the world of the Heian exquisites severely shaken. But even in this unlikely context as much attention is given to the warriors' panoplies as to their prowess:

> . . . Shigehira was second in command . . . and he was attired that day in a hitatare of dark blue cloth on which a pattern of rocks and sea-birds was embroidered in light yellow silk, and armor with purple lacing deepening in its hue toward the skirts.

Ihara Saikaku's novels, published in the late seventeenth century, present a different world entirely, bourgeois in its tastes and attitudes. But although a direct and explicit sensuality has replaced the languorous aestheticism or bloody heroism of the earlier works, Saikaku's descriptions of people differ little from those of his predecessors in emphasis on details of clothing:

> She wore her clothes with matchless elegance; underneath were purple-spotted fawns on a field of pure yellow, outside, the design of a hundred sparrows upon gray satin.

Through these literary expressions of highly diverse eras runs a single thread: the passion for "bright and elegant attire".[2] Taste in dress was clearly regarded more as a component than as a mere enhancement of physical beauty. And the loveliness of clothing was felt to consist not in its tailoring, which was simple and relatively unvaried, but in its harmonies of color and pattern—in other words, in the beauty of the fabrics and colors, the elegance of the designs, and the refinement with which these elements were combined.

The textile collection assembled by Nomura Shōjirō between 1883 and 1940 reflects his interest in the designs that ornament robes (*kosode*) worn by some of the most resplendent personages of the sixteenth through nineteenth centuries. According to Japan's Agency for Cultural Affairs, the Nomura Collection comprises 156 *kosode*, 100 screens on which are mounted some 120 partial *kosode*, 16 obi, 57 personal articles designated "bags", and 256 toilet articles and hair ornaments.[3]

It is the *kosode* and *kosode* screens that form the subject matter of this book, whose theme is the technical and aesthetic evolution of *kosode* design. Particular attention has been paid to the earlier *kosode*, of which the Nomura Collection contains an extraordinary number.

To Nomura Shōjirō's farsighted connoisseurship we owe the existence of this superb collection. His son-in-law and daughter, Shizuo Morris Nomura and Masako Nomura, have preserved the collection intact for the delight and erudition of future generations, and they have given us the opportunity to exhibit a selection of its abundant treasures to a Western audience. This book, too, owes much to their patient guidance and generous support. I am particularly indebted to Mr. Nomura, who provided exhaustive written recollections, personal interviews, and consultations. For the Nomuras' unfailing encouragement and frequent hospitality over the past six years I should like to offer my personal thanks.

The author, Amanda Mayer Stinchecum, is a fine scholar who commands extensive knowledge of Japanese textiles. She has succeeded admirably in making current Japanese textile scholarship accessible to Western readers. Her research in Japan was made possible by the Nomura Shōjirō Memorial Fund at the Japan Society, a fellowship from The Metropolitan Museum of Art, and the Japan Foundation. Monica Bethe has provided information and insights new to the Western reader on colors, dyes, and pigments. Ms. Bethe, who lives in Kyoto, is a dyer, weaver, and authority on Nō dance, and her firsthand knowledge of textile techniques, coupled with sensitive awareness of the significance of color in Japanese life, has contributed signally to this project. Mr. Alex Kerr did a fine bit of sleuthing concerning the elucidation of the *kosode* inscriptions.

The scope of this book necessitated consultation with many fine Japanese scholars who gave generously of their knowledge. They include Kitamura Tetsurō, Yamanobe Tomoyuki, Kirihata Ken, Kamiya Eiko, and Tokugawa Yoshinobu. Japan's Agency for Cultural Affairs has supported this project, as has the International House in Tokyo. My associates at Kodansha International commissioned the excellent photographs by Nishikawa Takeshi. Nobuki Saburo and Suzuki Takako at Kodansha International have worked tirelessly on this project since its inception, and Ichiura Makiko at Kodansha International in New York has efficiently coordinated communication with the Tokyo office. Imanaga Seiji, curator of textiles at the Tokyo National Museum, made the collection available for research and photography. The Nomura Shigeru family and Yoshida Shiyuichi, keeper of the Nomura family storehouse, allowed me to explore the documents therein during a few snowy days in 1982. We are also grateful to the National Museum of Japanese History in Sakura, which provided additional photographs for the book.

In this country Nobuko Kajitani, textile conservator at The Metropolitan Museum of Art, generously shared her great knowledge and gave much valuable time to ensure that unfamiliar and complex processes were clearly understood and described. Jean Mailey, also of The Metropolitan Museum of Art, gave unflagging encouragement and access to the Textile Study Room, of which she is curator. Louise Cort and Sondra Castile answered innumerable queries on textiles. Along with Ms. Kajitani, Ms. Mailey, Professor Paul Varley, and Alan Kennedy, they also read the manuscripts and gave good counsel. Junco Sato Pollack worked hard in the beginning stages of this project and made useful suggestions, particularly concerning the glossary. Sharon Rhoades Nakazato assisted us with translations. Colleagues at many institutions in this country abetted our research, most notably those at The Metropolitan Museum of Art and including scholars at The Fogg Art Museum, the Museum of Art Rhode Island School of Design, the Los Angeles County Museum of Art, The Minnesota Museum of Art, the Mills College Art Gallery, and the New York Public Library. To all these persons and institutions I extend my profound gratitude.

Most difficult to thank sufficiently are my associates at Japan House Gallery. Rand Castile conceived this project many years ago, and Maryell Semal, Mitsuko Maekawa, Hisayoshi Ota, and Alexandra Munroe have been imaginative and constant in their support of it. The book's felicitous design is the work of Kiyoshi Kanai, and its production was much expedited by Karen L. Brock, whose good efforts coaxed the manuscript into the Princeton University Computer. I am most grateful to Naomi Noble Richard, who grasped all the warps and wefts and edited the text into its final form.

The merits of this book are owing to the many people mentioned above. Any distortions or misperceptions that my distance from the authors in Japan may have occasioned remain my final responsibility.

MARGOT PAUL
Editor

A CREATIVE CONNOISSEUR: NOMURA SHŌJIRŌ

MARGOT PAUL

Fig. 1. Nomura Shōjirō.

Nomura Shōjirō (1879–1943) acquired the first robe in his collection at the tender age of thirteen, in an incident that reveals the nice mixture of enthusiasm, discrimination, and determination that characterizes the born collector. En route to visit an aunt in Nagoya, the young Nomura came upon a gorgeous robe of the early Edo period in an antique vendor's stall on the road to Nagoya Castle. In exchange for that robe he handed over all his travel money, leaving his mother no choice but to send him more money for his return to Kyoto. That robe is in the present collection; unfortunately, family records do not indicate which one it is.

This precocious acquisition enjoys distinguished company. Nomura recognized that the sixteenth through nineteenth centuries had seen the flowering of Japan's textile arts. Beginning in the seventeenth century government policy had segregated the country from foreign influences. Peace and prosperity had fostered the development of the applied arts. The social milieu spurred competitive consumption. In response to this conjunction of stimuli, textile designs became highly refined, luxurious, and uniquely Japanese. Occasional sumptuary restrictions were circumvented by the invention of more ingenious techniques and dazzling designs. During the late Meiji (1868–1912) and the Taishō (1912–26) periods, when Western tastes and techniques were dominant and the native arts seemed threatened, Nomura Shōjirō devoted himself to the study, collection, and preservation of the most beautiful robes from the age that had so recently ended.

His collection comprises 156 complete robes. Moreover, his perspicacity and imagination extended to preserving fragmentary but exceptional robes by mounting them on screens in such a way as to suggest the whole garment. The one hundred two-panel screens on which these precious fragments are displayed are an inspired contribution to the history of Japan and its arts. Nomura's connoisseurship is attested by his collection as a whole, which scholars recognize as one of the finest and most extensive assemblages of *kosode* ("small sleeves", the standard outer robe since the sixteenth century) of the sixteenth through nineteenth centuries.

Nomura Shōjirō (Fig. 1) came of a long line of cloth merchants named Iwanaga who lived near the Tokugawa castle compound in present-day Nagoya. Iwanaga Tei, his mother, was a spirited young woman; although it was considered unseemly, she was often to be found in the family shop, calculating prices for customers in place of the head clerk. Her parents sent her to Kyoto at an early age to be adopted by Nomura Akezu, a wealthy and childless tea ceremony master. When she grew up, Nomura Akezu found Tei a husband, whom he adopted as his heir and professional successor in accordance with Japanese custom. This marriage produced six children, of whom Shōjirō was the fifth born. But the traditional constraints of a tea master's wife were not for Nomura Tei. As soon as possible she delegated all household affairs to her eldest daughter and set about pursuing her two great passions, commerce and Kabuki.

Tei opened her first business in a small stall on the Kamo River, from which she could watch Kabuki actors rehearsing. There she sold antique cotton and silk wrappers for boxes or gifts (*furoshiki*). When a Westerner, misunderstanding Tei's ten outspread fingers, paid her ten *yen* for a *furoshiki* instead of the ten *sen* she was asking, Tei realized that there was money to be made in dealing with Westerners and directed her business accordingly. Her affairs prospered, and at the turn of the century she built a magnificent shop on Shinmonzen Street in the heart of Kyoto, near hotels patronized by Westerners.

There, in addition to antique textiles, she sold embroidered wall hangings, tapestries, and screens of her own design, decorated with abstract or pictorial renderings of classical Japanese and Chinese themes. Eventually Nomura Tei employed several hundred weavers and embroiderers on a large property she owned near the Golden Pavilion in northeastern Kyoto. Her clientele was almost exclusively Western. By the time Nomura Shōjirō was a teenager, his mother's thriving business occupied several sizable estates in Kyoto and engaged the efforts of the entire family. Her imperious, somewhat eccentric management is well remembered in her family. When pumpkins were in season, for example, she would buy them by the cartload, and till they were gone everyone ate pumpkins and rice. Those who complained went hungry. Tei was invalided in 1908 and died in 1916. The many vivid anecdotes about her still current in her family point to a strong-minded, unconventional, resolutely practical person.

Her son Shōjirō had inherited his mother's enterprising spirit. Deciding at seventeen to learn English, he persuaded Tei to send him to America for that purpose. Instead of money to pay his way, Nomura was given Japanese prints to sell, which plunged him into art dealing at an early age. A business associate of his mother placed him in a high school in Greenville, Illinois, and his experiences in this small midwestern town in the year 1896 made him a lifelong admirer of America.

On returning to Japan, Nomura apprenticed with art dealers who were business associates of his mother. Though Meiji Japan was engrossed by Western culture, Nomura made use of his family's business and professional connections to study classical Japanese art, going about to old temples to look at ancient statues. In his early twenties he started selling antiques abroad—fine portable objects, including *ukiyo-e* prints, Buddhist sculptures, and antique textiles. His business took him to Australia, China, India, and the United States, travelling steerage with valuable cargo. These voyages were hazardous as well as uncomfortable: many times Nomura's goods were stolen or seized by dishonest customs officials. Nevertheless, tenacity coupled with a head for business gained Nomura a small fortune. Dutifully he sent the money to his elder brother Kōjirō, the family accountant, who in 1907 lost all of Shōjirō's hard-earned money, along with most of the family's holdings, in ill-advised business dealings. Shōjirō's anger created a permanent family rift.

With his mother's encouragement and financial support, Nomura began again. In 1908 Nomura Tei built a combination shop and dwelling for him near her own on Shinmonzen Street (Fig. 2). Its facade was modelled after the prestigious Peers Club in Hibiya Park in Tokyo. Its sign read "S. Nomura". Inside, the store boasted high "palace style" ceilings and large rooms combining aspects of Western and Japanese architecture in a manner typical of the Meiji period. Its main room offered raised alcoves (*tokonoma*) and tatami spaces as well as carpeted floors, and textile fragments in black lacquer frames were hung on the walls. A bridge over an interior garden connected the public and private parts of the house. Nomura was greatly interested in architecture and a careful observer of architectural styles during his extensive travels.

The private rooms, where Nomura lived with his wife and daughter, were mostly in traditional Japanese style. But the house was so spacious that Nomura could devote one room to a full-size billiard table, bought on one of his trips abroad. Clearly, Nomura shared his mother's business acumen, for this novelty drew Western customers, who were fond of visiting him in the evening to play billiards and enjoy his Cuban cigars, scotch whisky, and delicacies from local restaurants served by his wife and daughter.

With great effort but in a relatively short time Nomura revived his family fortune by selling antiques to Westerners in his store in Kyoto and abroad. By his late twenties he had established business contacts in China, India, Australia and, most importantly, the United States. He held auctions at art societies, clubs, and galleries and had professional associates in New York, Boston, Chicago, and other cities.

By the beginning of the Taishō period Nomura was an internationally recognized dealer in Oriental art. In 1914 he wrote, in English, a study entitled *An Historical Sketch of Nishiki and Kinran Brocades*, which was published in Boston. At the time his business consisted primarily of antique textiles, particularly Buddhist pieces, including banners (*ban*), altar cloths (*uchishiki*), and priests' stoles (*kesa*). He was meticulous in his research, writing for his *kesa* detailed labels describing the type of cloth, place of origin, pattern, date, and size. Auction catalogues from his sales (all in 1915) at the Copley Society of Boston, the Buffalo Fine Arts Society, the Art Institute of Chicago, and the Anderson Galleries in New York still exist. An extraordinary collection of 120 "Ancient Chinese and Japanese *Nishiki* and *Kinran* brocades of 1400–1812", which he assembled, was sold to The Metropolitan Museum of Art in 1919 through Porter E. Sargent. The Metropolitan's collection was among the first to be enriched by Nomura's expertise. He loved to visit museums in the United States, and his two favorites were the Boston Museum of Fine Arts and The Metropolitan Museum of Art in New York.

Although Nomura's main interest was ancient textiles, his business included many other types of Japanese art. His auctions abroad included hundreds of *ukiyo-e* prints, porcelains, Buddhist sculptures, and small bronzes and lacquers; large works, such as screens, were handled in the shop in Kyoto. Other major dealers in Kyoto catered to the foreign market, but even in this sophisticated group Nomura was distinguished by his scholarly approach to textiles.

By the end of the Taishō period the scarcity of high-quality antique art and the problems of shipping large, delicate objects such as screens led Nomura to specialize more and more in textiles. He started with nineteenth- and twentieth-century kimono and wedding robes, which Westerners bought to display on kimono stands or to wear. Nomura also designed robes, evening clothes, and shirts for Westerners, as well as introducing them to an adaptation of the ordinary workman's coat, called the *happi* coat, and the *haori* jacket. All these were made up in the most sumptuous Japanese silks, which Nomura, who understood the fabric's structure, could drape and tailor to superb advantage. Ruth St. Denis, a pioneer in dress as well as in dance, visited his shop in 1925 and came away with a silk *happi* coat. The vast success of Nomura's *happi* coats and summer dress shirts spawned a host of cheap rayon copies, made by Yokohama exporters for the five-and-dime stores. Nomura used to say that these shoddy imitations ruined his line in about six months. Nevertheless, his business went from success to success, generating a branch store in Kobe and one near the Imperial Hotel in Tokyo. An aura of enchantment must have filled these shops, stocked with gossamer robes, fragrant incense, crystal jewelry, and small art objects unerringly chosen for their intrinsic beauty and their appeal to Westerners.

Almost all the considerable profits from his business went into Nomura's textile collection, which attracted visitors from all over the world. Nomura's guest book lists most of the prominent collectors who passed through Japan from the opening of his shop in 1908 until the late thirties. In it such luminaries as the then Prince of Wales wrote glowing comments on his generous hospitality and extraordinary textile collection. Mrs. Martin A. Ryerson, whose husband was a trustee of the Art Institute of Chicago, wrote in the guest book on 26 October 1921:

> Mr. Nomura has contributed greatly to the interest and pleasure of our stay in Kyoto. Our visits to his place, as much museum as shop, have supplemented admirably our sight-seeing among palaces and temples. They have given us insight into an important and fascinating branch of the art of old Japan which we could not have obtained without the Nomuras' kind explanations illustrated by the treasures of his beautiful collection.

The quality of Nomura's collection made other collectors, including many Americans, turn to him for advice. The Lucy T. Aldrich Collection (now in the Museum of Art, Rhode Island School of Design), which contains some of the finest Nō robes and *kesa* outside of Japan, owes much to Nomura's guidance and encouragement. Nomura even accompanied Aldrich to China in 1919 to search for classic Chinese textiles. The collection of Bella Mayberry, now in the Los Angeles County Museum of Art, contains sixty robe fragments of the seventeenth through nineteenth centuries, all framed under sleeve-shaped mats. Purchased from Nomura during a visit in 1917, they are early examples of this still-popular presentation technique.

An encounter with John D. Rockefeller, Jr., in 1921 evoked all of Nomura's tact and his scrupulous care to separate his art dealing from his art collecting. After viewing Nomura's private collection, Rockefeller asked to purchase the remarkable *noshi kosode* (Fig. 3) for donation to the Japanese government. But Nomura had spent years searching out the pieces of this robe and reassembling them, and he was enormously proud to have the robe complete save for one small square of the lower back hem. Furthermore, he had vowed never to sell any robe from his private collection. He resolved the conflicting demands of hospitality, patriotism, and principle by donating the robe to the Yūzen Society, which placed it on permanent loan at the Kyoto National (then Imperial) Museum. There it remains, designated an Important Cultural Property because of its extraordinary *yūzen* dyeing.

Clearly, Nomura Shōjirō played a formative role in the creation of important Western collections, public and private, in the early twentieth century. Although it is difficult to identify as such many of the pieces that came to this country through his shop, there is ample evidence of his connections with The Metropolitan Museum of Art, the Los Angeles County Museum of Art, and the Museum of Art, Rhode Island School of Design. He also numbered outstanding private collectors like Louis V. Ledoux among his friends and clients.

Nomura was one of the first Japanese collectors to pay serious attention to Japanese costume as a unique and endangered art form, deserving of study and in need of preservation. The focus of his collection was the beautifully patterned robes worn by women of the imperial court, the military class, the upper bourgeoisie, and the high demimonde from the sixteenth through the nineteenth centuries. By the sixteenth century the outer robe (*kosode*) had acquired the simple, standard shape still current in today's kimono, a shape admirably suited to the display of decorative designs. These designs were created to order for their elegant wearers. They might be painted by the most eminent artists, or dyed or embroidered to their designs by artisans of breathtaking skill. No expense was spared, for the design in a woman's *kosode* was the outward expression of her social position, fortune, and personality.

Before the modern era such *kosode* were handed down intact or made into mountings for precious scrolls or, occasionally, into covers and bags for treasured lacquers, ceramics, and Buddhist paraphernalia. During the Meiji period, however, many family collections were being sold, either out of economic necessity or else because of the vogue for all things Western. Contemporary scholars have remarked that Nomura collected at precisely the right

Fig. 2. Nomura Shōjirō's store.

moment, when the supply was relatively great and the demand small. From the Taishō period on, robes of the early Edo period and before were rarely available. Considering the devastation of wars and natural calamities in Japan, it is remarkable that these delicate objects have survived, and it is extremely rare to discover one today.

Nomura had considerable experience in the antique textile business and substantial funds to spend on collecting. Other textile dealers gathered around him and monthly brought their finest textiles to be auctioned privately. These auctions were formal affairs, with twelve to twenty dealers and collectors in black silk kimono seated around the perimeter of an austere tatami-mat room. Each one in turn would present treasured textiles for thorough inspection. Bids were registered in writing and competition was keen.[1] Nomura had a reputation for paying high prices for the finest classical robes and fragments.

One day a dealer brought Nomura an exquisite early *yūzen kosode* depicting all the great landmarks of Miyako (Kyoto) on an unusual deep yellow ground.

It was as splendid as any *rakuchū-rakugai* (scenes in and around Kyoto) screen of the same era. After negotiating a considerable price for the robe, the dealer promised to return with it in a couple of days. Several days had elapsed with no sign of robe or dealer, when Nomura heard that another collector, the president of the Matsuzaka store in Nagoya, had acquired a splendid robe of similar description. Nomura visited him in Nagoya and discovered that it was indeed the robe that he himself had been promised. His solution to this predicament was to propose a Shinto wedding between the "*yūzen* Miyako" robe and an exceptional cotton man's underrobe from his own collection, decorated with scenes of Edo (Tokyo) which Nomura considered to be in the style of Hiroshige. The president of Matsuzaka agreed to the marriage proposal.

The wedding ceremony took place in Kyoto in 1932, at Saami Restaurant, which dates from the Tokugawa period (1615–1868) and still occupies its original site in Maruyama Park. It was performed in formal Genroku era (1688–1704) style, by candlelight, with Inokuma Asamaro, director of the Kyoto National Museum, officiating in full Genroku era regalia. The traditional present (*yuinō*) that the groom gives to the bride to prepare for the wedding was Nomura's payment for the robe. The wedding guests were leading textile connoisseurs. After the ceremony the "bride" (Cpl. 40) and the "groom" (Cpl. 56) were packed into white cypress boxes together with ceremonial cloths and poems dedicated to their union. Since the Japanese bride traditionally enters her husband's family, the "*yūzen* Miyako" robe now belonged to Nomura.

Shinto belief acknowledges the existence of spiritual qualities in exceptional places and things as well as persons, and Shinto marriage between two such objects is an ancient tradition in Japan. Still, it occurs rarely, and this is the only time that two garments have ever been joined in matrimony. The wedding of these two robes was a recognition of their transcendent aesthetic qualities.

In 1912 the empress Teimei insisted on traditional costume for herself and her attendants at her coronation. From this time interest in native Japanese costume rekindled, with Nomura in the forefront of the revival. Together with one of his closest associates, Professor Ema Tsutomu, Nomura organized exhibitions, published books and periodicals, and held sketch classes at shrines to which artists were invited to work from historically accurate costumes modelled by geisha.[2] Occasionally Nomura and other collectors lent original robes for these sessions. Styles no longer extant were reproduced according to paintings and literary descriptions. The purpose was to provide artists with the opportunity to reinterpret classical genre painting from live models. Itō Shōha (1877–1968), Uemura Shōen (1875–1949), and Nakamura Daizaburō (1898–1947) were among those who frequently sketched and studied Nomura's collection. Nomura's happiest hours were spent, with his colleagues or alone in the middle of the night, studying every line of a beautiful robe; his favorite, perhaps, was the one painted by Hōitsu with a design of a flowering plum tree (Cpl. 52).

Nomura's first completed collection comprised rectangular fragments of early court ladies' robes with exceptional designs. They were mounted under sleeve-shaped mats and framed with glass, like the Mayberry pieces now in the Los Angeles County Museum of Art. Nomura called these mounted fragments *tagasode*, meaning "Whose sleeves . . . ?"—a well-understood poetic allusion to an unseen woman's presence.

Research on textiles of the Edo period led Nomura to an interest in the customs of the imperial and military aristocracies, including the complex etiquette of gift giving. He put together a collection of gift covers (*fukusa*), which were the outermost wrapping used in the most formal presentation ceremony. They were made of silk, usually with elaborate designs dyed, embroidered, or woven in the same techniques employed on contemporary robes. The gift

cover collection was donated to Mills College in 1953 by the Nomura family.

T he nucleus of Nomura's collections comprised robes worn by women of the imperial and shogunal courts and wealthy merchant families. Nomura began by collecting whole robes dating from the sixteenth through early eighteenth centuries, only later extending his search to robes of the eighteenth and nineteenth centuries. The 156 whole robes in the Nomura collection date mostly from the earlier period. Very different in style is the group of later robes that Nomura named *Goshodoki to Edo-doki* (Robe designs of the imperial court in Kyoto and the shogunate in Edo).

Along with intact *kosode*, Nomura bought fragments, always in hope of finding the remaining pieces and reassembling the original garment. *Kosode* might have been cut apart for a variety of reasons. It was the custom among the lay Buddhist population to make donations to Buddhist temples. These might include *kosode* that would be cut up and used for banners, altar cloths, and vestments. Dealers too cut up *kosode*, to sell the best pieces as bags, wrappings, and mountings for art works and family heirlooms. And some robes reached the market in such fragile condition that only parts were salvageable. Nomura was tireless in his search among these sources, uncanny in his ability to recognize pieces

Fig. 3. Nomura family at home, with *noshi kosode* hung on rack behind them.

Fig. 4. Robe in Cpl. 18 as Nomura found it in form of Buddhist altar cloth.

als describing customs and costumes had been published in the preceding Manji era (1658–61). Of particular interest is a Manji era manual called *Onnakagami* [Mirror for women], which pictures robes draped gracefully over racks. Nomura owned a comprehensive library of *hiinagata* books, including a rare dated set of the Kanbun era, now on loan to The Metropolitan Museum of Art in New York. By calling his screen-mounted collection *Hiinagata*, he acknowledged the *hiinagata* books as its inspiration.

Nomura was the first to affix actual robes to screens; in fact, he patented his design. His manner of designing these screens drew on two strands in the Japanese artistic tradition. In the large, open rooms of castles and palaces women often hung their robes on racks to air them or to create temporary partitions. Doubtless it was also a permissible way of showing off their treasured garments. Even in the open, for such festive occasions as flower viewing, cords would be strung and *kosode* draped over them, creating a temporary pavilion that offered privacy at the same time that it proclaimed the exquisite taste of its occupant. This custom, in turn, created one of the most popular themes of Momoyama (1573–1615) and early Edo (1615–88) painting: *tagasode* ("Whose sleeves . . . ?"). The central element of most *tagasode* screens is a gorgeous *kosode* casually draped over a rack, conjuring in the viewer's mind the woman who has just left it there.[3] Eighteenth-century *ukiyo-e* renderings of famous beauties include the woman herself, but their principal subject is still her costume—its pattern, drape, and flow.

Like the *tagasode* artists, Nomura draped his *kosode* over racks. Like the *ukiyo-e* masters, he disposed them across the golden backgrounds in pliant patterns that hint at the wearer's movements. He excluded from these compositions all boudoir accessories such as musical instruments, games, and perfume bags (which are present in most *tagasode* screens) and concentrated on the arrangement of the fabric. Contemporary designers and artisans have tried to make textile screens in the Nomura style, but none have succeeded in combining such exquisite examples of early *kosode* with such sophisticated graphic presentation. Nomura's screens are not utilitarian devices for preservation and display of fabrics but powerful and beautiful collages.

Creating them was the work of years. *Kosode* fabric that had been made into religious vestments, bags, or the like had to be unstitched and the pieces matched again like a jigsaw puzzle on the tatami floor of Nomura's studio. Both procedures were exacting and onerous. (Figure 4 is a photograph of the robe in Colorplate 18 as Nomura found it, in the

of the same *kosode* found several years apart, and masterly in reassembling these pieces with only the weave and the design for guides.

For splendid fragments whose complements were not to be found, Nomura created an inventive and appropriate mounting. Lacquer *kosode* racks (*ikō*) with metal fittings were executed in low relief and affixed onto the golden surfaces of two-panel screens measuring 175 cm. square. On each screen one or two fragmentary robes were mounted in such a way that they appear to be complete *kosode* draped over the racks. It must be emphasized that Nomura never cut up an intact robe in good condition; his purpose was to preserve, not to destroy. These screens and the 156 intact robes, along with obi, hair ornaments, and cloth bags, constitute the Nomura Collection, now owned by the National Museum of Japanese History in Sakura. Nomura dated the screen-mounted fragments, like the intact robes, from the sixteenth through the nineteenth centuries, with most of them assigned to the early part of this period.

The screen collection was completed in 1934. Nomura entitled it *Hiinagata*, after the catalogues of *kosode* designs issued mostly in the mid-Edo period (1688–1781). The earliest *hiinagata* books date from the Kanbun era (1661–73), but women's manu-

form of a Buddhist altar cloth.) Then a formally pleasing yet seemingly natural arrangement had to be devised that would at the same time allow the incomplete robe to suggest a complete one. When this had been achieved, assistants would remove the robe's lining, saving any inscriptions they might find, and mount the robe on mulberry paper to strengthen the delicate silk.

Next the screen was prepared: the gold-leaf squares or scattered gold particles applied and the trompe l'oeil lacquer rack with metal fittings made in a style consistent with the period of the robe and the taste it reflected. The rack, about one-quarter inch thick, was affixed to the screen following Nomura's precise instructions, and then the robe was pasted in place. A special starch- and water-based paste was developed for this by Nomura and a chemist associate, but the recipe is lost. No two screen compositions are alike, and if Nomura the perfectionist was dissatisfied with the smallest aspect of any one of them, it would be dismantled and done over.

The dating of textiles presents knotty problems, but Nomura was not content merely to own and enjoy. His approach to his collection was in part didactic. He wished to discover the history of Japanese textiles, and in his study he enlisted the aid of many scholars, collectors, artists, and dealers during the twenties and thirties. Among these were Ema Tsutomu, a distinguished anthropologist and president of the Society for the Study of Japanese Customs and Costumes, who wrote introductory essays for several of Nomura's portfolios; Inokuma Asamaro, director of the Kyoto Imperial Museum; and Yoshikawa Kampo, an anthropologist, costume collector, and advisor on costume for period films.

Most of the fabrics that Nomura searched out were without documentation of any kind, but *kosode* that had been donated to Buddhist temples on their owner's death were often inscribed on the lining or the presentation cover by one of the temple priests. The inscription noted that the robe was a gift, and might also record the date on which it was received and the Buddhist name of the deceased. Famous temples owned large numbers of these robes, and Nomura found some with linings and inscriptions still attached (see photographs in Appendix 1). The date of dedication does not, of course, tell us when the robe was made: it might be a garment of the wearer's youth or an heirloom from a previous generation. But at least the inscription would have provided a *terminus ad quem*. Unfortunately, to mount the robes smoothly it was necessary to remove the linings, and although Nomura carefully saved them, there is no record of which lining came from which robe. Nomura has ascribed the robes in Colorplates 19 and 28 to imperial ladies of the seventeenth century, and he preserved inscribed linings of about their periods; but an explicit connection between the specific robes and linings is missing. These linings from the screen-mounted *kosode* were recently made available for research, and perhaps some way will yet be discovered to match them to their robes.

Dating is simpler for robes created and signed by famous painters, like those by Sakai Hōitsu (Cpl. 52) and Matsumura Goshun (Cpl. 51). Moreover, the great families frequently kept careful records of their important possessions, whether preserved in the family treasure house or given as gifts. Appendix 3 contains an interesting study recently done by Kamiya Eiko on a group of early men's *kosode* owned and recorded by various families. Since the standard proportions of *kosode* changed over time, her measurements of these dated *kosode* provide valuable guidelines for the dating of similar undocumented garments.

Nomura dated some of the robes on his *hiinagata* screens to specific eras of the Edo period. In the absence of documentation such dating required careful inference from exhaustive research into such questions as the time of origin or greatest popularity of various decorative techniques. For example, a stencilled imitation (*kata-kanoko*) of fawn-spot resist dyeing (*kanoko shibori*) became popular about the Tenna era (1681–87), when strict sumptuary regulations forbade the wearing of the extremely labor-intensive and therefore costly allover resist-dyed patterns.

The *hiinagata* robe-design catalogues were also an aid in dating, since they give year and place of publication as well as depicting the most up-to-date designs of the time. Certain of these designs are credited in the catalogues to famous *ukiyo-e* artists.[4] In addition to creating actual *kosode* designs, *ukiyo-e* artists greatly influenced *kosode* decoration by creating prints of beautiful women wearing *kosode* whose patterns would be widely copied. Nomura dealt extensively in woodblock prints, and his familiarity with them allowed him to notice likenesses in design between a textile in his collection and a *kosode* in a print whose artist's dates, at least, were known. A few of his *kosode* are catalogued as being "in the style of" or "preference of" certain *ukiyo-e* artists.[5] We do not know, though, whether the dates he assigned are based on verifiable historical evidence or simply on design similarities.[6] He may likewise have used resemblances in weave structure to relate an undocumented *kosode* to one of known date.

More modern methods of analysis now permit surer and more refined dating, but Nomura's methods—technical and stylistic comparison of the unknown with the known—are neither invalid nor outmoded and become increasingly useful as more information is acquired.

With a thoroughness and lavishness unusual among textile collectors of his time, Nomura documented his entire collection in seven color portfolios, published by Unsōdō in Kyoto. They were among the first works of such scope to deal with Japanese textiles of the sixteenth through nineteenth centuries. Published in the order of completion of Nomura's collections, they include:

Tagasode hyakushū [Whose sleeves . . . ?—a series of one hundred], 1919
Zoku tagasode hyakushū [Whose sleeves . . . ?— another series of one hundred], 1930
Kosode to furisode [Short-sleeved and long-sleeved robes], 1927
Zoku kosode to furisode [Another series of short-sleeved and long-sleeved robes], 1932
Gosho-doki to Edo-doki [Robe designs of the imperial court in Kyoto and the shogunal court in Edo], 1932
Jidai kosode hiinagata byōbu [Antique *kosode* screens], 1939
Jidai fukusa [Antique gift covers], 1939

Several of these portfolios were given by the Nomura family to the New York Public Library, The Metropolitan Museum of Art, and the Library of Congress. They are collectors' items, as the editions were small and the portfolios popular among textile designers and collectors of the period. Each portfolio consists of large colorplates on unbound sheets. Particular care was taken to ensure clarity of detail, so that the reproductions would be valid documents for the study of the textiles. The portfolios were bound in specially selected and dyed silk, and some were encased in boxes of lacquered cypress wood embellished with gold calligraphy. They epitomize the twin facets of Nomura's connoisseurship: his concern for scholarship and his love of beauty. They do not, however, contain much text beyond their brief introductions and lists of colorplates.

In 1920 Nomura published the first comprehensive study of *yūzen*, a brush-resist dyed technique that is central to the history of eighteenth-century textile decoration. The book, *Yūzen kenkyū* [Study of *yūzen*], traces the history of the term and the technique in relation to social, political, and literary contexts. Although additional information has been discovered since its publication, this book remains a classic on the history of *yūzen*. Nomura's interest in *yūzen* continued throughout his life: he was a founding member of the Yūzen Society in Kyoto and collected superb examples of *yūzen* dyeing; he arranged several exhibitions of *yūzen* textiles and loaned many of his best pieces to an exhibition in Kyoto in 1919. In the two years before his death he was working on a book on the origins of painted resist techniques and the relationship between *yūzen* and Okinawan resist techniques.

In 1921 a young American named Helen Benton was introduced to Nomura. She had been inspired to study Japanese textiles by the collection of priests' stoles, assembled by Nomura, that had been shown at The Metropolitan Museum of Art in February 1920. She asked to study textiles with him, and Nomura offered to collaborate with her on a book on Japanese textiles in English. Nomura and Benton spent months together, discussing the entire history of Japanese textiles. In Nomura's guest book, in an entry dated October 1921, she describes their collaboration:

In the color maze of rich brocades, in the stalwart design of old kimonos, in the shadowy splendor of ladies now forgotten, we have felt the real heartbeat of Japanese Art. Mr. Nomura has unfolded to us the romantic secrets of the nameless craftsman's devotion, the undying artist's imagination, and the beauty-craving that ruled the hearts of the lavish and the brave.

Publication of their book was delayed until 1963, many years after Nomura had died and Helen Benton had become Helen Benton Minnich. Called *Japanese Costume and the Makers of Its Elegant Tradition*, it is written in a lyrical style, with many literary allusions and anecdotes animating the history of Japanese costume. It has captured the imagination and aroused the interest of Western textile scholars.

When Nomura had completed his one hundred *hiinagata* screens in 1934, all of them were exhibited at the Kyoto National Museum. This was his only collection to be shown complete to the Japanese public, and the occasion was one of the high points of his life. Another was the marriage in 1930 of his only child, Masako, to a young American lawyer of Japanese descent. Following Japanese tradition, Nomura adopted his son-in-law, who became Mr. Shizuo Morris Nomura.

Shortly after the exhibition of his collection in

1934, Nomura Shōjirō turned most of the details of his business over to his son-in-law and retired to a small house in Kyoto. The unsettled political climate and the looming threat of war with the United States made him depressed and reclusive. His whole life had been spent in professional and personal association with Americans, and when war broke out he was devastated. Nomura died not long thereafter at the age of sixty-four.

During the war the collection was stored at a farm outside Nara. In 1954, following the death of Nomura Shōjirō's wife, Shizuo Nomura returned to America with his family. A large portion of the collection he shipped by boat, in several installments, for storage at The Metropolitan Museum of Art. This he had been encouraged to do by Alan Priest, curator of the Department of Far Eastern Art at The Metropolitan from 1927 to 1963, who had met Shizuo Nomura and seen part of the collection during the Occupation. In 1956 Pauline Simmons and Alan Priest organized an exhibition at The Metropolitan of part of the Nomura Collection, including robes, obi, and hair ornaments. Pauline Simmons describes this exhibition in *The Metropolitan Museum of Art Bulletin* of February 1956, in an article entitled "Artist Designers of the Tokugawa Period". The exhibition was shown from 15 February to 15 May 1956 in cooperation with the Japan Society. The rest of the Nomura Collection of *kosode* and *furisode* was brought to New York in 1958 from Toronto, where some of the pieces had been shown at the Royal Ontario Museum in the same year. One screen, not a part of the collection of one hundred, remains in Tokushō-ji, the Nomura family temple in Kyoto.

The *hiinagata* screens and *kosode* collections were shown in their entirety for the first time by The Metropolitan Museum of Art from 4 November 1959 to 3 January 1960. The screens were skyed in three levels on the vast walls of the museum's galleries, the robes displayed on hanging racks and mannequins, together with a few Nō robes from the Ledoux family and other lenders. It was an outstanding exhibition, widely reviewed, and it made a profound impression on those who saw it. It is described in *The Metropolitan Museum of Art Bulletin* of December 1959, in an excellent essay by Jean Mailey entitled "Four Hundred Winters . . . Four Hundred Springs".

When the exhibition closed in 1960, the collection remained in New York City in storage. In the late sixties it came to the attention of the counsellor of Japan's Agency for Cultural Affairs, the late Kurata Bunsaku, and the commissioner, Adachi Kenji. The Agency for Cultural Affairs negotiated its return to Japan, partly by purchase, partly as a gift of the Nomura family. Several of the Nomura pieces were exhibited at the Tokyo National Museum from 16 October to 25 November 1973, shortly after their acquisition by the Agency for Cultural Affairs. The catalogue of this exhibition is entitled *Nihon no senshoku* [Japanese textiles]. The collection was stored at the Tokyo National Museum.

Pieces from the collection have occasionally been loaned by the Japanese government for exhibition. In the fall of 1980 and winter of 1981 several of the robes and *hiinagata* screens were shown in the "Great Japan Exhibition" at the Royal Academy of Arts in London. On the occasion of the publication of this book by the Japan Society an exhibition containing most of the pieces illustrated here will be shown at the Japan House Gallery in New York. The collection will be housed permanently at the National Museum of Japanese History (Kokuritsu Rekishi Minzoku Hakubutsukan) in Sakura, in a wing devoted to the art and culture of the Tokugawa period.

Textile scholars in Japan agree that the Nomura Collection is one of the largest and finest assemblages of early *kosode*. The largest collection of Japanese textiles is at the Tokyo National Museum, and the following public museums have fine collections of *kosode* or Nō robes or both: Eisei Bunko Foundation, Tokyo; Hatakeyama Museum, Tokyo; Itsukushima Shrine Treasure House, Miyajima; Kyoto National Museum; Okayama Art Museum; Suntory Museum of Art, Tokyo; Tokugawa Art Museum, Nagoya; Tōyama Art Museum, Kawajima; and Uesugi Shrine Treasure House, Yonezawa. The finest textiles, however, are rarely shown, because of the fragility of the ancient fabrics and the fugitive quality of some of the dyes. Since the Nomura robes and screens have been exhibited very little, they are in excellent condition. The Nomura Collection remains a testimony to one of the greatest artistic traditions of Japan and to Nomura Shōjirō, who devoted his life to its preservation.

KOSODE:
TECHNIQUES AND DESIGNS

AMANDA MAYER STINCHECUM

Chapter 1
EVOLUTION OF THE KOSODE

THE NOMURA COLLECTION

The Nomura Collection includes 156 *kosode* robes and 100 two-fold screens on which fragments of *kosode* have been mounted. It reflects the best in Japanese design and the highest achievements of the Japanese dyer's arts. During the period represented by the collection, from the late sixteenth to the mid-nineteenth century (and especially the first half of this time span), the decoration of *kosode*, or small-sleeved robes, was in the vanguard of creative design. Indeed, the most famous Japanese painters of the period did not scorn to decorate *kosode* fabric.

Even in a country where textiles are so highly regarded and eagerly collected, the Nomura Collection is unusual in its breadth, containing *kosode* worn by the court nobility, the military elite, the prosperous merchant class, and courtesans. As far as we know, most of these are women's garments, many having been presented to temples following the deaths of their wearers in payment for prayers for their departed souls. The collection also boasts a remarkable number of early *kosode*, dating from the late Momoyama and early Edo periods. Among them, *yūzen* dyeing is strongly represented, attesting to Nomura Shōjirō's particular interest in this refined technique of pictorial decoration.[1] In the Nomura Collection we see the fullest flowering of the art of the *kosode*, the forerunner of today's kimono.

HEIAN PERIOD

Although we tend to think of the *kosode* as the classical Japanese robe, the principal outer garment for all of society in all periods, it is in fact a relatively recent development in the nearly two thousand years of Japanese costume history. During the Asuka and Nara periods (552–645 and 645–794, respectively), when the influx of Chinese and Korean cultural influences was at its peak, court dress, appropriate to the imported ceremonies then popular, reflected that of the continent. But as ties with China weakened and diplomatic relations ceased at the end of the ninth century, a more characteristically Japanese form of dress evolved, in keeping with the native style of architecture. In the Nara period court ceremonies had been performed standing, as at the Tang Chinese court, but Heian courtiers carried out many of the ceremonies of their offices sitting on the floor.[2]

Although some elements of domestic architecture have altered further with successive waves of influence from the continent, the interiors of aristocratic dwellings that we glimpse in the painted handscrolls of the Heian and later periods differ little from those of a finely built traditional house of the nineteenth century. The *shinden* style of architecture emphasizes simplicity, openness to the outdoors, and undecorated surfaces of wood and woven straw. There is almost no furniture: for all their activities people kneel, sit, or lie on the straw matting. The lives of women, especially, were to a great extent enacted on the matted floors of the imperial palace and aristocratic mansions.

Clothing became stiffer and more voluminous, both men and women wearing many layers of solid-colored garments with large, loose sleeves open to their full width at the wrists. The stiff robes lent grace and an air of decorum to floor-seated figures, and multiple layers are still a virtual necessity in rooms open to the raw winter climate of central Honshū. The amplitude of men's dress was to some extent restricted by the practical requirements of their more active lives, but women of the highest rank often wore ten, twelve, even fifteen layers of robes, conventionally called the *jūni hitoe*, or "twelve-layered dress". The layers varied somewhat in cut and most artfully in color, each hue being carefully chosen to set off the others, with layer upon layer visible at the neck, front, and sleeve openings. The harmony of the whole was considered one of the most telling indications of a woman's sensibility. Due to the many foldings of so great a volume of fabric and to the fact that, except at the edges, only the top layer was visible, patterns were generally limited to small repeated motifs woven into monochrome silk twills.

The undergarments, characterized by a different form of sleeve, were called *kosode*, literally "small sleeve", in contrast with the "large-sleeve" (*ōsode*) outer garments. The reference, however, was not to the size of the sleeve itself but to the size of the wrist opening. In later periods even garments with long hanging sleeves (*furisode*) were considered a type of *kosode* because the wrist opening was small. As undergarments for the aristocracy, *kosode* were usually of white silk in plain or twill weave. Commoners, who were not allowed and could not have afforded either silk or "twelve layers", wore as their basic garment *kosode* made of bast fibers such as hemp or ramie and decorated with woven stripes and checks or simple dyed patterns. Even several layers of these *kosode* provided little warmth.

KAMAKURA PERIOD

By the end of the Heian period the social order had changed: power had slipped away from the civilian court into the harder hands of the provincial warriors, whose capital at Kamakura became the effective seat of government and gave its name to the period (1185–1333). Actual political authority was no longer a perquisite of birth but depended on economic and military strength derived from control of land rights and military retainers. This new military elite developed its own culture, more austere than that of the Heian aristocrats and less sedentary. Effectiveness and courage joined refinement and taste as the highest attributes of virtue.

With time, this culture came to influence that of the courtiers as well. Clothing for all but the most formal occasions became simpler, answering to the practicalities of a new and more active way of life. Courtiers and members of the higher military classes wore fewer layers of robes. As the number of outer garments diminished, the neckband and front of the one or more *kosode* undergarments were increasingly revealed and, in keeping with this new prominence, were sometimes patterned. Toward the end of the Kamakura period full-cut trousers known as *hakama*, previously concealed under layers of robes, now came to be worn over *kosode* by women of the ruling military class; women of the court adopted them for informal wear. Such simplifications in dress reflected the Spartan ideals as well as the more active life of the military class.

By this time bolder designs embellished the *kosode*, now highly visible. The *Kasuga Gongen reigenki emaki*, a handscroll painted about 1309, depicts women of the upper classes wearing elaborately patterned *kosode*.[3] One woman, shown napping, wears a *kosode* decorated at the shoulders and hem only, a style known as *kata-suso* (shoulder-and-hem) which became popular in the late sixteenth century.

Kosode were often worn one over another or covered by a looser robe, sometimes with the outer robe slipped off the shoulders and tied or held at the waist. Of the lower *kosode* only the shoulders and, when the wearer moved, the front hem area would be seen. It is likely, during this early period, that on some *kosode* only the areas expected to be seen would have been decorated. Even sixteenth-century *kata-suso* style *kosode* were sometimes patterned only at the front of the hem, recalling the origins of the form.

MUROMACHI PERIOD

During the Muromachi period (1333–1573) the center of political power, previously concentrated in the military government at Kamakura, again shifted. The cultural and aesthetic enthusiasms of the ruling Ashikaga shoguns distracted them from the business of governing. The reigning imperial house was by now so impoverished that one of the emperors lay unburied for six weeks after his death for want of money to pay funeral expenses. Strife between lesser feudal lords fragmented the country, and the breakdown of centralized government resulted in the Ōnin War, which for ten years (1467–77) devastated Kyoto, the imperial capital, and its environs. The fortunes of war blurred class boundaries, destroying former great houses and elevating brilliant soldiers of humble origin so that by 1582 Japan was ruled by Toyotomi Hideyoshi, who had begun his career as a common foot-soldier.

Paradoxically, incessant warfare encouraged trade and the formation of artisans' guilds and merchants' associations. The reasons are not far to seek: competing warlords needed military equipment for their campaigns as well as domestic equipment for their fiefs; the weakening of central control enabled provincial warriors to establish production centers and markets to their own advantage; and the very turbulence of the times both required and permitted the commercial classes to organize their interests. Thus the merchants, whose subculture in the Edo period was to transform Japan's urban society, began to acquire wealth, power, and status.

Social distinctions in dress also weakened during this period, and by the end of the fifteenth century all classes wore *kosode* as their principal outer garment except for the most formal ceremonies of the imperial court. Henceforth all of Japan's textile arts would be concentrated upon the *kosode*.

THE SHAPE OF THE KOSODE

In cut, the *kosode* has changed relatively little over the past eight or nine hundred years; paintings of the Late Heian period depict easily recognizable *kosode*. But although paintings can illuminate costume and textile history, a definitive description of the shape of the *kosode* must be based on actual garments. Kamiya Eiko has made a valuable study of twenty-three men's *kosode* of known provenance and date.[4] The earliest extant *kosode* was discovered in 1960 in the coffin of

Fujiwara Motohira (d. 1157) at Chūson-ji, a Buddhist temple in Iwate Prefecture.[5] It is too large for a man of Motohira's size and may have functioned as bedclothes. When found, it was spread under and wrapped around the remains without passing the arms through the sleeves. The robe differs from later *kosode* and present-day kimono in having narrow (25 cm.) tubular sleeves and no front overlap. This type of sleeve, with a triangular underarm section, allows greater freedom of movement and requires less material than a standard kimono sleeve; it is still seen today in the work clothes of farmers and fishermen.

No other *kosode* have come down to us from the Heian or Kamakura periods, but contemporary paintings suggest that the same kind of tubular sleeve, fully open at the wrist, was common to *kosode* of that time. Paintings of the fourteenth century, such as the *Kasuga Gongen reigenki emaki* and the *Ōeyama ekotoba* (in the Itsuō Art Museum, Osaka), show a partial sewing-up of the sleeve opening and a rounding of the sleeve into the curved shape that remained characteristic through the mid-Edo period (1688–1781).[6] This is the origin of the use of the sleeve as a pocket (*tamoto*, sleeve-pocket) seen in today's kimono.

The next oldest extant *kosode* bears a design of quails, chrysanthemums, and other plants and birds in white and red *tsujigahana* dyeing. Originally donated to the Hakusan Shrine in Gifu Prefecture, it is now in the Tokyo National Museum.[7] It is dated the ninth year of Eiroku (1566) and has the narrow sleeve and wide body typical of *kosode* of the late sixteenth and early seventeenth centuries.

The sleeve width (*sode haba*) is the distance from the seam between body and sleeve, or shoulder seam, and the cuff. The sleeve length (*sode take*) is the distance from the shoulder fold to the lower edge of the sleeve, the bottom of the sleeve pocket (see Appendix 3). Thus the *furisode* in Cpl. 44 is, in the Japanese sense, a long-sleeved (rather than a wide-sleeved) garment.

The twelve next earliest *kosode* examined by Kamiya belonged to Uesugi Kenshin (1530–78), one of the most powerful feudal lords of the Muromachi period. They are preserved at Uesugi Shrine in Yamagata Prefecture, and form one of the most important groups of documents for the study of sixteenth-century textiles.[8] These garments all display narrow sleeves, wide body with approximately equal back and front widths, wide front overlap, and long neckband (relative to the size of the wearer as estimated by Kamiya from the breadth of the *kosode* back and the width of the sleeves).

Kosode have always been worn with the left side lapped over the right. The cut of the garment has changed little since at least the sixteenth century, and *kosode* of this early period as well as the modern kimono consist of the following seven pieces (see Appendix 4): body (*migoro*), two pieces, each extending from center front opening to center back seam; sleeves (*sode*), two pieces; overlap (*okumi*), two pieces; neckband (*eri*), one piece. It is characteristic of Japanese clothing construction to cut all pieces from a single length of cloth in such a way as to waste no fabric. This cutting layout also permits cut pieces to be sewn back together into a single length when the fabric is to be washed and stretched.

The proportions of the parts of the garment and the average woven width of the cloth have changed significantly as the *kosode* developed to its present form (see Appendices 3, 4). *Kosode* of the late Muromachi and Momoyama combine a wide overlap, back, and neckband with narrow sleeves. By 1700, however, the width of the *kosode* back had decreased, from an average 37.6 cm. to 30 cm. The woven width of cloth had also decreased: early *kosode* cloth was woven about 41 cm. wide, compared with the 36 cm. that is standard for kimono today.[9]

The woven width of the cloth and the width of individual garment pieces together determine cutting layout. In the early *kosode* the wide neckband and narrow sleeves must have been cut from a single width, and the wide overlaps from another single width bisected diagonally (see Fig. 4-1, Kamiya's reconstruction of cutting layout for the *kosode* dated to 1566). But with an increase in sleeve width, sleeve and neckband could no longer be cut from a single width. A new cutting layout became necessary, with the neckband and overlap taking one full width and the sleeves another (Fig. 4-2). According to Kamiya's findings this change in cutting layout must have taken place by the second half of the seventeenth century, for the *kosode* belonging to Tokugawa Mitsukuni (d. 1700) reveals the wide back of the earlier style and the wide sleeves of the later one. These sleeves plus the neckband could not have been cut from a single width of cloth, hence the new cutting layout, which is still used today.

A systematic study of the width of textiles woven for clothing between the mid-sixteenth and early eighteenth century would be most helpful in dating *kosode* and textiles woven in other periods. Although various scholars have commented on changes in textile width and on differences between textiles woven in Japan and those imported from China, no one has consolidated all the findings or attempted to draw conclusions from available data.

KOSODE IN THE
NOMURA COLLECTION

Virtually all extant *kosode* dating before the mid-nineteenth century—and all those in the Nomura Collection—were worn by the ruling and moneyed classes. Farmers and laborers wore their clothes to rags—we have almost none from before the late Edo period (1781–1868).

Another accident of history limits *kosode* of known provenance and date almost exclusively to men's garments. So far as can be determined, however, the Nomura Collection comprises mostly women's. During the late Muromachi and the Momoyama periods men and women wore very similar clothing, and in the early years of the seventeenth century the distinction was still not clearly drawn. Hashimoto Sumiko's study of a pair of eight-fold screens in the Tokugawa Art Museum, Nagoya, probably painted in the Kan'ei era (1624–44), indicates the strong similarity between men's and women's garments at this time.[10] During the mid-Edo period (1688–1781) men's clothing became more subdued, but it was probably not until late Edo that its decoration was restricted to the dark colors and patterns of checks, fine stripes, or small flecks we see today.

There are two main reasons for the lack of women's *kosode* of known date and provenance. First, a woman's *kosode* was often recut to conform to changing styles, either by the original owner or by her heirs, while men's were more frequently preserved in their original form. Second, men's garments were often formally presented as gifts to their subordinates or preserved by their families as mementos, and such dispositions would be recorded in family documents. Since in feudal society women ranked far lower than men, their clothing was not apt to be similarly cherished. Commonly, when a woman died, one of her garments would be presented to the temple where she had worshipped, in return for prayers for her salvation. Many of these garments were inscribed on the lining with the woman's posthumous Buddhist name and the date of presentation, but once donated they would be cut up for priests' vestments (*kesa*), altar cloths (*uchishiki*), or temple banners (*ban*), and in the process the original inscriptions might be lost or separated from the fabric. Even those inscriptions that remained attached tell us only the date of death of the garment's owner; the *kosode* itself might have been made in her youth or even handed down to her from an earlier generation.

Several *kosode* inscriptions, collected by Nomura, have recently been discovered in Kyoto (see Appendix 1). Unfortunately, in the process of making the screens they were removed from their *kosode* and stored separately, so that we can only conjecture what information they might have provided for the early history of *kosode*. Nevertheless, it is to the credit of Nomura Shōjirō, given the somewhat primitive level of contemporary textile studies, that these materials were preserved at all. They cannot help us date these particular *kosode*, but they indicate the esteem in which the garments were held and the kind of information that might yet be found on other garments.

Chapter 2
THE WEAVING INDUSTRY

THE WEAVING OFFICE

The annals of the Chinese kingdom of Wei record a tribute from Japan of silk textiles in A.D. 243, and plain-weave silk fragments excavated from a tomb site in Fukuoka dating to the beginning of the Common Era are believed to have been woven from locally produced fibers.[1] Not until the fifth and sixth centuries, however, when large numbers of skilled artisans came to Japan from China and Korea (with the introduction of Buddhism), did Japanese weavers begin to employ the complex weaving and dyeing techniques necessary to create the kinds of fabrics preserved in the Shōsō-in repository in Nara since the eighth century. Throughout the Asuka (552–645) and Nara (645–794) periods frequent missions carried trade goods to and from the continent, and large quantities of silk textiles entered Japan. Much of the silk clothing worn by members of the court was imported, or made in Japan by Chinese or Korean weavers. Taxes in the form of silk cloth, yarn, or floss, specified in the Taika Reform Edict of 646, indicate the importance of domestic silk production at that time. By the eleventh century, when the extravagance of Heian court dress had reached its zenith, a complete set of formal court robes for a woman of high rank could require more than 40 rolls of silk, equivalent to 480 meters of present-day kimono fabric.[2] Although most of this must have been produced domestically, imported Chinese textiles, especially those requiring great skill, such as compound twills and gauzes, were eagerly sought after.

The Weaving Office (Oribe no tsukasa), a subdivision of the Ministry of the Treasury (Ōkurashō), was in the eighth century put in charge of the weaving and dyeing of the finest quality textiles for court use, managing the skilled artisans working in various provinces. But by the tenth century artisans attached to this office were weaving in their own homes.[3] The Weaving Office had lost its monopoly over their output, and by 1048 it had become necessary to issue an edict forbidding the private production of luxury fabrics. This was apparently without effect: powerful families now employed their own artisans and even filled orders from the court, which naturally brought the privately employed artisans into conflict with those of the Weaving Office. From the end of the Heian period the activity of the latter was greatly reduced, and orders for the emperor's clothing were officially executed by the Imperial Clothing Office (Gofuku dokoro) in the Ministry of Central Affairs (Nakatsukasashō). The final blow to the official weavers came in 1246, when fire destroyed Orite-chō, the district they inhabited west of the imperial palace. The production of luxury textiles was taken over on a private basis by court retainers (toneri), who had settled in the adjacent district and learned the arts of making cloth from the weavers nearby.[4]

RISE OF THE CLOTH GUILDS

At the same time demand for Chinese fabrics continued to rise, and Japanese weavers began to copy complex Chinese weaves. The remaining weavers of the Imperial Clothing Office also accepted private orders, so that the distinction between government and private enterprise became increasingly tenuous, eventuating in an independent artisan class. Regular cloth markets were held, not only in Kyoto, the capital, but also in Nara and Kamakura. In 1274 a guild (za) of brocade makers was established under the protection of the Gion Shrine in Kyoto.[5] By the early fifteenth century organization of the textile arts extended to guilds of artisans and merchants engaged in various aspects of textile production in Kyoto and Nara,

some under the protection of the great Buddhist temples there.

At the same time wholesale and retail trade became clearly separated, with wholesale brokers beginning to emerge as powerful magnates. This group would form the pillars of the townsman (chōnin) class which was to change the nature of Japanese urban society in the Edo period (1615–1868).[6] Trade with Ming China, carefully licensed and controlled by the shogunal government, grew rapidly: 919 double-length rolls of silk twill, brocade, damask, and gauze; 60 finely embroidered robes; a damask pillow appliquéd in velvet; a gauze-weave mosquito net decorated with gold leaf; and other rare items came from China in 1406 and 1407.

DISPERSAL AND GROWTH OF THE WEAVING INDUSTRY

The Ōnin War, which ravaged Kyoto from 1467 to 1477, dispersed the weaving industry hitherto concentrated there. Artisans fled the capital for protection in the Buddhist temples of Nara, in Shinto shrines, or in the castle towns of powerful provincial clans. With the destruction of Kyoto, however, the techniques of some of the more complex weaves were lost. By the end of the fifteenth century figured gauze (ra) and some twills were no longer being woven. But many of the toneri weavers, hired by wealthy merchants of Sakai, settled in that growing port city near present-day Osaka, through which passed much of the trade goods from the continent and Southeast Asia. There they came into contact with the newest imports and strove to learn the techniques of making them, especially the softer-textured silks such as crepe and figured twills and satins.[7]

Not until the seventeenth century, however, did these weaves become an integral part of kosode design. They were preceded in fashion by plain-weave silks (nerinuki), whose production was monopolized by the weavers of the nerinuki za (nerinuki guild).[8] With the ending of the Ōnin War and the rebuilding of Kyoto many of the weavers who had fled to Sakai returned to the capital. There they established themselves in the Nishijin district, just west of the imperial palace, where an active silk-weaving industry has continued to flourish to this day. They wove for the court as well as for private customers. The guilds, which had formed originally under the protection of powerful manors or religious institutions, had become semi-independent bodies. Ultimately the guild monopolies gave way, broken in the late sixteenth century by decrees establishing "free markets and free guilds" (*rakuichi, rakuza*), which allowed merchants to trade outside the guild monopoly. New trade associations formed, however, centering on the wholesale merchant, with a complex organizational structure and system of apprenticeship.

Silk yarn and fabrics continued to be produced not only in the capital but in the provinces as well. Local daimyo had encouraged textile production within their own domains since the Ōnin War, offering physical protection and a ready market to artisans who chose to work for them. By the middle of the Muromachi period twenty-two provinces were producing silk, though not of the finest quality. The best silk yarn was still being imported from China in large quantity, and toward the end of Muromachi there were merchants who specialized in Chinese silk yarns.[9] Shogunal edicts of 1604 and 1635, however, asserted a monopoly of the sale of imported raw silk, which must have further encouraged local production.[10] Nevertheless, undyed silk yarns and fabric from China continued to be of major importance to domestic weaving and dyeing of the highest quality textiles until the late seventeenth century, when restrictions on the importation of white silk fabric and silk yarns further promoted domestic re-

gional production. Centers of silk production spread eastward from central and western Japan. Such towns as Kiryū in the province of Kōzuke (present-day Gumma Prefecture) and Ashikaga in Shimotsuke (Tochigi Prefecture) competed with Nishijin for the luxury silk market.

INTRODUCTION OF COTTON

Cotton had been imported from the continent at intervals since the Nara period, but not until the fifteenth century was the demand for it marked; at this time it was probably imported primarily from Korea.[11] Tradition dates attempts at domestic cotton cultivation from the sixteenth century, but in fact it probably did not begin to flourish until the Edo period. Because it provides greater warmth than the bast fibers and is so much easier and cheaper to raise, process, and dye, cotton gradually replaced hemp and ramie as the chief clothing material of the lower classes. Fine bleached ramie in time became a luxury fabric, the perquisite of the court and the higher levels of the military and mercantile classes. Its crisp and cool feel rendered it particularly suitable for the unlined summer *kosode* known as *katabira* (Cpls. 33, 37, 44).

Chapter 3
WEAVE STRUCTURES AND FABRICS

A woven fabric structure is one in which one set of "parallel elements that run longitudinally in a fabric [warps] are crossed at more or less right angles and interworked by transverse elements [wefts]".[1] All three of the basic weave structures—plain, twill, and satin—are well represented in the Nomura Collection.

PLAIN-WEAVE FABRICS IN THE NOMURA COLLECTION

Plain weave (*hira-ori*; see Fig. 2-1) is the simplest woven structure, in which "each weft passes alternately over and under successive warp units, and each reverses the procedure of the one before it".[2]

Nerinuki

Nerinuki is a plain-weave silk characterized by warps of raw (unglossed) silk and wefts of degummed (glossed) silk; the latter are often thicker than the former.[3] The warps give crispness to the fabric but are brittle and eventually deteriorate before the weft yarns; the glossed wefts add luster and body. *Nerinuki* is relatively simple to weave, and its uniformly flat surface is especially suited to the delicate ink painting typical of late Muromachi and Momoyama *tsujigahana kosode* (Cpls. 1, 2, 4). It was widely used for *kosode* in the sixteenth century and is represented in some of the earliest pieces in the Nomura Collection (Cpls. 1–4).

Bast Fibers

Another plain-weave fabric common in the Nomura Collection is the ramie cloth used for summer *kosode* (*katabira*). Ramie (bot. *Boehmeria nivea* Gaud., J. *chōma* or *karamushi*, also called China grass) is of the nettle family. It is a bast fiber, that is, produced from the fibrous layer between the bark and inner pulp of the plant's woody stalk. Many bast fibers have been woven in Japan—ramie, hemp (bot. *Cannabis sativa*, J. *asa* or *taima*), and banana fiber (bot. *Musa basjoo Sieb.*, J. *bashō*) are among the most common.[4] Hemp and ramie were widely used for commoners' clothing until the spread of cotton cultivation in the eighteenth century. Of the bast fibers used in Japan, ramie yields the finest and longest filament and has long been cultivated there, especially in Okinawa, Fukushima, and Niigata prefectures, for the highest quality summer clothing (see Cpls. 33, 37, 44).

Chirimen Crepe

Crepe (*chijimi*) is a plain-weave fabric, of any fiber, characterized by a crimped texture produced by the use of highly twisted wefts and/or warps. *Chirimen* (hereafter referred to as *chirimen* crepe) is a type of silk crepe in which the twist direction of the wefts changes with every two weft yarns (Cpls. 34–36, 40–43, 46, 47, 53). *Chirimen* crepe, one of the fabrics introduced from China in the sixteenth century, came into prominence in Japan during the latter part of the seventeenth century with the development of *yūzen* paste-resist dyeing techniques, which permitted extremely detailed decoration in an unlimited range of colors. The highly pictorial designs that came to characterize *yūzen* dyeing were set off to best advantage by the textured, matte surface of *chirimen*. Figured satin continued to be used but was usually confined to *kosode* decorated with *shibori* (see Chap. 4) and embroidery, as its clearly patterned surface and high luster distract from an elaborately detailed, brushed design.

TWILL WEAVES

Twill (*aya*) is the second of the three basic weave structures. In plain weave each weft yarn passes over one warp yarn and under the next; this numerical order is abbreviated 1/1.[5] Passing a weft yarn over or under two or more warps at a time creates floats, and a fabric containing floats is called a float weave. A twill, or twill weave, is a float weave distinguished by a diagonal alignment of successive floats, creating in its simplest form diagonal ribs on the surfaces of the fabric. Many numerical orders are possible, but one of the commonest in this collection is the 3/1 warp-faced twill, in which one warp passes over three wefts, then under one, then over three, etc. The weaver creates it by passing one weft shot (individual weft thread) under three warps, over one, under three, etc. (Fig. 2-2). The surface, or face, of the fabric shows predominantly warp yarns; the reverse shows predominantly weft yarns and is described as a 1/3 weft-faced twill. (Less specifically, such a fabric is also called a four-harness twill.)

Figured Twill and Saya

Three/one warp-faced twill weave forms the basis for figured twill (*mon aya*), often used for men's *kosode* and sometimes for women's as well. *Mon aya* may be described as a warp-faced twill ground with a weft-faced twill figure (Fig. 2–3; Cpl. 2, right); its reverse is a weft-faced twill ground with a warp-faced twill figure. The opposite relationship between face and reverse also constitutes a figured twill. A related structure is *saya*, a 3/1 warp-faced twill figure on a plain-weave ground (Fig. 2–4), whose reverse is a 1/3 weft-faced twill figure on a plain-weave ground. Both figured twill and *saya* fabrics were primarily monochrome, often further decorated by other techniques (see Chap. 4).

SATIN WEAVES

Unfigured Satin

The third of the basic weave structures is satin (*shusu*). Like twill, satin is a float weave, but distinguished from twill by the *intermittent* diagonal alignment of floats, which creates satin's characteristic smooth surface unbroken by diagonal ribs. The longer the float, uninterrupted by ties of the opposite set, the smoother and more lustrous the surface. The most typical satin structure is 4/1 warp-faced satin (five-harness satin) (Fig. 2–5). Seven/one warp-faced satin (eight-harness satin) came into use slightly later (Fig. 2–6). Like the twills described above, the two surfaces of a satin are dissimilar, the one displaying the reverse structure of the other.

Plain (unfigured) satins were often used for richly embroidered or painted *kosode* in the mid- and late Edo periods (1688–1868), and to a lesser extent in early Edo (1615–88) (Cpls. 26, 27, 52).

Monochrome Figured Satin

By far the most popular of the figured silks imported from China in the sixteenth century, monochrome figured satin (*rinzu*, structurally a damask weave) replaced *nerinuki* as the most commonly used *kosode* fabric about the beginning of the following century. The crisper *nerinuki* had suited the more voluminous garments of earlier times, but the softness of satin was more appropriate to the drape of the now-fashionable *kosode*, which followed the lines of the body. It also lent itself better to the decorative techniques and finely detailed designs then gaining in popularity. Satin was probably also more practical and durable than the rather brittle and fragile *nerinuki*, a consideration for the growing number of wealthy merchants eager to parade their newly gained financial ascendancy over the daimyo, samurai, and court nobility. Most of the figured satin used for *kosode* of the Edo period is five-harness satin, a 1/4 weft-faced satin figure on a 4/1 warp-faced satin ground (Fig. 2–7; Cpls. 3, right, and 6).

Saya Pattern

Almost all of the figured twills and satins in the Nomura Collection are woven in *sayagata*, or *saya* pattern (Fig. 2–8), probably so called because the pattern is typical of the *saya* fabrics (twill-weave figure on plain-weave ground) first imported from Ming China. A type of diagonal key-fret pattern, the *sayagata* is derived from continuously linked swastikas and is usually woven with superimposed flowers such as the orchids and chrysanthemums shown here.

Chapter 4
THE BASIC DECORATIVE TECHNIQUES

Two classes of substances are used to color fiber of any kind: dye, which is soluble in water or other liquids (with or without the action of other chemical substances) and therefore penetrates the fiber; and pigment, which is not soluble in water and adheres to the surface of the fiber. Most dyes are extracted from vegetable sources, and vegetable dyes are the ones most commonly used in Japan. Pigments are for the most part derived from minerals.

IMMERSION (DIP) DYEING

A number of basic techniques were employed to decorate *kosode* i.e., immersion dyeing, painting, *shibori*, applied gold or silver leaf, embroidery, and paste resist. Immersion dyeing (*tsuke-zome*) is the fundamental method used to dye an entire length of cloth or a batch of yarns a single color. When the dye has been extracted from its source and the dye bath prepared, the cloth or yarn is immersed, sometimes repeatedly, until it has acquired the desired shade. Then it is removed, rinsed, and dried. In many cases, however, the dye extract by itself will not penetrate the fabric to produce the required color but must be aided by a metallic salt, or mordant, and sometimes by an additional acid or alkali.[1] Sometimes the cloth is placed in the mordant bath prior to the dye bath and sometimes afterward, depending on the nature of fiber, dye, and mordant and on the cultural or individual predisposition of the dyer.

PAINTING

The term "painting" has been used to refer to two distinct modes of decoration: brushing in a previously outlined pattern and background with dyes and mordants; and freehand painting with carbon ink and pigments, using a calligrapher's brush (*kaki-e*). The process of brushing dye over a whole piece of cloth or a background area is called *hiki-zome*; filling in a design outlined in resist paste is called *iro-sashi* (or *iro-zashi*). Early attempts at *hiki-zome* tended to produce a somewhat uneven, streaky effect compared with dip dyeing. The blossoming of urban *chōnin* (townsman) culture during the late seventeenth century created a demand for a method of decoration that took less time than *shibori* and did not thicken and stiffen the fabric as embroidery did. *Hiki-zome* was perfected in response to this demand.

Freehand painting (*kaki-e*) was usually done in the black ink used for calligraphy and painting (J. *sumi*, made from lampblack or pine soot) and in vermilion (J. *shu*, mercuric sulfide, also called cinnabar). Highly calligraphic line quality characterizes the best *kosode* painting of the Momoyama period (1573–1615), such as the grapes and grape leaves on white background in Colorplates 2 and 3, left. During the middle (1688–1781) and late (1781–1868) Edo periods renowned artists decorated *kosode*, creating priceless masterpieces to be worn in the streets. The Nomura Collection boasts two fine examples by the painters Matsumura Goshun (1752–1811) (Cpl. 51) and Sakai Hōitsu (1761–1828) (Cpl. 52).

SHIBORI

There are two ways to create a dyed pattern on a dip-dyed textile. The simplest is to paint or print the pattern over the dipped background color, but the resulting hue will be mixed. The other way, and the one most often used in Japan, is to reserve the pattern areas, that is, to protect these areas in some way so that the dye does not penetrate them, thus obtaining a white pattern against a dyed background. The converse is also possible, namely, reserving the entire background so that only the pattern areas are exposed to the dye. This type of dyeing technique is called resist dyeing, and *shibori* is one of the four major resist techniques common in Japanese dyeing, along with paste resist, stencil dyeing, and *kasuri* (*ikat*). *Kasuri* is not represented in the Nomura Collection and therefore will not be discussed here.

In *shibori* the area to be reserved is "squeezed" (*shiboru*) or pulled into three-dimensional form, then bound or clamped off to protect it from contact with the dye. The more tightly the reserved area is compressed, the more completely it will be reserved. The whole fabric is then immersed in the dye bath, removed, dried, and the squeezed areas released.[2] They will appear reserved in white, with a slightly blurred outline, against the dyed background. As a result of compression the reserved areas will also be somewhat raised and surrounded by radiating wrinkles, and these textural effects may be exploited as decorative elements.

Shibori may be accomplished by binding, stitching, or folding and clamping the areas to be reserved. Although these closely related techniques are all based on one physical action—squeezing or pinching part of the fabric away from the rest to prevent dye penetration —there is no satisfactory English term that comprises them all. "Tie-dye" has been widely used as the equivalent of *shibori*, but the term is at once too narrow and too broad.[3] The term *shibori* covers resist techniques that do not involve binding or tying, such as folding and pressing between clamped boards.[4] Furthermore, some writers use "tie-dye" to refer to *ikat* techniques and textiles, in which not fabric but yarns are resist dyed before weaving, often but not necessarily by tying or binding.[5] For the sake of clarity I have retained the use of the Japanese term *shibori*. *Shibori*, or *shibori-zome* (*shibori* dyeing), first appears in documents of the seventeenth century; during the six-teenth century *kukushi* (from *kukuru*, to bind) was in common use.[6]

Kanoko Shibori

In applying a bound resist, a strong, relatively unabsorbent thread or fiber is used to tie off the pattern area. During the Momoyama and Edo periods hemp was often used for this purpose; today dyers often use strips of vinyl. *Kanoko*, or *hitta*, *shibori* is a form of bound resist widely used in *kosode* of the Edo period. Closely spaced small (ca. 8–10 mm.) circles in diagonal rows are reserved by folding successive bits of the fabric into quarters along the bias and binding them tightly with thread; the tip of each bit of fabric is left unbound so that an eye-like dot in the center of each reserved circle will take the dye. The fabric is then immersed in the dye, dried, and the bindings undone. Since the dye cannot penetrate the binding, the result is a pattern of tiny white (undyed) circles with a small dot of the dye color in the center of each. Fabric for use in *kosode* is then slightly steamed, leaving the crimped texture caused by the binding. This type of *shibori* is designated *kanoko*, meaning "fawn-dot", because of its resemblance to the white-dappled coat of a fawn (Cpls. 3, 7, 8, 9, 12, 14). The term *hitta* is sometimes used for similarly produced but slightly larger, rectangular dots covering the entire surface of the *kosode*, but *kanoko* and *hitta* are not consistently differentiated. I have used the former term throughout.

Among earlier *kanoko*-decorated *kosode* an occasional tie would be insufficiently tight, allowing the dye to seep into that circle. When the dyeing was completed, these unintentionally colored spots were whitened with face powder (*oshiroi*), which consisted primarily of white lead. The lead turns black with age, and as a result many seventeenth-century *kosode* contain black spots among the white *kanoko* circles. These occur rarely after the early Edo period, when *kanoko* dyers had reached a high level of expertise.

Stencilled Kanoko

Kanoko shibori was a slow, exacting process, which could produce only a limited number of extremely expensive *kosode*. To meet the growing demand for such *kosode*, not only among the court and military aristocracy but among the newly wealthy merchant commoners as well, dyers developed a stencilled imitation, stencilled *kanoko* (*kata-kanoko*, or *suri-hitta*). Resist paste was applied through a stencil, then the fabric was dip dyed. When the dye had dried, the paste was removed, leaving a pattern of white spots. The central eye-like dot in each white spot was then painted in by hand. On some garments, in order to approximate the characteristic texture of true *kanoko shibori* the fabric was laid wrong side up on a semihard wax surface and each dot pressed into the wax with a blunt tool (*uchidashi kanoko*). Certain clients, however, may have preferred the regular pattern and smooth surface produced by stencilled *kanoko*. Some later examples of stencilled *kanoko* omit the central dot entirely.[7]

It has long been held that stencilled *kanoko* developed in response to the stream of sumptuary laws promulgated during the seventeenth century, especially those issued in 1682 and 1683 by the rigidly moralistic fifth shogun, Tokugawa Tsunayoshi (ruled 1680–1709). These forbade the use of overall *kanoko* (*sō-kanoko*), in which an entire *kosode* was completely covered with closely spaced *kanoko dots*.[8] The so-called Keishō-in *kosode* (preserved at Gokoku-ji, Tokyo), however, suggests that stencilled *kanoko* was in use before this time. This garment has been accepted by Japanese scholars as belonging to Keishō-in, mother of Tsunayoshi and concubine of Tokugawa Iemitsu (1604–51).[9] Keishō-in died in her eighties in 1705, but the large scale of the design motif and the wide hanging sleeves (*furisode*) suggest that she wore this robe when relatively young, between the late Kan'ei (1624–44) and Manji (1658–61) eras. The design of the *kosode* features a single plum tree that spreads up the right side of the back and spreads its branches across both shoulders. The trunk and branches are executed in *kanoko*; to the left and below the branches is plain black background, while the rest of the background is *kanoko* on red. Some of the plum blossoms are also in *kanoko* on a red ground; the remainder are heavily embroidered in red silk and gold. The *kanoko* spots are suspiciously regular in size and alignment for hand-tied *shibori*, and not one has been corrected with white lead powder. In addition, evenly spaced vertical lines appear in the *kanoko*-on-red background area, strongly suggestive of the lines produced by overlapping of stencil repeats. Although we are not absolutely sure how the *kanoko* spots on the Keishō-in *kosode* were made, leading textile scholars tentatively accept it as the earliest extant example of stencilled *kanoko* of known provenance.[10]

Stitch-Resist Shibori

Stitch resist (*nuishime shibori*) has perhaps the broadest application of the basic *shibori* techniques.[11] It is represented in the Nomura Collection by *kosode* of the sixteenth through nineteenth centuries. Stitch resist is used primarily to reserve relatively small design elements; for larger reserved areas, variants of stitch resist called capped *shibori* and tub resist

(see below) are generally employed. A small motif to be reserved is outlined with a row of very fine stitches (sometimes only a few threads of the fabric per stitch), which are drawn up tightly, as in shirring, and knotted to keep them from slipping. The bit of fabric "squeezed" into three-dimensional form by the shirring is then tightly wound with thread to protect it from the dye, and the whole fabric is dipped in the dye bath. When the dye has dried, the shirring and winding threads are removed. The minute size of the stitches on some pieces and the delicacy of the silk fabric make this extremely painstaking work. Some of the finest *shibori* pieces of the Momoyama period (1573–1615) still retain, unintentionally, fragments of the hemp threads used in the stitching.

The dye will not have penetrated the thread-wound area nor the deepest recesses of the shirred folds, but it will have seeped into the looser parts of the folds. The result is a design element reserved in white, surrounded by a row of tiny white dots and beyond these by radiating lines in pale tones of the background color. These radiating lines blur the outline of the design. All *shibori* is characterized by blurred outlines; stitch resist is distinguished by the row of fine holes left by the needle around the perimeter of the reserved area. Both *kosode* in Colorplate 1 display typical lines of stitch-resist dots in the veins and outlines of the leaves and in the stems of the flowers.

Capped Shibori

To reserve a medium-sized solid-colored area, the outline of the area is first stitched off, the stitches are drawn tight, and the whole area to be resisted is wrapped with waterproof bamboo sheath which is tightly bound before dyeing. This version of stitch resist is called *bōshi* (capped) *shibori*, because the bound portion resembles a hat.

Tub Resist

To reserve a large background area, a more elaborate version of stitch resist was sometimes employed. In tub resist (*oke-zome*) the area to be reserved was first stitched off, then placed inside a tub with a close-fitting lid and the lid clamped shut, with the areas to be dyed hanging outside the tub.[12] The whole length of fabric, including the tub, was then immersed in the dye bath, but only the sections left outside the tub would absorb the dye.

Somewake, meaning literally "divide by dyeing", denotes a design element rather than a technique. It describes *kosode* in which the background has been divided into two or more color areas, which are then decorated in various ways. The various background colors may be produced by tub resist or, for smaller areas, by capped *shibori*. Colorplate 9 illustrates a good example of a *somewake*, or divided ground, *kosode*. Here the area to be reserved in white was first stitched off and clamped or wrapped and the *kanoko* spots tied; then the whole piece was dipped in red. When this was completed, parts of the red and white areas were stitched off and clamped or wrapped and the fabric dipped in black. The term *somewake* usually refers to *kosode* of the so-called Keichō style, named for the Keichō era (1596–1615) in which it was developed, and less often to *kosode* of later periods. In the *kosode* at right in Colorplates 2 and 3 the white wave crests are reserved by *bōshi shibori* against the black background. The third basic *shibori* technique, that of folding and clamping, is not represented in the Nomura Collection.

Pinch Dyeing

Pinch dyeing (*tsumami-zome*), one of the most difficult types of *shibori*, was used when delicate and complex forms were to be dyed on a reserved ground. The areas would be stitched off and tightly bound, and the dyer would then dip only the section to be colored into the dye bath, carefully holding away the portion to be left white. In this way different pattern areas could be dyed in different colors. Pinch dyeing, which is only used to create dyed pattern on reserved ground, is one of the most exacting types of *shibori*.[13]

Shibori may be one of the oldest decorative techniques in Japanese fabrics. Certain eighth-century fragments are probably the oldest extant examples, but written records hint at a much earlier beginning.[14] The third-century annals of the Chinese kingdom of Wei (see p. 26) record tribute from Japan of *nishiki* (usually translated "brocade" but meaning silk cloth woven of many colors) and *hanpu*.[15] The latter, which means "spotted or dappled cloth," could refer to *shibori* or *ikat* or to some more primitive dyeing method.

APPLIED METALLIC LEAF

Gold or silver leaf (*suri-haku*, literally "rubbed leaf"), particularly popular during Momoyama, lent to the surface of *kosode* a soft gleam far more appealing than the somewhat garish gold embroidery used in later eras. In the sixteenth and seventeenth centuries it was most often applied in small-scale, repeated patterns, many of which were derived from the *yūsoku* (court) patterns of the Heian period (794–1185). The earliest

dated *tsujigahana* pieces, temple banners made between 1528 and 1530, combine silver leaf with *shibori*.[16] Metallic leaf had been used to decorate clothing in Japan at least since the Heian period, but when a new method of application was developed in China during the Ming dynasty, this was adopted by the Japanese.[17]

A stencil cut with the desired pattern was laid over the silk, and adhesive applied through the stencil. The exact composition of this adhesive has been lost, but it was probably a rice-flour base mixed with some substance containing sugar to keep the paste flexible when dry. The stencil was then removed, and the leaf pressed onto the pattern of paste on the fabric; when the adhesive had dried, any leaf not adhering to it was brushed away.

The physical properties of the adhesive make applied leaf (*surihaku*) the most perishable of the decorative mediums, and many *kosode* that originally had large areas covered with metallic leaf patterns now bear only traces. The fish-net pattern in gold leaf on the "golden waterfall" *kosode* (Cpl. 16) is now mostly missing, but on the black *kosode* patterned with blades of grass (Cpl. 14) the allover pattern of short horizontal lines of gold leaf is well preserved.

EMBROIDERY

Freedom and subtlety of execution in form, color, and detail, plus a richly textured and lustrous surface distinguish embroidery (*nui*) from the other textile arts. Unrestricted by the grid of warp and weft, and free from the structural complexities of polychrome woven patterns, embroidery has been a vehicle of pictorial expression on costume in Japan since at least the Nara period (645–794). With the devastation of Kyoto and its nascent weaving industry in the fifteenth century, embroidery became a substitute for some of the more elaborate float-weave textiles whose technique was derived from China (*kara-ori*, literally "Chinese weaving"). This is clearly illustrated by the *uchikake* (outer *kosode* worn as a cloak) at Kōdai-ji, Kyoto, said to have belonged to Kita no Mandokoro, wife of Toyotomi Hideyoshi (d. 1598). Here embroidery renders a woven pattern widely used since the Heian period: *kikkō hanabishi*, or tortoise-shell diaper enclosing floral lozenges.[18] In this example, however, the diaper pattern is irregularly overlaid with embroidered cloud forms. Such a design would be practically impossible to render on a loom.

Float-Stitch Embroidery

Sixteenth-century Japanese embroidery was much influenced by imported embroideries from Ming China. The tightly twisted silk embroidery yarns used in the Muromachi period and earlier were replaced by the untwisted floss found in Chinese work of that time. Momoyama embroidery is remarkable for its profusion of plant motifs and its lush texture, so thickly and densely packed that the forms seem padded. This is accomplished in long float stitches (*watashi nui*) of untwisted floss anchored to the base fabric only at the edges of the embroidered shape. Only at these points do the embroidery yarns appear on the reverse of the fabric, thus creating a dotted outline of the design on the obverse. Yarn of a contrasting color—often no more than a single strand—used to depict the veins of a leaf, the stamens of a cherry blossom, or the feathers of a quail, may serve as couching, holding down the float stitches at intervals, but floats two or more centimeters long attached only at their end points are not uncommon.[19]

In contrast with Ming Chinese practice, sixteenth-century Japanese embroiderers did not use metallic embroidery floss (threads wrapped in gold or silver leaf-covered paper) but frequently filled the spaces between embroidered motifs with *surihaku* (rubbed leaf) for a more subtly gleaming effect. (Decoration that consists solely of embroidery with rubbed metallic leaf is called *nuihaku*.) Neither *watashi nui* nor *nuihaku* is included in the Nomura Collection. Many but not all of the extant examples have been handed down as Nō costumes.

Edo Period Embroidery

By the end of the Momoyama period embroidered forms had shrunk to the small-scale motifs seen in Colorplates 5–9. The float stitch (*watashi nui*) gradually fell into disuse, and the tighter satin stitch (*hira nui*) and long-and-short stitch, which pass across the reverse as well as the face of the fabric, filled in the shapes of the flowers, leaves, birds, and auspicious symbols common to embroidered *kosode* of the Edo period (1615–1868).[20] These, like Momoyama embroideries, were executed primarily with untwisted silk yarns; twisted yarns rarely recur before the mid- to late Edo periods. During early Edo metallic embroidery thread came into use. Because it could not be passed through the cloth without damage, it was always laid on top of the fabric and couched down at intervals with silk thread. In the early years of the seventeenth century metallic threads were used sparingly, usually only one or two threads couched together; Colorplate 8 illustrates this early style with stems and leaves of bamboo and mandarin orange delicately outlined with gold thread. Colorplates 20, 26, 29, 32, and 33, from the mid-Edo period, display a much more luxuriant use of gold, with thread after thread couched side by side for the richest possible effect.

TSUJIGAHANA: A COMBINATION OF TECHNIQUES

The word *tsujigahana* conjures up images of white flowers floating on a dark background, of trees and grasses delicately painted in ink, of insect-bitten leaves and dew-laden camellia blossoms modelled with ink shading. It is one of Japan's finest and most distinctive contributions to the textile arts—not a particular technique but a number of techniques in the service of a unique aesthetic.

Shibori is the primary means of creating *tsujigahana*, supplemented most often by free-hand painting (*kaki-e*) in ink or cinnabar and by metallic leaf, less frequently by embroidery. Secondary, dark, and cool colors predominate: much green, both light and dark; purple; light and dark blue. Red is the exception rather than the rule, in direct contrast with contemporary *nuihaku* robes. Motifs are overwhelmingly floral, often in combination with geometric forms. The three *tsujigahana kosode* in Colorplates 1 and 2 illustrate a number of these features.

Tsujigahana was usually applied to plain-weave *nerinuki* silk. Sometimes figured satins or twills were used, but their textured surfaces obscure delicate ink painting and disrupt the cohesiveness of *shibori* designs. Furthermore, the richness of these surfaces, especially satin, conflicts with the impression of lightness conveyed by the best *tsujigahana*.

The reader should keep in mind that what we now call *tsujigahana* may bear little or no relation to what was originally meant by that word.[21] Yamanobe Tomoyuki, the eminent textile authority, has pointed out that the name *tsujigahana* was probably first applied during the Meiji period (1868–1912) to the sixteenth-century textiles described above and illustrated in Colorplates 1 and 2, left. No prior records mentioning *tsujigahana* can be connected to any extant garments. What evidence we have for the nature of *tsujigahana* is indirect, disconnected, and contradictory.

Painted handscrolls of the twelfth century, such as *Shigisan engi emaki* and *Ban Dainagon ekotoba*, depict commoners wearing boldly patterned *kosode*.[22] Some appear to be of woven checks, but most were probably dyed using basic resist techniques, including *shibori*. Some Japanese scholars trace the origins of *tsujigahana* to the lower classes.[23] They argue as evidence that *shibori*, as the most elementary method of resist dyeing, was probably employed by the lower classes since early times; that stiff bast-fiber fabrics did not lend themselves to elaborate woven patterns; that complex woven or embroidered patterns required more time and skill than the lower classes disposed of; and, in conclusion, that it was natural for the poor to employ simpler means of decoration.

But the only convincing pictorial evidence for the use of *tsujigahana* by commoners is the screen painting *Maple Viewing at Takao* by Kanō Hideyori, usually dated to the second half of the sixteenth century.[24] The screen shows two groups of commoners, men and women, drinking *sake*, making music, dancing, and enjoying the brilliance of the maple leaves. Both the woman at the far right of the right-hand group and the man in the center of the left-hand group appear to be wearing *kosode* of dark red or purple decorated with patterns of white flowers. Although paintings afford uncertain evidence for textile techniques (as opposed to motifs, designs, or colors), these two garments are so similar to the purple-ground *tsujigahana kosode* shown in Colorplate 1, left, that they may well have been intended as depictions of what we know as *tsujigahana*. Furthermore, the wistaria pattern clearly visible on the female figure is so common in extant examples of *tsujigahana* as to lend considerable credence to this interpretation.

Of the many literary references to *tsujigahana* only one, a fourteenth-century poem about a woman of Katsura (*Katsura no onna*) connects it with the lower classes.[25] The poem reads:

Haru kaze ni	In the spring wind,
wakayu no oke o	Holding
itadakite	A bucket of sweetfish,
tamoto mo tsujiga	Bending the flower
hana o oru ka na.[26]	On her sleeve of *tsujigahana*.

If we accept the translation given above, the poem tells us only that *tsujigahana* was worn by commoners at the end of the fourteenth century; it does not tell us what kind of fabric was meant by the term.

Paintings such as the *Kasuga Gongen reigenki emaki* (dated to 1309) attest that the upper classes also wore elaborately dyed fabrics, and literary sources of the fifteenth, sixteenth, and early seventeenth centuries associate *tsujigahana* with the military aristocracy, not with commoners.[27] All of these literary sources, however, describe garments quite other than what we today know as *tsujigahana*. First, they speak of *tsujigahana*-decorated *katabira* (an unlined summer garment, usually of ramie). But not a single extant *tsujigahana* garment is a *katabira*, suggesting that whatever these early sources meant by *tsujigahana*, it was not what we mean by it. Furthermore, a number of the medieval documents also associate *tsujigahana* with the color red, and we have seen that red is atypical among the textiles now known as *tsujigahana*. Finally, although bast fibers such as hemp and ramie, of which *katabira* are usually made, are not completely unsuitable to *shibori*, their stiffness does not lend itself easily to the finely detailed stitch resists (*nuishime shibori*) characteristic of *tsujigahana* as we know it today.[28]

A number of *kosode* and other garments in the decorative mode known today as *tsujigahana* have come down to us. These were originally owned by such sixteenth-century warlords as Uesugi Kenshin (1530–78), Toyotomi Hideyoshi (1536–98), and Tokugawa Ieyasu (1542–1616).[29] But none of these *tsujigahana* garments are *katabira*. Conversely, four *katabira* belonging to Uesusgi Kenshin survive, but none of them resemble what we call *tsujigahana*.[30]

The discrepancy between early references to *tsujigahana*, which associate it with red flower-patterned *katabira*, and the *shibori*-dyed silks we call *tsujigahana* today has not been adequately resolved by any of the current hypotheses. For the present the name remains a puzzle, but the works are nonetheless glorious.

PASTE RESIST

Paste resist is one of the four principal Japanese methods of resist dyeing, along with *shibori*, *kasuri* (ikat), and stencil dyeing. The use of paste-resist technique employing a stencil is exemplified in the Nomura Collection only in the form of stencilled *kanoko* (*kata-kanoko*).[31]

To create designs using paste as the resist medium, the basic technique is to make an underdrawing of the design on the fabric, apply the paste to the area to be reserved (whether design or background), and then apply the dye. There are several paste-resist processes, which vary more or less in the composition of the paste, the method of applying the paste and dye, and the exact steps of the dyeing process. Since the paste-resist technique best represented in the Nomura Collection is *yūzen* dyeing (*yūzen-zome*), it is this dyeing process that will be explained in detail below.

Yūzen Dyeing

We find the earliest references to *yūzen* dyeing (*yūzen-zome*) in late seventeenth-century sources. Kirihata Ken, in a study of early *yūzen* dyeing, quotes ten of these, some literary (such as the works of Ihara Saikaku), others reportorial in tone.[32] The *Genji hinakata*, a design book published in 1687, names twenty-seven different types of dyeing, attesting to the fever of dyeing activity and the wealth of techniques being explored at the time.[33] Among these is *yūzen* dyeing.

Since these early references provide few details of actual methods, much of our account of early *yūzen* dyeing techniques is based on current practices. With these in mind, the reader will better understand the salient characteristics of the earlier pieces as well. The *yūzen* process, then, as it is employed today, includes the following steps. First, the silk is stretched straight between tensors or lightly pasted to a board. Then the underdrawing is painted onto the white silk with a fugitive blue liquid derived from the flower (*aobana*) of the *tsuyugusa* (or *ōbōshibana*, bot. *Commelina communis*, a plant of the spiderwort family). This blue is easily rinsed away with water. Next, the underdrawing is traced over with narrow lines of resist paste, which protects the cloth beneath it from the dye and allows much less bleeding than the *shibori* process. The resulting sharp-edged fine white lines not only separate one color area from another but also impart a decorative quality of their own, which is as typical of *yūzen* dyeing as a softly blurred outline is of *shibori*. In Colorplate 42 these lines are clearly visible, detailing the pine and willow branches and the waves in the river and outlining each stone along the riverbank. Although the use of resist paste to create fine white lines is one of the most important characteristics of *yūzen* dyeing, this technique considerably antedates the emergence of *yūzen*, as a number of Muromachi and Momoyama examples show.[34]

The resist paste is composed primarily of glutinous rice. Today zinc dust is added to make it more visible to the craftsman; in the past fugitive reddish liquids extracted from sappanwood (*suō*) or purplish juices from beefsteak plant (*shiso*, bot. *Perilla frutescens* Brit., var. *crispa Decne.*) were used for this purpose. The paste is applied much like decorative frosting to a cake, squeezed from a cone of heavy paper that is permeated with water-resistant persimmon tannin and sometimes tipped with a small metal nozzle. (The dark brown paper is the same as that used for making stencils.) Resist paste may also be applied with a pointed stick; this produced a finer line than the tube method but is no longer practiced today.

When the paste has dried, the entire surface of the cloth is brushed with *gojiru*, a liquid extracted from soybeans that have been presoaked in water. This inhibits the bleeding of the dyes as they are brushed on the cloth. After allowing the *gojiru* to dry, the dyer brushes the coloring medium (*iro-sashi*) onto the design outlined on the silk, which has been attached to bamboo tensors and placed over a small charcoal brazier to speed drying of the colors. He uses a small, flat brush cut at an angle or a soft-pointed calligraphy brush. The pattern areas are then thickly covered with a slightly different rice paste containing lime and salt, and the dye for the background color brushed over all with a thicker brush (*hiki-zome*). Several applications may be necessary to achieve the desired shades in both design and background, and each application is allowed to dry before the next is applied. Mordant may be brushed on before, after, or between applications of color, depending on the chemical properties of the dye being used. Madder red (*akane iro*), for example, takes better on premordanted cloth, whereas sappanwood red (*suō*) should be mordanted between coats of dye. During the seventeenth century brush dyeing came to replace most dip dyeing. Since brush dyeing did not soften or dissolve resist paste, as did long or repeated immersions in a dye bath, it permitted many more colors and shades to be used in a design.

The crisp outlines and sharply defined color areas produced by *yūzen* dyeing were particularly suited to the detailed pictorial themes that came into favor at this time. In addition, repeated sumptuary prohibitions of gold embroidery and overall *kanoko* designs further stimulated the development of *yūzen* dyeing.

At the completion of dyeing the fabric is steamed, which sets the protein, esters, and calcium in the *gojiru*, thus rendering the dyes fast. All the resist paste is then carefully washed off in cold water, and the fabric is blocked into its original shape (crepe, the fabric most commonly used for *yūzen* dyeing, loses its shape easily when damp). Final details are added in embroidery and pigments.

A book of *yūzen* designs published in 1688, *Gosho imayō yūzen hiinagata* (called *Yūzen hiinagata*), describes in its introductory notes a number of features of early *yūzen* dyeing.[35] It is apparently the only early source to remark on contemporary techniques. The author notes first of all that the designs are "according to one's taste". This refers not only to the great variety of themes found in *yūzen* dyeing but, more importantly, to the complete freedom of expression in design and execution. Woven polychrome designs were subject to the rectilinear limitations of warp and weft and, like polychrome *shibori*, were exceptionally difficult to do, but the *yūzen* dyer could employ ten colors as easily as two. Calligraphic line quality and painterly shading of tones, only approximated by embroidery, were facilitated by the *yūzen* technique, although it must be noted that in expressiveness of line *yūzen*, in which the colors are applied by brush within resist-paste outlines, could not equal freehand painting (see Cpls. 35, 36, 39, 40).

Next the *Yūzen hiinagata* describes two alternative methods of reserving the design area: one, applying resist paste over the underdrawing, which created sharply defined forms; the other, *shibori*, which left softly blurred edges. If *shibori* was used, the underdrawing was made afterward.[36] Then metallic leaf or *kanoko* (probably stencilled *kanoko*) was added, and the design brushed on in dyes and pigments. Here we have the defining characteristics of *yūzen-zome*: the use of resist paste and the brushing of the dyes onto the design (referred to as *e*, a picture). Fabrics with metallic leaf in combination with *yūzen* dyeing are rare. The famous *noshi kosode* (with a pattern of stylized strips of *noshi*, or dried abalone) once belonging to Nomura Shōjirō and now in the collection of the Yūzen Historical Society, Kyoto, displays both of these features, but it is of a much later period.[37] In modern *yūzen* dyeing with synthetic coloring mediums the pattern areas are brushed in first, then covered with resist paste, and finally the background color is brushed on. The *Yūzen hiinagata* indicates a different order: the reserving of the pattern areas with resist paste or *shibori*, then the dyeing of the background color, and finally the brushing in of the pattern.

Enumerating the virtues of *yūzen-zome*, the *Yūzen hiinagata* mentions that fabrics of all types retain their softness after dyeing, and that the dyes remain fast in water. We can deduce from this that many dyeing processes in use at the time stiffened the fabric and/or were not colorfast.

Early *yūzen* dyeing was further characterized by shading (*bokashi*), of which the many-colored maple leaves in Colorplate 36 are good examples. This type of shading was executed with a flat brush; synthetic pigments are used for shading in present-day *yūzen* dyeing (and rarely elsewhere), but in the early pieces pigments and dyes may have been used interchangeably.[38] *Bokashi* is also the name given to the purple and blue inkblot-like spots on the same garment, but these were created by *shibori* and must have been dip dyed rather than brushed on.

The treasured dye safflower (J. *benibana*, bot. *Carthamus tinctorius*), one of several sources of vivid red, is conspicuous in many *yūzen*-dyed *kosode*, but only in the embroidery. Although frequently used for dip-dyed *kosode* (Cpl. 20), it cannot be employed in any paste-resist process, because the paste would disintegrate under the repeated immersions necessary to produce the characteristic rich red.[39] For areas of *yūzen*-dyed red color, other sources of red are employed.

On the basis of the early design books (*hiinagata bon*, the fashion magazines of Edo society) we can say that a number of motifs distinguished early *yūzen* design. Roundels, lozenges, poem papers, fans, and other framing devices were often scattered over the surfaces of the *kosode*. These contained smaller motifs, especially flowers or plants but also utensils, landscapes, and subjects from classical literature. Many motifs, although simple visually, contained literary allusions, visual puns, or riddles.[40]

The term *yūzen* derives from the name of a fan painter active in Kyoto at the end of the seventeenth century. Contemporary sources, beginning with the novelist Ihara Saikaku (1642–93), note the activities of Miyazaki Yūzensai the fan painter and proclaim the popularity of his designs. These designs were first published in 1686 and 1687, not by Yūzensai himself but in books that presented them as "Yūzen-style".[41] In the following year a certain Yūjinsai Heki Tokueimon Kiyochika, apparently a student of Yūzensai, published the design book *Gosho miyako imayō yūzen hiinagata*, based, according to Yūjinsai, on the designs of Miyazaki Yūzensai.[42] Yūjinsai commends these designs as preserving the elegant traditions of the past while appealing to the most contemporary tastes. This encomium probably refers to Yūzensai's presentation of traditional motifs within framing devices, a composition clearly derivative from fan paintings. Kirihata observes that although Yūzensai relied heavily on literary and verbal allusions, his designs did not incorporate characters, which were so important a part of earlier, Kanbun era (1661–73), designs but which Saikaku had declared old-fashioned. Yūzensai himself, as far as we know, published only one book of *kosode* designs, *Yojō hiinakata* (*Yosei hiinakata*, 1692).

There is no evidence that Yūzensai pioneered *yūzen* techniques. On the contrary, many of these, as well as many of the characteristic motifs, were already in use prior to his time. It was more likely his particular aptitude for design that drew attention to his work, and the combination of certain techniques with his designs became known as *yūzen* dyeing (*yūzen-zome*). Eventually these dyeing techniques themselves came to be called *yūzen*.

The earliest example of *yūzen* dyeing of known provenance is a hanging scroll that depicts Murasaki Shikibu, author of the *Tale of Genji*, at Ishiyamadera. The scroll, in the collection of the Tokyo National Museum, is inscribed "Fifth year of Kyōho [1720], in Kaga".[43] Other contemporary sources confirm that *yūzen* dyeing was produced in Kaga Province, present-day Ishikawa Prefecture, during the same period that Miyazaki Yūzensai's designs were all the rage in Kyoto. Kaga *yūzen* (also called Kaga-*zome* or *okuni-zome*) reportedly featured intricate patterns dyed in many colors, but the attributes of early Kaga *yūzen* and its relation to the development of *yūzen* dyeing in Kyoto are not clear. What is today called Kaga style *yūzen* features highly contrasting deep colors such as purple, green, deep red, and blue; purple and light blue *shibori* areas resembling inkblots and extensive use of shading are also typical. The maple-leaf-trellis *kosode* in Colorplate 36 clearly illustrates these features. The overwhelming majority of extant early *yūzen kosode* display similar characteristics, but it is unlikely that all were in fact produced in Kaga. Since the meaning of "Kaga *yūzen*" is uncertain, the term is best avoided. The earlier distinctions among polychrome dyeing methods that utilized resist paste applied freehand are now subsumed under *yūzen* dyeing.

Chaya-zome

Chaya-zome, or *chaya-tsuji*, refers to a dyeing technique employed for summer *katabira* made of fine ramie, in which extremely detailed designs were executed in indigo on a white background (Cpls. 44, 45). Although the term is associated with a Kyoto dyer of the seventeenth century, Chaya Sōri, no examples survive from that time and we have no idea of the characteristics of this early *chaya-zome*. Most if not all of the extant pieces date from the eighteenth century or later. *Chaya-zome* employs resist paste, much like *yūzen* dyeing, but the process differs in several important respects: (1) the resist paste is applied to the background, leaving the pattern areas exposed to the dye; (2) to protect the pristine whiteness of the background, the paste must be applied to both sides of the fabric, and the outlines of the resisted areas must match perfectly on face and reverse; (3) the pattern is invariably vat dyed, not brushed, because the chemical properties of indigo make it difficult to achieve even color with brush dyeing.

The *katabira* in Colorplates 44 and 45 is dyed two shades of indigo; after several dippings in the dye bath the areas intended to be light blue are covered with paste, and the cloth is again immersed repeatedly until the desired darker blue is obtained. The fine blue-and-white stripes that make up the roofs of buildings and the brushwood fences in Colorplate 45 may have been achieved by etching through the paste with a sharp tool. The even finer blue lines depicting fishnets, planks of bridges, and hillocks of snow were drawn in after dyeing with indigo wax, which is pigmentized indigo in crayon form. Under close examination its color can be seen to be muddier, even a shade greener, than the blue of the vat-dyed indigo areas. Sometimes pale yellow is applied to parts of the background, probably with a brush, as in Colorplate 45. In addition, there are often discreet touches of embroidery in colored silks and gold couching.

Chaya-zome cannot be duplicated today, for the composition of the rice paste has become a mystery. It must be adhesive enough to withstand repeated immersions in the indigo vat without any bleeding of the dye at the edges of the resisted areas, but it must also remain moderately flexible, so that it does not crack. The paste application alone must have taken months for the finer pieces. Clearly these were luxury garments affordable only by the wealthy, and in general they seem to have been worn by women of the military elite as summer *kosode*. It has been said that the wearing of *chaya-zome katabira* was restricted to the women of the six provincial branches of the Tokugawa house, but this has not been documented.[44]

Chapter 5
EARLY KOSODE DESIGN:
LATE MUROMACHI AND EARLY MOMOYAMA

MOMOYAMA TASTE

For a century after the conclusion of the Ōnin War in 1477 Japan continued to be torn by conflicts among powerful feudal barons, and the period is aptly referred to by Japanese historians as *sengoku jidai*, "the era of the country at war". In Kyoto the impoverished throne continued to exist, as did the Ashikaga shogunate which had governed Japan, at least nominally, since 1336, but both had become virtually powerless. Centralized government disintegrated, and the provincial clans that grew to power far from Kyoto fought each other to the knife for control of the country.

By the latter part of the sixteenth century the number of contending daimyo had greatly diminished, and unification under a strong, centralized military leadership was under way. The first of the three great military leaders who ultimately reduced Japan to order and rule was Oda Nobunaga (1534–82); his deposition of the last Ashikaga shogun in 1573 marks the beginning of the Momoyama period (1573–1615).[1] Neither Nobunaga nor his general and successor, Toyotomi Hideyoshi (1536–98), took the title of shogun. That remained for Tokugawa Ieyasu (1542–1616) in 1603. Ieyasu's final victory in 1615 over a great coalition of rivals, including Hideyoshi's son and his adherents, marks the political end of Momoyama and the beginning of the Edo period.

The new military aristocracy spawned by the wars brought a new aesthetic to Japan. These were self-made men, confident and aggressive. Their tastes ran as much to bold forms, brilliant colors, and rich textures as to the restraint, astringency, and understatement that had permeated Muromachi style. Nobunaga's castle at Azuchi, on the shore of Lake Biwa near Kyoto, was the first example of a new type of architecture and the major source of a new style in the visual arts. The seven-story edifice, begun in 1576 and completed in 1579, contrasted sharply with earlier secular architecture, in which smaller, brighter rooms had permitted a more intimate display of subtler art works. The new structures combined the functions of fortress and grand residence, and the decoration of their vast, dark halls required bold forms, large formats (sliding screens, wall panels, folding screens, and coffered ceilings), and a lavish use of color on gold leaf, not only to demonstrate the wealth of their patrons but to reflect the gleam of lamplight in dark spaces. Kanō Eitoku (1543–90), one of the greatest painters of the period, painted screens for Nobunaga in 1574, as well as murals in Azuchi Castle. After Nobunaga's assassination he painted for Hideyoshi at Osaka Castle. Neither Azuchi nor Hideyoshi's three castles long survived their masters, but in the folding screen of cypresses (in the Tokyo National Museum), attributed to Eitoku, sweeping brushstrokes of thick, rich color create bold forms outlined against a gold-leaf background. These paintings exemplify the new spirit of the Momoyama age.

The dualism of Momoyama taste, found in the contrast between castle halls and tea huts, is equally apparent in the other arts. Neither the Nō theater nor the tea ceremony were new in Momoyama, but both were taken up with unbounded enthusiasm by the military elite and molded by its taste. The gorgeousness of castle decoration had its parallel in Nō costumes, just as the refinement of the tea ceremony is also embodied in the delicate designs of *tsujigahana*.

DESIGN COMPOSITIONS

Textile arts reached their zenith in the Momoyama period. By the end of the fifteenth century *kosode* had emerged as standard dress for all classes and both sexes. Unlike the voluminously folded outer robes of earlier times, the simple shape and plane surface of the *kosode* made a natural field for elaborate designs, thus stimulating important developments in the textile arts, both in technique and in decorative style. Late Muromachi and early Momoyama *kosode* design employs two basic compositional types: (1) motifs more or less evenly disposed over the whole garment, and (2) the division of the *kosode* surface into fields, each of which might be embellished with contrasting smaller motifs.

Allover patterns (Cpl. 9) originated in the woven repeat patterns (*yūsoku moyō*) used in the clothing of the court aristocracy from Heian times onward. They might densely cover the fabric, or they might be freely but evenly scattered over its surface, leaving considerable background visible. The purple-background *tsujigahana kosode* (Cpl. 1, left) and the white *tsujigahana kosode* with painted grapevines and *shibori*-dyed lozenges, illustrated in Colorplate 2, left, are good examples of this latter type.

Kosode in which the decoration occupies distinct compartments were worn at least as early as the beginning of the fourteenth century. In the *Kasuga Gongen reigenki emaki* a sleeping woman wears a white *kosode* decorated in red across the shoulders and at the hem.[2] The red areas have undulating borders and are sometimes described as a shoreline or tide-pool form (*suhama*), sometimes as a cloud form. This decorative mode, known as *kata-suso* (shoulder-and-hem), probably has a practical origin: when the *kosode* was worn as an undergarment, all that would be seen of it was the hem (when the wearer moved) and the shoulders (when the outer robe was slipped down, as we see it elsewhere in the same scroll). Other modes of compartmentalized design probably originated in equally practical considerations: when prominent areas of a *kosode* became worn, the garment was taken apart and the worn areas exchanged with less worn, less conspicuous parts of the same garment. What had begun as thrift continued as style. Extant garments of the period as well as those seen in numerous sixteenth-century portraits exhibit sleeves differing in fabric or decoration from the body (*sode-gawari*, exchanged sleeves), right side differing from left (*katami-gawari*, exchanged halves), or broad horizontal bands or checkerboard blocks of different patterns (*dan-gawari*, alternating bands).

The *tsujigahana kosode* in Colorplate 1, right, appears to be of *dan-gawari* type, although the brown-and-white checked band has been pieced into the whole and we do not know the original composition of the *kosode*. The red-and-white *tsujigahana kosode* patterned with camellias and Chinese bellflowers (Cpl. 4) is also a version of *dan-gawari* composition.[3] Horizontal compositions or stripes are typical of *kosode* design during late Muromachi and early Momoyama. Vertical elements are deemphasized, imparting an air of majestic stability and repose to the figure of the wearer. This dominant horizontality breaks down at the beginning of the seventeenth century, when diagonal and vertical elements introduce a new dynamism into *kosode* design.

MOTIFS

In late Muromachi and throughout Momoyama the popular *kosode* motifs were primarily botanical. Lozenge and diaper patterns sometimes appear as a foil to flowers and plants, but less often than in later eras. Animals and birds occur infrequently. Although some motifs, such as the phoenix in a paulownia tree, derive from Chinese prototypes, and the grapevines seen in Colorplate 2 owe their popularity to Japanese fascination with this exotic, most of the motifs in this period reflect the foliage of Japan's changing seasons.

Men's and women's garments were not clearly differentiated by color, motif, or design. According to the Jesuits who came to Japan in the latter half of the sixteenth century, men and women alike wore bold patterns and bright colors and there was little if any distinction according to age or class.[4] Although almost all of the *kosode* in the Nomura Collection are said to be women's garments, delicate *tsujigahana* like that seen in Colorplates 1–4 occurs frequently on robes belonging to men and in portraits and other paintings of men as well as women.[5]

EMBROIDERED DESIGNS

*K*osode design of the late Muromachi period, after the Ōnin War had disrupted Kyoto's weaving industry, exploited the arts of the embroiderer and dyer. Necessity, however, was not the only inspiration: embroidery's relative ease of execution, the freedom of expression it permits, and the example of embroidered fabrics imported from Ming China in the sixteenth century all contributed to its popularity and inspired Momoyama artisans to create a characteristically Japanese form. As in other mediums, generous, large-scale designs are typical of the period, carried out in long, loose stitches of untwisted silk floss that form a soft, glossy padding on the surface of the cloth. Red was by far the most popular color for embroidery; as many as three shades of safflower red (*beni*) might be used in a single *kosode*.

EMBROIDERY AND METALLIC LEAF DESIGNS

*M*omoyama embroidery is quite different in feeling from its Ming prototype, which employed a considerable amount of twisted yarns as well as gold and silver threads made of silk yarn wrapped with thin strips of metal-leafed paper.[6] Whether Japanese artisans had not yet mastered the art of making leaf-wrapped thread or Momoyama taste rebelled at the flashiness of metallic yarns, gold and silver threads are not found in sixteenth-century Japanese embroidery. Instead, *kosode* makers enriched their embroidered and *shibori*-dyed designs with the subtler sheen of applied metallic leaf. Because metallic leaf is difficult to apply to areas wrinkled by the *shibori* process, it is more often seen with embroidery alone. This combination—embroidery with metallic leaf, called *nuihaku*—was extremely popular and forms one of the two principal decorative modes of early Momoyama *kosode*. Early examples of *nuihaku kosode* show a passion for total ornamentation, with gold or silver leaf filling all the areas between heavily embroidered motifs. *Kosode* solidly paved with decoration in this manner came later to be called *ji-nashi* (without background).

At first *nuihaku kosode* were apparently worn mainly by women.[7] Their gorgeousness, however, recommended them as costumes for the Nō drama, and doubtless they appealed to the ostentatious tastes of Nō's military patrons. Until the late fifteenth century costumes worn on the Nō stage were usually presented to the actors by their patrons from their own wardrobes. This practice continued during the sixteenth century, while at the same time the conventions of Nō costumes gradually evolved, with particular types of fabrics and designs becoming appropriate to each role.[8] Possibly because the brilliantly colored, gold-enriched *nuihaku kosode* made their way so readily into theatrical wardrobes, relatively few have come down to us as everyday apparel. There are none in the Nomura Collection, although this may be due more to Nomura's greater interest in dyeing than to the scarcity of *nuihaku kosode*.

Later Muromachi and Momoyama *nuihaku kosode* show a more sophisticated application of metallic leaf, employing stencils to create delicate patterns. Due to the fragility of the leaf itself, and to the fact that the medium with which it was applied has grown brittle with age, much of the original leaf has fallen off early *kosode*, leaving traces that can be seen only with a magnifying glass. In Colorplate 6, a detail of a late Momoyama *kosode*, bits of gold leaf are barely visible on the black background, which was once covered with evenly spaced horizontal lines of leaf in the so-called mist (*kasumi*) pattern. Gold leaf commonly rendered the small repeat motifs also seen in the woven silks of earlier periods, but there is at least one piece, decorated in leaf alone (*surihaku*), whose design is on the generous scale associated with early Momoyama.[9]

TSUJIGAHANA DESIGNS

Tsujigahana design shares with early *nuihaku kosode* certain formal similarities: the rendering of natural motifs as decorative patterns and the division of the background into contrasting pattern fields. In effect, however, they are markedly different, with *tsujigahana* offering a light crispness in place of the heavy luxuriance of embroidery and metallic leaf. What we now call *tsujigahana* flowered during the early years of the sixteenth century and was produced only until the beginning of the seventeenth. The earliest dated examples are the temple banners of 1528–30,[10] but their combination of *shibori* with silver leaf suggests that they were not among the earliest attempts at a new genre but represent some intermediate stage. *Shibori* is the essential and sometimes the sole technique of *tsujigahana*, but it is also found in combination with painting; with gold or silver leaf; with metallic leaf and painting; and with painting, leaf, and embroidery.[11]

Two of the five examples of *tsujigahana* in the Nomura Collection are decorated with *shibori* alone (Cpls. 1, left, and 4, left). The purple-background *kosode* with white flowers in Colorplate 1 represents the most easily executed form of *tsujigahana*, the pattern reserved in white against a dyed background. Similarly patterned *kosode*, which appear to be *tsujigahana*, are depicted in the late Muromachi period painting *Maple Viewing at Takao*.[12] The *tsujigahana kosode* in Colorplate 4, left, also employs *shibori* alone, but is far more complex in both technique and design. Here *shibori* is used in two different ways: to separate the red background areas from the white, and to separate pattern from background. The latter can be done by reserving either pattern or background, and Colorplate 4 demonstrates both procedures. Chinese bellflowers are reserved against undulant bands of red (now mostly faded to brown), using capped (*bōshi*) *shibori* and stitch-resist (*nuishime*) *shibori*; these are the primary *shibori* methods used in *tsujigahana*. To dye the camellias red and green against the white ground, however, required the protection of the entire background area from the dye, a much more difficult process. The touches of *kanoko* that decorate an occasional petal and form the dewdrops (or possibly insect holes) on the leaves likewise demonstrate a more subtle design sense as well as a more advanced skill.

Certain Japanese scholars hypothesize that *tsujigahana* fabrics with reserved designs, being the simplest to execute, were also the earliest, succeeded by those with reserved grounds.[13] Between the development of the reserved design and that of the reserved background fall those fabrics in which a reserved design on a dyed background is supplemented by painting in ink and small areas of color. Although this chronology may be correct, the scanty available evidence does not provide a firm basis for dating undocumented *tsujigahana* pieces. By the close of the sixteenth century, when both techniques had been mastered, they were employed simultaneously (Cpl. 4).

Two distinct styles of painting often seen in *tsujigahana* are perfectly illustrated in the Nomura Collection. In Colorplate 1, right, the camellias and wistaria represented in the lower band have been reserved in white against a green background, with additional color and ink applied by hand. The camellia blossoms and some of the leaves were outlined in ink with a fairly even line; then shading was added to some of these forms, again in ink, to bring them into shallow relief. The even ink outline and the precise, schematic shading create a highly stylized representation, tightly and almost mechanically painted, with no freedom of expression evident in the ink line or the forms.

This style of representation is seen also in a body of paintings, primarily handscrolls, executed in black ink and occasional touches of pigment on white and known as *hakubyō-e* (paintings on white).[14] These, executed from the late Kamakura through the Edo periods, usually illustrate the *Tale of Genji* or other classical narratives (*monogatari*). Like their subjects, their style derives from the brilliantly colored *yamato-e* handscrolls of the Heian period (794–1185). Their narrative content requires prominent depiction of the human figure, but gardens, flowering trees, and landscapes also play an important role, evoking the changing seasons and the emotions associated with them in Japanese poetry. In one scroll, the *Hakubyō Genji monogatari emaki*, dated to 1554, wistaria and various autumn flowers and grasses are depicted in *hakubyō* technique. Here the shading of the leaves and even the dewdrops closely resembles that seen in the Nomura fabric (Cpl. 1, right) and in numerous related examples of *tsujigahana*.[15] Although in the Nomura piece only the camellias are heightened with ink, many other *tsujigahana* fabrics display chrysanthemums, wistaria, and other flowers as well as camellias in the same technique.[16] Dewdrops are also clearly visible in another painted handscroll, the *Matsuhime monogatari emaki*, dated to 1526.[17]

The flowers and leaves depicted in *hakubyō* style, with its heavy black shading and frontally displayed forms, suggest not so much real plants as highly stylized ones carved in shallow relief. Camellias depicted in shallow relief appear frequently in lacquer and lacquered carved wood in the Kamakura-*bori* style —notably cosmetics boxes and portable cases for books of the Kamakura (1185–1333) and Muromachi (1333–1573) periods.[18] This kind of representation derived from Chinese prototypes, as did that of insect-bitten leaves, which reached Japan from China in the bird-and-flower paintings of the Southern Song dynasty (1127–1279).[19] These elements seem to have been incorporated into *hakubyō* painting at least by the early years of the sixteenth century and adapted to textile decoration by 1566.[20]

The relationship between *hakubyō* paintings and the painting in *hakubyō* style that embellishes *tsujigahana* textiles is unclear. Some *hakubyō-e*, the *Hakubyō Genji monogatari emaki*, for example, are known to have been copied from older scrolls as a pastime, but it is unlikely that the freehand painting in *tsujigahana* was done by amateurs.[21] Professional painters, not necessarily highly skilled, probably painted the stylized and rather mechanical flowers and foliage found in *tsujigahana*. Certainly a close connection exists between *hakubyō* painting and the flowers, insect-eaten leaves, and dewdrops carefully shaded in ink on the Nomura *kosode* and other *tsujigahana* fabrics, but the exact nature of that relation remains to be determined.

The second style of brushwork seen in *tsujigahana*, freer and more painterly, is exemplified in the fruit-laden grapevines and the little pine trees that ornament the white-ground *kosode* in Colorplates 2 and 3, right. The ink line, more fluid than in the *hakubyō* style, varies in thickness according to the pressure and angle of the brush; it conveys at the same time a vivid impression of the living plants and a vigorous expression of the artist's energy. The ink-wash shading is also more subtle, imparting a real sense of solid roundness to the clustered grapes and crisp texture to the broad leaves.

This style, when applied to the creation of paintings rather than the decoration of *kosode*, is called *suiboku-ga* (ink painting) and is directly related to the art of calligraphy. The brushes and ink used are identical, and the resulting line is similarly fluid and expressive. It is closely based on Song Chinese prototypes and reached its apogee in Japan during the Muromachi period, when Song models dominated Japanese art. The Momoyama period brought an increase in scale, with the typical Muromachi hanging-scroll format giving way to large screens and wall paintings. The style continued vital, in the hands of the same masters (Hasegawa Tōhaku, Kanō Eitoku, and Kaihō Yūshō, among others) who also created the brilliantly colored gold-leafed screens for which the period is known.[22]

It was natural that this complementary aspect of the Momoyama aesthetic should find a place, albeit a small one, in the textile arts as well. In the form of masks and temple banners, paintings on cloth have been handed down from the Nara period, preserved among the Shōsō-in treasures. But one of the most remarkable early items of painted *clothing* is a fourteenth-century divided skirt (*hakama*) dedicated to the Kumano Hayatama Shrine, Wakayama Prefecture, painted with plants and birds of the seashore.[23] In assurance and freedom of expression this is more than equalled by the grapevines and pines of the Nomura *kosode*, probably the finest extant example of *suiboku-ga* style painting on a *tsujigahana* textile.[24] Although painting as a textile art attained its ultimate verisimilitude of detail and refinement of color in the *yūzen* dyeing of the Edo period, it never again displayed the simplicity, freedom, and expressive vigor found in this *kosode*.

None of the *kosode* discussed above contains either foil or embroidery. Nomura may have felt that the lightness and delicate strength conveyed by *shibori* and ink painting better expressed the ideal qualities of *tsujigahana*. Motifs are primarily but not exclusively floral; fans, birds, and animals adorn some *kosode* and *kosode* fragments termed *tsujigahana* by leading scholars. But *tsujigahana* is not an exact term, and there are many *kosode* whose claim to be called by that name remains problematical.

Chapter 6
TRANSITION TO THE EDO PERIOD:
THE KEICHŌ STYLE

NEW FABRICS

As the sixteenth century drew to a close, *tsujigahana* began to yield to a new decorative mode in the textile arts. Perhaps the most important factor contributing to this development was the popularity of new fabrics introduced from China: figured satin and twill (*rinzu*, *mon aya*, and *saya*), and *chirimen* crepe.[1] For the delicate effects of *tsujigahana* and the heavy *nuihaku* designs of late Muromachi and early Momoyama, the even texture of *nerinuki* provided the perfect surface, but it stood stiffly away from the body in a manner reminiscent of the multilayered robes of earlier periods. With the increasing importance of the *kosode*, simple and narrow in form, the new fabrics, which draped softly over the body, acquired a special appeal. By the Tenshō era (1573–92) *chirimen* was woven for the first time at Sakai (although it was not widely used till the late seventeenth century). *Rinzu*'s softness and luster had more immediate appeal, and by the Keichō era it was being produced at Nishijin in Kyoto.[2]

NEW APPLICATIONS OF OLD TECHNIQUES

In *tsujigahana* designs *shibori* was the principal technique, supplemented by embroidery, painting, and metallic leaf, but in the new mode of decoration the versatility and lightness of *shibori* was much more equally balanced by the richness of embroidery and metallic leaf. *Shibori* became a means of defining areas to be decorated with embroidery or leaf rather than creating by itself, as in the earlier *tsujigahana*, the petals of a flower or the dewdrops on a leaf. Within this new balance of embroidery, leaf, and *shibori* the subtlety of ink painting was lost, and its role in *kosode* decoration declined. The better to set off the gleam of leaf and the bright colors of embroidery floss, backgrounds were often dyed a dark color such as purple (in many extant examples faded to walnut brown) or deep crimson.[3]

DATING

Later generations called this new mode the Keichō style, and the garments themselves Keichō *kosode* or Keichō-*gire* (cloth), after the Keichō era (1596–1615) when this new sensibility first made its appearance. Firmly dated examples of Keichō *kosode* are extremely rare, and genre paintings of the sixteenth and seventeenth centuries, which so lovingly depict the details of *kosode* design, cannot be dated with any degree of precision. This precludes a documented chronology of the Keichō style. Nevertheless, within the Nomura Collection alone, a stylistic progression is perceptible, from *kosode* that clearly reflect early Momoyama features to others that anticipate the so-called Kanbun style.[4] Even though features characteristic of several putative stages often coexist within one garment, making it impossible to put the extant examples into unequivocal sequence, we can still infer a stylistic order, from the mature Keichō style to those pieces closest to the succeeding Kanbun style. The Keichō era is conventionally considered as a part of Momoyama cultural history, but the

Keichō style probably persisted well into the Kan'ei era (1624–44) of the Edo period.[5]

Among the meager dated material is a portrait of the wife of Shinohara Kazutake, dated to 1598, which shows her wearing a *kosode* divided into areas of gold-patterned crimson and other areas of ink-painted designs on undyed ground. There is also a priest's stole (*kesa*) made from a woman's *kosode*, which depicts fan shapes filled with embroidered flowers and surrounded by metallic-leaf motifs; this was probably dedicated to Zuisen-ji in Kyoto in 1595, along with some examples of *tsujigahana*. Although we cannot reconstruct the entire *kosode* from this small fragment, we can infer that the Keichō style had reached its typical form by that date. The *kesa* and the portrait seem to represent an early phase of the new Keichō style. An altar cloth (*uchishiki*) made from fragments of a *kosode* in a more mature phase of the Keichō style was dedicated to Shinju-an, a subtemple of Daitoku-ji (Kyoto), in 1639. Of course, the *kosode* from which this altar cloth was made may have been much earlier in date, but stylistically it seems consistent with a late phase of the Keichō style.[6]

MAIN FEATURES OF THE KEICHŌ STYLE

The Nomura Collection, although it contains no *kosode* illustrating the very early stages described above, is rich in examples of the mature Keichō style and its transition to the succeeding style of the early Edo period (Cpls. 2 and 3, right; 4, right; 5–11; 13; 14). Three main features characterize the mature Keichō style, although not all three are unfailingly present in all examples: (1) the use of figured satin (*rinzu*) or other soft figured silk; (2) the division of the background into areas of black, red, and white by means of stitch-resist *shibori* (Keichō *kosode* are often referred to as Keichō *somewake*, or divided background); (3) complementary decoration of these areas with small motifs in embroidery and gold leaf and somewhat larger motifs in *kanoko* (fawn-dot) *shibori*.

Shibori and, to a much lesser extent, embroidery and leaf had been used to render *tsujigahana* designs, but in the Keichō style they are applied in a new manner and to very different effect. In *tsujigahana* stitch-resist *shibori* was used to divide the *kosode* into color fields for further decoration and also to define individual design motifs. In the Keichō style stitch-resist *shibori* serves primarily to define large, irregular color fields; for smaller-scale motifs such

as leaves, flowers, and trees *kanoko* is used. The entire surface (not merely certain details, as in *tsujigahana*) is then embellished with very small motifs in embroidery and gold leaf, completely filling the ground; hence this type of *kosode* was also called *ji-nashi*, "without background". Usually the gold leaf is confined to the black areas and the *kanoko* to the red; embroidery spans red and white fields and sometimes extends to the black as well.

Late Muromachi–early Momoyama designs are essentially two-dimensional. This quality is asserted by the surface interest of rich embroidery and gold leaf, by the close juxtaposition of patterns, and by the random placement of scattered motifs, which denies the potentially three-dimensional quality of the space.

The horizontality that dominated sixteenth-century *kosode* design gives way to a more dynamic structure of diagonals and verticals. The predominantly rectilinear color fields typical of early Momoyama *kosode* have been transmuted into areas of irregular shape and size whose curvilinear outlines are reinforced by curvilinear embroidered or *kanoko* forms. These motifs are no longer neatly confined to a single color area but may spread organically over two or more, as if growing from one into the next. The stitch-resist *shibori* areas are abstract shapes suggestive of some generalized organic form such as a leaf or a wave, but the tiny embroidered motifs depict specific plants and birds. Disjunctions in scale among the areas defined by stitch-resist *shibori*, the patterns executed in *kanoko shibori*, and the smaller embroidered and metallic-leaf motifs create a suggestion of three-dimensional space.

There is a close correspondence between motif and technique in the Keichō style: stitch resist defines large abstract color areas, *kanoko* and embroidery depict medium-sized and tiny representational motifs respectively, and metallic leaf is used for small repeat, or diaper patterns. This usage contrasts with *tsujigahana* and *nuihaku* (embroidery and metallic leaf), in which these techniques are used freely throughout the design. The significant interplay of forms and decorative techniques in the new style is very different from that found in the more homogeneous stability of the earlier modes.

Visual Ambiguity

The counterpoint of *shibori*, embroidery, and metallic leaf is used to create not only a new sense of space but also a provocative ambiguity of form new in Japanese textile design. Deliberate ambiguity, exploited in the mid-and late Edo periods in the form of rebuses and riddles, appears for the first time as an important aspect of the Keichō style.

EXAMPLES FROM THE NOMURA COLLECTION

The mature Keichō style and its transition to the succeeding Kanbun style of the early Edo period are well illustrated in the Nomura Collection. Representative *kosode* are discussed here to demonstrate this stylistic progression. Two examples of the mature style embody the features described above. Colorplate 5 reveals certain affinities with *tsujigahana* sensibility—in the prevailing horizontality of the composition, emphasized by the irregular band of black across the shoulder area, and in the lightness of feeling lent by the buoyant pale blue and white cloud forms. Strong diagonals are present but are stabilized by the horizontal elements. The limited use of *kanoko shibori* also links this *kosode* with the earlier decorative mode. In the detail (Cpl. 6) we see clearly the busy counterpoint among the large abstract forms created by stitch-resist *shibori*, the fine pattern created by embroidery and gold leaf (traces of gold leaf are visible on the mountain-like black areas), and the separate, underlying pattern of key fret and plum blossom woven into the figured-satin ground. This lively interplay presents a marked contrast to the calm strength of earlier Momoyama design. The embroidered motifs are much smaller than those of the earlier period, but they utilize the same loose stitches of untwisted floss passing back and forth across the surface of the fabric, giving to these vegetal motifs a painterly feeling quite unlike the tightly stitched, precisely detailed quality of middle (1688–1781) and late (1781–1868) Edo embroidery. The divided ground (*somewake*) is very different from the compartmentalization of the early Momoyama period: the several color areas are irregular in size, shape, and placement. Straight lines are not entirely absent from the composition but are interrupted by other elements. And while the traces of gold leaf are restricted to the black areas, embroidery bridges the red and white. These flowers, plants, and trees, in themselves completely two-dimensional, cluster together in miniature landscapes given the illusion of depth by the overlapping *shibori* shapes. Precisely because a *scene*, and not simply a *pattern*, is implied, the disjunctions in scale are more disturbing than those in *tsujigahana* designs. The crenellated roundels (*yukiwa*, a conventionalized snowflake form) in pale blue, red, and white may be intended to represent winter in this depiction of the four seasons, for the flowers of spring, summer, and autumn abound.

Formal ambiguity makes its appearance here. In the detail seen in Colorplate 6, for example, the grotesque white form in front of the black triangle can be interpreted either as a cloud obscuring the base of the black mountain or as one of the curiously shaped rocks common in Ming Chinese landscape painting and in Japanese gardens. Seen as a rock, it provides a backdrop for the flowers and grasses bending in front of it. The white area at center right can be read as a cloud or as a pond whose bank is lined with pines and flowering shrubs. Such visual punning becomes more obvious in later examples.

In several respects the *kosode* in Colorplate 8 resembles that in Colorplate 5: the background is divided into color fields (here, black and red, with pale blue and white for secondary forms); the black and white *shibori* areas are abstract (although some suggest large leaves or plumes), while the embroidered motifs can be identified specifically; and the red grounds are decorated with embroidery and the black with gold leaf. But there are also significant differences, the most immediately apparent being the change in composition. A sweeping arc begins with the black sleeve at left, curves across the black neckband and continues downward and toward the left, following the two large white "leaves" and the black one below them in a dynamic arrangement of powerful curving diagonals. Except for the unobtrusive, delicately embroidered stems of the bamboo and the ribs of the fans, every form is curvilinear, the successive arcs of fans, black garment yoke, and "leaves" reinforcing each other. In purely formal terms this *kosode* is a vertical composition, best seen on a standing figure, while that in Colorplate 5 exhibits the calm horizontality of many sixteenth-century portrait paintings of seated figures.

Differences are also evident in individual design elements. *Kanoko* (used minimally in the *kosode* in Colorplate 5) plays an important role in decorating the surface in Colorplate 8. The embroidered motifs are larger here and somewhat more tightly worked, with more open space between them. Couched gold threads have been used with great restraint to outline many of the smaller motifs. It is often categorically asserted that gold thread was not used in embroidery of the Momoyama period; although it does not seem to be a feature of the compartmentalized designs typical of early Momoyama, it does occur in a number of examples of the Keichō style. The disjunction in scale is more conspicuous in Colorplate 8; the fans dwarf the bamboo and mandarin orange (*tachibana*), and all in turn are overpowered by the white and black plume-like shapes that may be intended as chrysanthemum leaves. Such disjunctions, in combination with the more open feeling, give a stronger sense of spatial depth, albeit a confused and inconsistent one.

These two examples from the Nomura Collection display between them the main features of the mature Keichō style: the use of figured satin (*rinzu*); division of the background into areas of red, white, and black; and complementary decoration of these areas with *kanoko*, embroidery, and metallic leaf. Secondary characteristics, including crowding of the surface with contrasting patterns, ambiguity of form, and disjunctions in scale, are also evident.

As the Keichō style approaches the early Edo aesthetic, the undecorated, open area between individual motifs continues to expand and is consciously used as a positive element of the design. Larger areas of white contribute to the lighter feeling. The black, red, and white background areas take on more concrete but still generalized forms, while spatial and formal ambiguity is deliberately exploited. Embroidered motifs increase in size, giving more weight to the meaning of each. Horizontal elements have disappeared from the design of the *kosode*, and curves, verticals, and diagonals determine the composition of the whole. Although at this stage *kosode* composition still appears without cohesion, some examples exhibit the beginnings of a pictorial approach to design in which the whole *kosode* is treated as a canvas unified by a strong central element. Another aspect of this unifying approach is evident in the use of auspicious themes based on certain combinations of motifs primarily Chinese in origin. In the early Edo period (1615–88) this preference for thematic unity engulfed the whole field of design: allusions to classical court literature, pictorial themes derived from Buddhist art, and themes associated with specific occasions or places joined auspicious motifs as topics for *kosode* decoration. The transition to this new mode can be glimpsed in the next four examples.

The *kosode* in Colorplates 7 and 9 are closely related to those in Colorplates 5 and 8, but the unadorned background area has increased considerably; the organic red, white, and black shapes are no longer merely surfaces on which to spread motifs but have become meaningful parts of the design. There is a tendency for one color to dominate, to be seen as the background, against which the other two colors as well as the embroidery, *kanoko*, and gold leaf are interpreted as pattern. But there is as yet no clear separation of background and pattern, a distinction that emerges with greater definition in the early Edo period. In the *kosode* seen in Colorplate 9 the black areas, which appear to be part of the background,

take on pictorial meaning as the form of a leaf or a rock emerges. There is increasing abstraction in the smaller forms defined by stitch-resist *shibori*, and a greater sense of design as an interplay of those abstract forms.

Formal and spatial ambiguity plays a role in both these examples of the Keichō style. In Colorplate 7 the paulownia blossoms and leaves depicted in *kanoko* beneath the large pine bough, also in *kanoko*, are shown hanging from the pine branch like wistaria, a common motif. Just as the black form immediately to their left can be seen either as background or as a leaf-shaped design element, the dripping blossoms read as both paulownia and wistaria. This equivocal rendering of forms becomes extremely popular in the later seventeenth century.

Shibori areas and embroidered motifs overlap so that one form, by covering another, appears to be in front of it, creating a three-dimensional effect. The disjunction in scale seen before is more skillfully employed here to convey a sense of objects in space: the two pairs of cranes and tortoises in Colorplate 7 are almost lost under the giant leaves and pendent blossoms, but the disproportion also makes them—especially the cranes surrounded by an empty red field—seem occupants of a distant world. The miniature embroidered pines on two white cloud-like areas at the left side are glimpsed as if through a window into a separate space, and yet the texture of the embroidery brings them back to the frontal plane of the *kosode* surface.

The *kosode* in Colorplate 10, by carrying further certain tendencies seen in the four *kosode* discussed above, presents the beginnings of a different sensibility and allies itself more obviously with the so-called Kanbun style, characterized by a single sweeping curve or diagonal from shoulder to hem, which was prevalent during the Kanbun era (1661–73) (Cpls. 16–20). Limiting the main color areas to black and white simplifies the composition; the surface seems to separate into white background and black pattern, with small embroidered pictorial accents. Although the black area is covered with the short gold-leaf hatchings called *kasumi* (mist) pattern, open space is a far more significant design element than in any *kosode* we have seen earlier. The whole surface is organized as a unified design based on one strong vertical form, which acquires added force from being rendered in black.

But this *kosode* stills falls within the broad boundaries of the Keichō style, although it seems to be a late example of that style. The black and white areas defined by stitch-resist *shibori* (*nuishime shibori*) have become completely abstract, allowing for a freer interpretation of the formal ambiguities they present. The bold black shape reads at first glance as an enormous tree, a pine from whose branches hang heavy clusters of wistaria and other flowering vines. Its lower quarter, however, becomes an inlet of the sea—on its right a white island bordered with bamboo and pines from which a solitary crane rises, on its left a pine-sheltered white beach fringed with blossoming cherry trees. Identical gold-leaf lines represent mist on the tree and ripples on the water. (The pine-sheltered shore, a recurrent theme in Japanese art, recurs in the Nomura Collection on an eighteenth-century *katabira* [Cpl. 37]). The marked increase in size of the individual embroidered motifs is a further indication that this piece is of somewhat later date than the four previous examples.

Thematic content links the five *kosode* thus far discussed with early Edo *kosode* design, in which a combination of images presented a particular theme, sometimes in the form of a rebus (see Cpl. 30). At the left side of the large white area in Colorplate 10 is a cluster of hexagonal forms embroidered in gold. This pattern is known as a tortoise-shell diaper (*kikkō*), from its resemblance to the markings on the shell of a tortoise. Crane, tortoise, bamboo, and pine—symbolic of endurance and long life —came into Japanese art from Chinese painting. Usually they were depicted in combination, although not always all four together; during the Momoyama period crane, tortoise, and pine constituted a popular theme in painting and the decorative arts. Their connotation of longevity must have made them especially appealing to the warlords who patronized the arts, men whose lives were continually at risk in battle and intrigue. In later periods these auspicious motifs were combined with others of Japanese origin and frequently employed in the decoration of *kosode*, especially those worn on felicitous occasions. The tortoise-shell diaper in this *kosode*, the miniaturized pairs of tortoises and cranes in Colorplate 8, and the bag of treasures painted on one of the fans in Colorplate 7 were perhaps included to emphasize the auspiciousness of the other motifs depicted and only secondarily for their design value.

Colorplate 11 represents another late variation of the Keichō style. The tricolor divided background, the contrast between the abstract forms of the *shibori* stripes and the specifically descriptive embroidered elements, and the use of gold leaf (now barely visible) on the black areas locate it within the Keichō tradition. But the strong verticality of the sawtooth bands, the clear spatial organization, and the increased size of the embroidered pines and tree peonies indicate a place at the end of this development,

even though this *kosode* is less suggestive of Kanbun style composition than some of the other pieces discussed above (Cpls. 7–10).

BLACK-BACKGROUND KEICHŌ KOSODE

A third group of *kosode* in the Nomura Collection is strongly akin to the Keichō style and parallels it in development but lacks one of its main features, namely, the division of the background into areas of black, red, and/or white by means of stitch-resist *shibori*. All *kosode* in this group have black backgrounds patterned in embroidery, metallic leaf, *kanoko*, and capped (*bōshi*) *shibori* and display most of the other characteristics of the Keichō style; I have termed them black-background Keichō *kosode* (Cpls. 4, right; 12; 2 and 3, right; 13). In spatial organization all but the first of these are closer to early Edo *kosode* design than the other Keichō *kosode* we have examined. A fifth example (Cpl. 14) reveals early Edo style composition, but the techniques employed relate it closely to this group.

The use of a plain-weave silk ground links the *kosode* in Colorplate 4, right, with early Momoyama; despite the overwhelming predominance of figured satin until the latter part of the seventeenth century, plain-weave silks continued to be used occasionally. This *kosode* also echoes early composition in its close and even distribution of embroidered flowers and *kanoko* cloud forms; there is no dynamic, no attempt to organize the space. Originally the entire black surface was covered with gold leaf in small repeat patterns, including mist, various diaper patterns, and overlapping circles, making it a typical *ji-nashi* (without background) *kosode*.

The *kosode* in Colorplate 12 is of figured satin (*rinzu*) and has small embroidered motifs and traces of gold leaf covering the entire black background in typical Keichō style. But the simple diagonal arrangement of the embroidered elements, so strongly emphasized by the woven bamboo fence reserved in capped *shibori* and *kanoko*, a motif not common in Momoyama design, is indicative of a later date.

By comparison, the black-background *kosode* in Colorplates 2 and 3, right, is much more complex in both composition and imagery. Here we can see the beginnings of pictorial treatment. Unlike the abstract *shibori* areas in more typical Keichō pieces, the large white shapes here are clearly recognizable as mountain, wave, and pine-bark lozenge (*matsu-kawa-bishi*). Formal ambiguity is more extreme here than in any preceding example: the white mountain at the upper right slopes down to become the crest of a wave, an image repeated in the lower half of the garment. The white areas thus represent both mountains and water. In addition, the pine-bark lozenge motif defined by the lower boundary between white and black areas not only outlines the mountain and wave forms but also hints at pines growing on the mountainside. There are traces of gold leaf, but it was sparingly applied.

This pine-covered mountain swept by waves represents an entirely new kind of thematic treatment. As Kirihata Ken has demonstrated in his commendable study of literary themes in Japanese textiles, the illustration of subjects from classical Japanese and Chinese poetry was not uncommon in Heian court costumes, but the practice seems to have died out in the Kamakura period.[7] By the second half of the seventeenth century literary allusions and written characters were again common in kosode designs, but evidence for their use between the end of the Heian period and that time is unclear. Besides this one, the earliest of its kind in the Nomura Collection, Kirihata has found only three examples of late Momoyama period textiles that illustrate literary themes.

The wave threatening to engulf the pine-mountain is an image found in two poems in Japan's best-known poetry anthology, the Kokinwakashū, compiled in 905:

Ura chikaku	The snow that falls
furikuru yuki wa	Near the shore
shiranami no	Looks as if the white waves
Sue no Matsuyama	Might cover
kosu ka to zo miru.[8]	Pine Mountain of Sue.

Kimi o okite	If I left you,
adashi kokoro o	Turning
wa ga motaba	My fickle heart elsewhere,
Sue no Matsuyama	Surely the waves would cover
nami mo koenamu.[9]	The Pine Mountain of Sue.

Sue no Matsuyama, Pine Mountain of Sue, was probably in Michinoku, the northernmost part of mainland Japan (Honshū), but its precise location is unknown.[10] The first poem is a nature simile: the snow swirling in the wind near the seashore looks like the waves of the sea rising so high as to cover even the famous Pine Mountain of Sue. In the second poem nature becomes a metaphor of the poet's constancy in love—a figure of speech no less familiar in Western languages. The image of waves sweeping over Pine Mountain of Sue (Sue no Matsuyama) recurs in later anthologies of Japanese poetry, and is alluded to as well in the Tale of Genji, a highly popular source of themes for kosode design in the late Edo period (1781–1868).[11]

The white mountain peak in the Nomura kosode suggests snow; so do the large kanoko roundels, whose shape very closely resembles the crenellated snowflake roundels (yukiwa) (cf. Cpl. 27) common in later seventeenth-century kosode design. The unsure outlines of these kanoko roundels probably reflect the dyer's inexperience at creating a snowflake shape in kanoko. In the conjunction of mountain, wave, and pine-bark lozenge lies the clue that this design represents Pine Mountain of Sue; the two snow images confirm us in reading it as a specific allusion to the first of the two poems quoted above. A more apt visualization of a theme is hard to imagine: the wave merging with the snow-covered mountain, the name of the mountain implied by the pine-bark lozenge outline, and the kanoko roundels suggesting falling snow—these are at once an unforced expression of the poem and a harmonious design.[12] The subtlety of this interpretation is necessitated by the ambiguity and allusiveness of the motifs, qualities central to Japanese literature since the Heian period, and to painting and architecture as well, but new to textile arts in the Keichō style.

The black-background kosode in Colorplate 13 retains the small-scale embroidered motifs, the filling of the entire surface with gold leaf, and the limited palette of the Keichō style, but, as in the two previous examples, capped (bōshi) shibori is used to create specific and recognizable forms. Here, not only shibori but also embroidery renders the crenellated snowflake roundels. The design is considerably simplified: the number of different motifs is sharply reduced, and although the background is covered with gold leaf in the mist (kasumi) pattern, it is not crowded with densely packed embroidered motifs creating an allover effect. A large area is left free of embroidery and shibori, and the verticality of the design is stressed by the triple row of flowering vine scrolls at the left. The composition is slightly weighted on this side, and although only a part of the garment is visible, it clearly displays the asymmetry that so strongly characterizes early Edo kosode design.

The last piece in this group (Cpl. 14) really belongs to the Edo period and will be discussed further in that context, but the means of rendering the design of giant blades of grass or bamboo leaves are typical of black-background Keichō kosode. The gold-leaf mist pattern covering the entire background, the small scale of the embroidered shapes relative to those in kanoko, and the limitation of the palette to black, white, red, gold, and touches of green are all familiar features. But there is no mistaking the emergence of a new style and a concept of pattern and background different from what preceded it. Here the *kosode* is treated as a canvas on which the pattern is painted in bold strokes. The background is not simple absence of pattern but a positive value in the composition: the unpatterned space (the area covered with gold leaf alone) is emphasized by the clear-cut asymmetry of the pattern, which in turn requires that space to set it off. The gold leaf, because it is not a part of the cloth itself, brings the background forward into the same plane as the pattern, creating an ambiguity seen in other Keichō *kosode*. But in Colorplate 14 this is the only ambiguity, and the gold leaf that creates it is so different in scale from the blades of grass that we continue to see it as background at the same time that we recognize it as pattern.

In the early years of the Edo period metallic leaf falls into disuse, that particular ambiguity disappears, and we see pattern clearly set upon background.[13] This in turn leads the way to a more literal form of pictorial representation that accompanies the development of *yūzen* dyeing and is the most pervasive trend in Edo *kosode* design.

Chapter 7
DESIGNS OF THE EDO PERIOD

THE YEARS OF TOKUGAWA RULE

After a century and a half of almost continual warfare the year 1615 ushered in an age of political stability that was to last nearly three hundred years. In that year the diminishing number of contenders for supreme power was finally reduced to one: Tokugawa Ieyasu. Having succeeded to power after Hideyoshi's death in 1598, Ieyasu defeated a vast coalition of enemies at the battle of Sekigahara in 1600, received the commission of shogun from the emperor in 1603, and made himself absolute ruler of Japan by destroying the last of Hideyoshi's family at Osaka in 1615. The village of Edo (present-day Tokyo) in eastern Japan, which was first one of Ieyasu's strongholds, after his victory at Sekigahara became his permanent headquarters and the seat of the shogunal government as well.[1] The 253 years during which Tokugawa Ieyasu and his descendants governed Japan are known as the Tokugawa or Edo period.

Ieyasu and his successors directed their civilian policies toward creating and maintaining a stable hierarchical society with themselves at its apex. The security of the government was construed as depending on the stability of society. It is significant that in many, if not most, Tokugawa edicts and directives the word *change* is an object of prohibition and a synonym for *revolt*.

To prevent change, Ieyasu and his successors proscribed Christianity, excluded foreign traders (save for a handful of closely confined Chinese and Dutch), and finally, in 1639, "secluded the country" against all foreigners and foreign influences. All domestic policy was directed to the same end. The division of classes—in descending order, samurai, farmers, artisans, and merchants—was made rigidly unbreachable and hereditary.[2] The samurai, now largely shorn of warlike employment, were removed from their domains to live on stipends in castle towns. The merchants and artisans in castle towns and commercial centers were made subjects of the shogunal government. The daimyo (great lords) were required to maintain establishments in Edo, to live there parttime, and to leave their families there as hostages when they returned to their domains.

These policies allowed the Tokugawa regime to maintain itself in power till 1868. They also allowed the foreign arts, ideas, and technical skills that had made their way into Japan during the late Muromachi and the Momoyama periods to mature into a culture distinctively Japanese. But they produced as well certain unanticipated and unwished-for results. Peace and order created conditions favorable to economic growth; agricultural production and domestic commerce increased markedly. But economic prosperity entailed proliferating luxuries and rising prices, and to the samurai, now living in towns on fixed incomes, it brought poverty and debt. So, too, did the obligation to spend time in Edo, which spurred social competition and conspicuous consumption. Even many daimyo lived perennially beyond their incomes. The government responded with repeated ineffectual sumptuary regulations designed to keep the samurai out of debt and all classes "in their places". Increasing economic distress and social unrest led to intermittent decrees cancelling all samurai debt to merchants. But the economic anomalies (as the government saw them) only worsened, and by the eighteenth century the financial power of the merchants was breaking down social constraints. By marriage, by the peculiarly Japanese custom of adoption, and by employment in government, merchant families were joining at least the lower ranks of the samurai class.

The flourishing economy created a growing class of townsmen (chōnin), comprising wealthy merchants, the artisans who produced the goods they sold, and entertainers (including actors, singers, and dancers). Inevitably, as the samurai grew poorer and the merchants and artisans richer, the patronage of art and luxury goods, literature and the theater began to shift from the samurai to the chōnin. Kyoto, the seat of the imperial court, was still the center of tradition and refinement, but the court, living on an allowance from the shogunate, was poor by comparison with the wealthy townspeople of Edo and Osaka. Although occupying the lowest level of the social order, the new, urban rich did not imitate the court aristocracy or the military elite but set a style of their own, in the enjoyment of which they were joined by those samurai who could afford it.

The principal scenes of the new culture were the licensed pleasure quarters—Yoshiwara in Edo, Shimabara in Kyoto, Shinmachi in Osaka. Sexual enjoyment was only one of the pleasures offered here; other attractions were theater, music, dance, dining and drinking parties, gambling, bathing, and the accoutrements of these activities, including beautiful clothes. Courtesans competed in elegance and wit and numbered among their clients the most modish and the most accomplished men of their day—novelists, poets, playwrights, painters, and print makers. Their records of this "floating world" (ukiyo), so called for the transience of its pleasures, express the daring and the vitality of urban culture in the Edo period.

STYLISTIC DIVERSITY IN THE VISUAL ARTS

The visual arts of the Edo period exhibit a number of most diverse trends. The Kanō school developed a distinctively Japanese fusion of Chinese style monochrome ink painting with the highly colorful traditions of yamato-e. This is a decorative style, characterized by bold forms, rich colors, energetic brushstrokes, and sweeping rhythms; we first saw it in the paintings of Kanō

Eitoku and Kaihō Yūshō in the Momoyama period. The ink paintings of the nanga, or bunjinga (literati painting), school, which drew their inspiration from Chinese literati painting of the seventeenth and early eighteenth centuries, offered an escape from the bourgeois values that informed chōnin culture.

The rimpa style, which might be called the later Japanese decorative style, originated in the collaboration of calligrapher Hon'ami Kōetsu (1558–1637) and painter Tawaraya Sōtatsu (?–1643?). In contrast with the Kanō decorative tradition, in which composition tends to be crowded, execution polished and representational, and motifs Chinese in origin, rimpa painting revived themes from the Japanese classical literature of the Heian and Kamakura periods and emphasized strongly asymmetric placement, liberal use of open space, and radical patternization of natural forms. The rimpa school takes its name (rin-pa) from the last syllable of the name of Ogata Kōrin (1658–1716), a later master who not only directly influenced kosode design but himself painted kosode in ink and colors.

Ukiyo-e, "pictures of the floating world", is usually associated in the West with woodblock prints. Originally a melding of many painting styles and techniques, it vividly depicted the pleasures of the urban world for the delectation of its inhabitants. Ukiyo-e artists paid great attention to surface detail and especially to clothing, whose rapidly changing splendors in the Edo period made it a most rewarding subject for popular art.

A literal realism influenced by Western works of art that trickled into Japan through the tiny Dutch settlement at Nagasaki is embodied in the Maruyama school. Its founder was Maruyama Ōkyo (1733–95), whose style influenced kosode design of the later Edo period and who himself made underdrawings for yūzen-dyed kosode.

William Watson has written that the style of the Kanō school of painting, by imposing on traditional elements a "characteristic pattern of curving masses and sweeping perspective alternating with passages of exquisite detail", epitomizes "the art of the new age in nearly all its forms, whether quintessential and expressive or craftsmanlike and repetitive".[3] This is true of the best design of the period, and especially of the textile arts of the seventeenth century—of the Kanbun (1661–73) and Genroku (1688–1704) eras. But by the second half of the eighteenth century strength of expression had faded from kosode design, and in general the best examples from the late Edo period consist solely of "passages of exquisite detail".

THE KANBUN STYLE

The Keichō style, as we have seen, evolved toward greater clarity of design, in which the *kosode* is treated as a single field patterned with one bold subject asymmetrically placed. The design as a whole is thematic, and often auspicious in meaning. The use of *shibori* to divide the ground into abstract shapes of various colors, which are then treated as background areas to be further decorated with embroidery, metallic leaf, and *kanoko*, has been largely replaced by *kanoko* alone, filling large, representational forms sometimes defined by stitch-resist *shibori*. Increasingly, the background is left unpatterned.

No sharp stylistic break divides the Keichō style from the succeeding Kanbun style, so called because it reached stylistic maturity during the Kanbun era (Cpls. 14–22). The new style is characterized principally by strongly asymmetric composition that utilizes the entire *kosode* as a single field of design. In back view one main pattern element extends from a sleeve across both shoulders and curves down the opposite side. Forms are large and bold and usually weighted on the right side of the design field. There is a clear opposition between background and pattern, with most backgrounds light (often white) in color. Pattern is executed in *shibori* and embroidery, including gold thread, while metallic leaf and painting (*kaki-e*) drop out of use. The design's theme is often a subtle allusion to a well-known episode in a classical narrative, a poem from one of the imperial anthologies, or a Nō play, with written characters from the text sometimes included. To maintain one's status as an urban sophisticate, it was essential to be able to identify such recondite allusions and rebuses. This literary pastime, a proof of stylish (if sometimes superficial) erudition, was not the preserve of the aristocracy—the townsmen were now its most enthusiastic devotees.

Design Books

In conjunction with thematic content there appears a tendency toward pictorial representation, which gains strength with the development of *yūzen* dyeing during the Genroku era (1688–1704). It is during this period that fashion as we know it (as opposed to style) comes into play for the first time. To define fashion as the prevailing custom in dress is inadequate, for fashion comprises an element of rapid change that implies both a strong desire to be up-to-date and a commercial exploitation of that desire, both of which involve a competitive spirit.

That spirit, which incited the nouveaux riches townspeople to vie passionately for the newest and best of everything, is an important part of the blossoming urban culture. The emergence of fashion is evident in the publication, in 1666–67, of the first in a long series of printed books of *kosode* designs, *On-hiinakata* [Patterns, or Models].[4]

These *hiinagata bon* (design books, pattern books) are a rich source of information on changing *kosode* designs, colors, and decorative techniques after the middle of the seventeenth century and consequently are of particular relevance and value to a thorough understanding of the Nomura Collection. Unfortunately, a systematic comparison of these materials with individual *kosode* in the Nomura Collection is beyond the scope of this discussion, and I must leave this important task to future studies of the subject.

Of almost 200 *hiinagata bon* that were published between the Kanbun era (1661–73) and the Bunka-Bunsei era of the early nineteenth century, about 120 different titles are extant. The new pictorial designs that utilized the entire *kosode* as a single design field required more ingenuity on the part of the *kosode* designer than did the earlier styles, which relied heavily on the division of that field into compartments decorated with a limited range of discrete motifs.[5] The *hiinagata bon* provided a repertoire of ready-made patterns, useful alike to the customer, who could choose among them, and to the artisan, who could copy them. They enabled the *kosode* industry to respond to the growing demand for fresh and ingenious designs. Of course, the design books also increased the chances of meeting someone wearing the identical *kosode*, a social discomfiture that the consort of Hideyoshi would not have encountered.

The demise of the *hiinagata bon* in the early decades of the nineteenth century is due in great part to the decline of *kosode* design into certain fixed motifs, themes, and compositions—primarily the restriction of pictorial elements to the hem or lower skirts of the *kosode*. These developments, as well as the focusing of interest on the elaborate obi and the accompanying popularity of small repeat designs, stripes, and checks, gradually eliminated the craving for innovative design. The last design book to be published, *Mansai hiinagata*, was an 1820 reprint of a 1724 original, *Tōryū moyō hiinagata tsuru no koe*.[6]

Examples from the Nomura Collection

The evolution of the Kanbun style was gradual; it is reflected in many transitional examples such as the black-background Keichō *kosode* (Cpl. 14) discussed above and the *kosode* illustrated in Colorplate

15. Its asymmetrical composition, bold, curvilinear forms depicted in *kanoko* and embroidery, and unifying theme of flowing water and chrysanthemums all link the *kosode* in Colorplate 15 to the Kanbun style. But the dark coloration, the use of gold leaf in addition to gold embroidery, and the filling of every bit of ground with small-scale patterns reflect the previous Keichō style. The *kosode* in Colorplate 14 is closer to typical Kanbun composition, but again its detail relates it to the earlier style.

The white satin *kosode* in Colorplate 16 is unusual not only in its boldness of conception, delicacy of execution, and interpretation of its theme but also because it displays elements of several styles at once. The golden waterfall plunges the length of the *kosode* against a white background reserved by *shibori* (possibly *oke-zome*, tub resist); *shibori* was likewise employed to reserve the white flowers that dot the rocks from which the waterfall spills. The use of *shibori* and the fine ink drawing that details the stream and spray of the water recall *tsujigahana* fabrics. The more abstract black forms of the craggy rocks above, the gold-leaf pattern superimposed on the black, and the gold-leaf fishnet diaper that originally covered the entire white ground (still clearly visible on the right sleeve) are vestiges of the Keichō style. Although the overall composition is strongly asymmetrical, it is a bit stiff and lacks the sweeping curves of the mature Kanbun style seen in Colorplates 17 and 18. The combination of waterfall and chrysanthemums in Colorplate 16 alludes to the Chinese legend that long life awaits one who drinks of a stream into which dew has dropped from chrysanthemums growing along its banks. This theme was popular in the seventeenth century, particularly, for obvious reasons, among the military class. It is found in two plays for the Nō theater, of which the military elite were keen patrons. But the basin into which the water streams is unique in representations of the theme; here it may be a tray in which the cut chrysanthemums are to be arranged, an interpretation that miniaturizes the waterfall and brings it into the realm either of man-made objects or of fantasy.

By contrast, the *kosode* in Colorplate 17 epitomizes the pure Kanbun style. Nothing dilutes the simplicity of the conception or the power of its expression. The white area on the left suggests the yawning space under the bridge, whose two-dimensional representation reinforces the emphatic contrast between ground and pattern. Leaping up around the base of the pilings, curling waves provide an effective counterpoint to the diagonal of the bridge and vertical of the pillars. A frequent subject of Edo period design, the bridge over the fast-flowing

Uji River recalls the bleak final chapters of the *Tale of Genji*, which are set mainly in Uji, several miles southeast of the capital. Uji Bridge was a favorite subject for screen paintings as well as for lacquer ware during the Momoyama and early Edo periods. The screens usually depicted a broad riverside scene, but a pair of lacquered hand-drums in the Kyoto National Museum are much closer in composition to the Nomura *kosode*, showing only close-up views of the bridge and the swirling waters beneath.[7] A design very similar to the one on the Nomura *kosode* appears in the pattern book *Shinsen on-hiinagata*, published in 1667.[8]

Broad-brimmed hats looped together with gold cord and overflowing with dark blue and black chrysanthemums decorate the *kosode* in Colorplate 18. Originally the chrysanthemum petals were outlined with gold leaf, still used at this time to complement the rich gold embroidery. As in the Uji Bridge *kosode*, undecorated space is effectively exploited.

The presence of traits characteristic of earlier periods in Kanbun style *kosode* does not necessarily imply that the garments are early in date. Composition and technique place the *kosode* in Colorplates 20 and 21 clearly within the Kanbun style; their Keichō elements point not to an early date but to an archaizing tendency. The diaper pattern in Colorplate 20 also appears in Colorplate 16, rendered there in gold leaf as allover background for the golden waterfall. On the red satin *kosode* in Colorplate 20, however, the diaper constitutes an embroidered design rather than a metallic-leaf background—a design we can interpret either as a fishnet or as curling waves with crests of heavier gold embroidery. The *kanoko* area suggests foaming water, which is consonant with either reading, but toward the hem it separates from the curving crests and thereupon becomes a simple abstract shape. This kind of formal ambiguity is, as we have seen, a common element in the Keichō style. The black-background *kosode* in Colorplate 21 suggests the earlier style in its choice of colors (blue has been added to the standard Keichō combination of black, red, and white) and in the small scale of the embroidered flowers, but the hard-edged, tight embroidery, the mannered, nervous lines of the streamers, and the use of the *takara zukushi* (myriad treasures—a congeries of auspicious objects) motif support a later dating.

A further stylistic development is incorporated into the design of another black-background *kosode*. Chrysanthemums and flowing water (*kiku-sui*) are the theme of the *kosode* in Colorplate 22 (cf. Cpl. 15), but here the rising waves and the giant blossoms half-submerged in them threaten to engulf the whole design field. Without the smaller, embroidered chrysanthemums, we would have a sparse composition in typical Kanbun style; the use of gold leaf to outline all the *kanoko* areas even suggests a date early in the sequence. But the embroidered chrysanthemums filling in some of the space appear more in keeping with later seventeenth-century design and are probably later additions.

Origin and Patronage

According to popular belief the Kanbun style appeared suddenly, a result of the great Meireki and Kanbun fires which devastated Edo and Kyoto respectively in 1657 (year 3 of the Meireki era) and 1661 (year 1 of Kanbun). Vast numbers of *kosode* were burned, and to replace them quickly, it is said, *kosode* makers devised the large-scale designs and open composition that left much of the surface undecorated.[9] We have seen, however, that the Kanbun style did not appear suddenly but evolved gradually from the preceding Keichō style.[10] Furthermore, the *kanoko shibori* and lavish embroidery that embellished the Kanbun style were in themselves extremely time-consuming, so that the new style could not be considered a labor- and time-saving device. Finally, although the destruction of so much property, including clothing, must have made people more receptive to a new style, the number of surviving Keichō and Momoyama pieces suggests that this was not because nothing remained from the earlier periods.

Both the sudden appearance of the Kanbun style and its association with the "slight vulgarity typical of urban taste"[11] are notions contradicted by a number of extant order books from a Kyoto clothing shop, the Kariganeya, established by the ancestors of the great painter Ogata Kōrin.[12] The Kariganeya order books preserve almost five hundred drawings of *kosode* designs entered between 1661 and 1678, with notations on the type of material, colors, and techniques to be used for each. In addition, there are notes but no illustrations for orders placed in 1646 (year 3 of Shōho).

Although not official purveyors to the imperial palace or the shogunate, the Kariganeya made robes for Yodogimi (Hideyoshi's mistress); for Tokuko, the wife of the second shogun, Hidetada; for her daughter Kazuko (later called Tōfukumon-in), consort to the emperor Go-Mizunoo; and for Kazuko's daughters. Orders from Tōfukumon-in and her household are illustrated in the book dated to the first month

of 1661 (year 4 of Manji), entitled *On-gachō*.[13] These *kosode* designs display the sweeping forms, asymmetric composition, and bold use of empty space that characterize the Kanbun style. They were selected in Kyoto before the Kanbun fire by women of the highest rank; it is unlikely that the Edo fire four years previously, or a need to economize, would have affected these ladies' design choices.

The preference of such exalted patrons for typically Kanbun style designs does not prove that these designs were worn exclusively by women of the very highest social class. Extant Kanbun garments range considerably in quality and tastefulness, but only in later periods does it become possible to infer the class of the wearer from the design of the robe.

The Kariganeya order books contain a great wealth of information about *kosode* designs and decorative techniques in the seventeenth century. A systematic comparative study of these order books, the printed design books (*hiinagata bon*), and extant *kosode* of the period would be of immeasurable value to the history of Japanese textiles and costumes.

THE TWO CURRENTS IN GENROKU STYLE

The sumptuary laws of the second and third years of the Tenna era (1682 and 1683), although not the first to be passed in the Edo period, were especially severe, reflecting the moralistic preoccupations of the ruling shogun. They prohibited both the manufacture and the wearing of gold-figured gauze (*kin sha*), gold embroidery, and allover *kanoko* decoration.[14] Recurrent promulgation of such edicts indicates that they were not strictly observed, but although the tradition of sumptuously decorated *kosode* persisted into the eighteenth century, it was gradually overtaken by a preference for clothes conveying a feeling less of opulence than of lightness and wit. It is not clear whether this new taste grew up in response to sumptuary decrees or was simply a natural reaction to a surfeit of richness. Whatever the cause, these two opposing traits clearly manifest themselves in the exuberance of Genroku period (1688–1704) *kosode*.[15] Whereas the thickly textured luster of embroidery and *shibori* on satin embody a past tradition, the matte finish of crepe and the delicate pictorial representation of *yūzen* dyeing are continuing elements in *kosode* design even today.

EARLY GENROKU SUMPTUOUSNESS

*K*osode of the early Genroku era, corresponding very roughly to the last decade of the seventeenth century, retain the asymmetric composition of Kanbun, but the suggestive empty space of the earlier era has gradually filled up with an energetic proliferation of forms reaching across the center back of the *kosode* (Cpls. 23–29, 32, 33). In the opulent style of this period gold and silver embroidery is no longer restricted to fine outlines of flowers and other forms but is laid down in bands three or four threads wide or covers the entire surface of a flower. The three *kosode* in Colorplates 23, 24, and 25 reflect the vigor of the Kanbun style in the thrusting pattern that arcs across the shoulders and down the lower right side. The center of gravity of the design still falls on the right shoulder and sleeve but a new secondary focus has appeared in the lower skirt, suggesting a downward shift in emphasis. Silver and white plum blossoms (Cpl. 23), windblown chrysanthemum leaves (Cpl. 24), and cresting waves (Cpl. 25) reach out to fill the void found in earlier designs. In Colorplates 32 and 33 that empty space has almost vanished in the luxuriant spread of pattern across the dark background, but the basic structure of the Kanbun composition remains.

Although preserving the large, dramatic forms and to some extent the sweeping curves of the earlier style, the *kosode* in Colorplates 26 and 27 have abandoned the interplay of decorated surface and empty background in favor of a heavily textured surface. The primary center of gravity of the composition has dropped perceptibly, from the shoulder and sleeve area to just above the waist. The embroidery is more densely packed, giving even the smallest forms a careful, precise, even hard outline in place of the earlier softer surface. Each of these *kosode* contains selected characters from a famous poem in one of the classical anthologies, along with motifs that cleverly incorporate the imagery of that poem, thus at one stroke proclaiming the literary and fashion acuity of the wearer and challenging that of the onlooker. The luxurious, swaggering, competitive spirit of Genroku could hardly be more graphically expressed.

EIGHTEENTH-CENTURY SENSIBILITY

*A*s the Genroku era entered the eighteenth century, the weight of the composition shifted from the shoulder area to the lower half of the *kosode*. This displacement was fostered by a progressive increase in the width of the obi and in the elaborateness with which it was tied. Both these developments had the visual effect of cutting the *kosode* in half at the waist. Designers responded by interrupting the pattern at the waist, or by using different designs for top and bottom. The decoration of the upper half became gradually sparser, until only the skirt was patterned. At the same time motifs lost the boldness associated with the Kanbun and Genroku styles, and allover designs of comparatively delicate scattered motifs again gained popularity as an alternative to leaving the upper half of the *kosode* unpatterned.

The *uchikake* (outer robe) in Colorplate 28 exhibits a new kind of stasis in its composition of opposing diagonals. At the same time it implies a downward motion, which appears much more emphatically in the *kosode* seen in Colorplate 29. In both, dramatic diagonals maintain some of the strength of the earlier designs, but the scale of the whole has shrunk, as if seen from a greater distance. The tightness of the embroidery is visible in the highly twisted thread outlining the purple, red, and white chrysanthemums in Colorplate 28 and in the red satin stitch defining the cherry blossoms in Colorplate 29.

A rebus decorates the black *kosode* in Colorplate 30: embroidered plum blossoms, a single oversized bamboo leaf, and the character for "pine" (*matsu* or *shō*) together form the auspicious combination of motifs called *shōchikubai* (pine-bamboo-plum), which eventually becomes a standard theme for wedding garments. Although the *kosode* in Colorplate 30 still retains a degree of asymmetry, the strong kinetic force of seventeenth-century design has been lost. The weight seems evenly balanced between upper and lower parts of the composition, foretelling the separation between top and bottom patterns that appears in Colorplate 31. The more delicate sensibility at work in the *kosode* in Colorplate 31 is characteristic of eighteenth-century design, and the use of gold leaf instead of embroidery, unusual for this period, gives a sense of lightness to the whole.

The black and white *katabira* design (Cpl. 37) of pine-fringed islands linked by arched bridges also recalls the curving asymmetric composition of Kanbun and Genroku, but the distance of the landscape from the viewer, the restrained use of gold embroidery, and the careful attention to the wood grain of the bridges is more in keeping with an eighteenth-century aesthetic. A heavily decorated *katabira* of bold design (Cpl. 33), the epitome of earlier Genroku opulence, presents a striking contrast, a clear demonstration of the difference between the sensibilities of the seventeenth and the eighteenth centuries.

YŪZEN DESIGNS

In order to follow the evolution of the second, and perhaps more important, trend in Genroku and mid-Edo *kosode*, we must consider some early examples of *yūzen* dyeing. The use of paste-resist techniques to reserve portions of a design in white while the unprotected areas absorbed the dye had been known for some time, but it was not until Genroku that *yūzen* dyeing as such came into its own. It is characteristic of *yūzen* that (1) the background is brush dyed, not dip dyed, (2) resist paste is used to define motifs and color areas and to protect the design from the background dye, and (3) the design is brushed in, using pigments as well as dyes. Stencilled *kanoko*, probably developed before the middle of the seventeenth century, often supplements the *kosode* decoration of early Genroku, possibly in response to recent sumptuary laws. But as a more fully pictorial representation replaced the abstract qualities of seventeenth-century design, *yūzen-zome* and the closely related *chaya-zome* usually stood on their own or were complemented by a restrained use of embroidery in gold and colors (Cpls. 35, 36, 38–45). The precursors of *yūzen-zome kosode* that display the full-blown Genroku style in bold, downward-moving designs also reveal a rather broad use of resist paste and a number of transitional characteristics (Cpls. 32–34). Although the undyed waterfalls, shoreline, and unpatterned cherry blossoms and leaves in Colorplate 33 have been reserved by a paste-resist technique, this *katabira* was probably vat dyed and thus is not, strictly speaking, an example of *yūzen* dyeing.[16] Again, on the *kosode* in Colorplate 32 it is only the waterfall and possibly the embroidered white drum-heads that have been reserved with resist paste. Both garments employ *kanoko shibori*, and on the *katabira* stencilled *kanoko* was used for the blue flowers.

Landscapes and Cityscapes

It was not until the creative force of the Kanbun style faded and a lighter, airier design sense emerged, in the eighteenth century, that *yūzen* dyeing came into its own and its potential was fully realized. Its capacity for free, delicate pictorial expression brought with it a wide range of themes entirely absent or only hinted at in earlier *kosode*.[17] The human figure, conspicuous by its absence from previous textile decoration, now makes its entrance, thanks to the more literal pictorial representation permitted by the new technique. Usually figures inhabit a city scene, going about their business in the shops and the streets, on bridges and riverboats (Cpls. 40, 42). The fine white lines defining forms and minute details, the subtle shading (*bokashi*) of hand-applied pigments, the wide range of colors in both dyes and pigments available to the *yūzen* dyer, and the matte finish of *chirimen* crepe are perfectly suited to scenes of naturalistic or narrative content. When, in the late Edo period (1781–1868), a literal realism gripped the visual arts in the wake of Western influence, its effect extended to embroidery as well (Cpl. 54).

Landscape was another common theme for *yūzen*-decorated *kosode*. In both *tsujigahana kosode* of the Momoyama period and *kosode* in the Keichō style landscape elements were often embroidered or painted within a roundel or a fan-shaped cartouche, as if glimpsed through a small window. But with the advent of *yūzen* dyeing the scene expands to fill the entire *kosode*, and we are treated to precisely identifiable views of Kyoto (Cpl. 40) and the Tōkaidō (the road between Kyoto and Edo) (Cpls. 41, 42). Other famous scenic spots, which formed a distinct and popular category in Japanese painting and prints, lent themselves equally to *yūzen* dyeing: among the most familiar are the Yoshiwara (the pleasure quarters of Edo) and the Eight Views of Ōmi, a Japanese version of a theme traditional in Chinese landscape painting.[18] Certain combinations of landscape motifs become associated with particular scenes or chapters from classical literature, lending a literary air to *kosode* design.

Landscapes in Chaya-zome

The gaily colored *yūzen* scenes are related to contemporary genre painting, whose principal subject was the everyday lives of common people, and *yūzen*-dyed robes were probably worn by women of the *chōnin* class. The more austere blue-and-white of *chaya-zome* recalls the fine, even black lines on pure white seen in *hakubyō* painting. These *katabira* of the finest ramie became, in the eighteenth century, standard summer attire for the ladies of the shogunal court. The cool fabric is complemented by its cool color scheme, sparsely accented with bright touches of gold and colored embroidery. Idyllic landscapes suggesting respite from the steamy urban summer were the preferred subjects. Water is an important element in these landscapes—refreshing streams flowing through hilly countryside (Cpls. 44, 45) or seaside scenes of boats and fishing nets. Rustic summer villas silently awaiting some elite entourage dot the landscape. Autumn flowers and grasses or snow-laden bamboo and pine evoke cooler seasons. Often these *katabira* were worn under a heavily embroidered *koshimaki* that was slipped off the shoulders and tied around the waist with a sash (Cpl. 49); the heavy ornateness of the *koshimaki* would have emphasized by contrast the crisp freshness of the *katabira*.

Everyday Objects as Motifs

In addition to landscapes with or without human beings, objects of everyday use such as utensils for the tea ceremony or flower arranging, toys, tools (especially those related to weaving), books, architectural elements, and furnishings associated with classical literary themes were adapted to *yūzen* designs. Inanimate objects had, of course, appeared on Kanbun *kosode*, for example, the basin, the bridge, and the flower-filled hats in Colorplates 16, 17, and 18, respectively. But the flexibility of *yūzen* dyeing encouraged a dramatic expansion of subject matter in the mid-Edo period. In the sheer crepe *kosode* in Colorplate 39 various types of river barriers —weirs, gabions, retaining walls made of barrels— compose stylized decorative bands showing the fine white lines and shaded colors typical of *yūzen* dyeing. These alternate with horizontal bands of solid color, created by stitch-resist *shibori* and representing water. Details of the barriers are hand-painted in carbon ink. The still-life designs also comprise combinations of certain auspicious motifs, which became formulaic in their predictability, especially for ceremonial wear.

Yūzen Composition

In composition *yūzen kosode* echo those decorated with *shibori* and embroidery. From the florid asymmetry of the early Genroku style, which recalls Kanbun composition in its strength and its emphasis on the upper half of the *kosode*, there is a gradual shift downward in the design's center of gravity, reflecting the growing size and importance of the obi. The two *kosode* in Colorplates 35 and 36 are typical of the best *yūzen* work of this period, and both utilize compositional devices that persisted well into late Edo. The trunk of the cherry tree (Cpl. 35) functions formally as a strong unifying vertical and pictorially as a support for the profusion of blossoms and ranks of poem slips concentrated above and below the waist. Colorplate 36 provides another

solution to the design problem posed by the obi: a living fence of maple branches sprouting colorful leaves distributes the pattern evenly over the *kosode* surface, becoming slightly sparser around the waist. Such an allover pattern—as opposed to a single vertical subject—suffers little from interruption by the obi. Although no actual trellis appears in the design, the chrysanthemums in the yellow twill *kosode* (Cpl. 38) are similarly disposed along horizontal-vertical coordinates, here supplied by the ranks of blossoms and rows of stems. The unusual combination of *yūzen*-dyed leaves and simple flowers executed in stitch-resist *shibori* with no further detailing emphasizes the soft forms of the blossoms and the crispness of the plants.

The *kosode* in Colorplate 43 is dated to 1740 (year 5 of Genbun) according to an inscription on silk pasted onto the back of the screen, which may have been a part of the original garment lining. The insistent diagonals, the divided tricolor background, and the manner in which the distinct background areas become an element of the pattern are all distant echoes of the Keichō (1596–1615) style, as are the flowers growing from one to the other of the background areas. But the light delicacy of execution and color are typical of the later period. The flattened form of the chrysanthemums is characteristic of *rimpa* design, and the unusual combination of plovers and autumn flowers suggests a literary allusion, although none has been identified.

LATE EDO DESIGNS

The *rimpa* manner appears again in Colorplate 46, a fine example of late Edo delicacy. Morning glories on a bamboo fence— another variation of the trellis theme—cover the lower two-thirds of this *kosode*; its upper part is unpatterned, a composition common by the mid-eighteenth century. Both the flattened style of the morning glories and the motif itself suggest *rimpa* influence, especially the work of Sakai Hōitsu (1761–1828), a late follower of Ogata Kōrin. Hōitsu's splendid plum tree (Cpl. 52), painted in ink and pigments on white satin, is a perfect balance of design conventions and artistic vitality; it is one of the masterpieces of the Nomura Collection.

Rimpa style also informs the rippling blue stream that curves through a field of bush clover in an *uchikake* that combines *shibori*, *yūzen* techniques, and embroidery (Cpl. 48). Less finely executed, but striking in design and imaginative in its combination of techniques is the *kosode* in Colorplate 53, in which wistaria blossoms and pine needles are reserved in white against a deep blue ground. This technique, popular in the first part of the eighteenth century but persisting long after that, especially in *kosode* made for women of the military class, is known as *shiro-agari* (finished in white), because no color was added to the reserved areas except for discreet touches of embroidery. Here it is balanced by the painted wistaria leaves and by the screens as well.

Matsumura Goshun (1752–1811), a painter contemporary with Hōitsu and of comparable eminence, created the *kosode* design in Colorplate 51. Goshun has treated the robe as a hanging scroll on which to render, in ink and light colors, a mist-wreathed mountain landscape in literati (*nanga*) style.

On the whole, nineteenth-century *kosode* design fluctuated between extreme restraint, epitomized by small-scale motifs restricted to the hem and sometimes the lower part of the sleeves, and bursts of flamboyance not always in the best of taste. The spectacular cycad palms flanking an earthen bridge (Cpl. 54) are reminiscent of early Edo design in the scale and vividness of their conception. But they betray a much later vision in the concentration of pattern on the lower part of the *kosode* and, even more, in the pedantic adherence to detail in the bark of the trees and the suggestion of a painting translated into embroidery seen in the careful texturing of the bridge. Because of its exotic subject and large, vivid design, this stunning example of nineteenth-century eclecticism would probably have been worn only by a courtesan. The white figured-satin *furisode* (Cpl. 55) profusely decorated with a design of half-lowered blinds and fans (evocative of erotic passages from classical narrative tales), on the other hand, was part of a wedding ensemble, along with an identically patterned red robe that is also in the Nomura Collection. The tight, hard-edged embroidery in a large variety of stitches is typical of the period, as is the vulgar surfeit of technical virtuosity no longer under the control of a refining sensibility. Nevertheless, we cannot help but be impressed by the exuberance of the curtain streamers, moving as if someone had just passed beneath them, leaving behind the carelessly dropped fans.

The early years of the nineteenth century, the two eras known jointly as Bunka-Bunsei (1804–30),
are sometimes described as a period of extravagant bad taste preceding the sumptuary edicts of the Tempō era (1830–44). These harsh restrictions, intended to prevent the further impoverishment of the military class, were to reinforce an oppressive austerity in clothing that lasted into the twentieth century and still casts its shadow on traditional dress. The edicts passed in the name of economic reform prohibited all manufacture, sale, or wearing of silk. Cotton had become a part of the Japanese economy by this time and was gradually replacing the indigenous bast fibers such as hemp and ramie for the clothing of the poorer classes. But those who could afford silk circumvented the laws, as the *juban* (under-kimono, worn by both sexes) in Colorplate 56 shows. This *juban*, a man's undergarment, would not have been visible when worn except for small areas around the hem and at the cuffs that might be revealed while the wearer moved. The surface of the *juban*, which is of gray cotton broadcloth, is solidly embroidered in silk twist with scenes of Edo in the manner of the *ukiyo-e* artist Andō Hiroshige (1797–1858). The concealed pleasures of this garment do not end, however, with the subtly colored views of city life. Its lining is brilliant yellow silk satin, embroidered in gold with crests across the shoulder area and wave-swept rocks on the skirt. Whichever side of this fully reversible garment was worn uppermost, all would have been covered by a dark and somber *kosode*, perhaps patterned with a fine stripe in two shades of gray. The repressiveness of the Tempō Reform and the sober period that followed help to account for the wild extravagance of the wedding *furisode* of Colorplate 55, worn on one of the few occasions—even after the severity of the Tempō era had lapsed—when colorful dress was permitted.

In order fully to appreciate the *kosode* in the Nomura Collection as works of art, we must consider the combination of imaginative powers, technique, and prevailing taste that transcended the framework of period style to create each particular one. To such an appreciation this essay is only preliminary—an attempt to describe *kosode* designs and the techniques with which they were made and to establish a tentative chronology of style.

COLOR:
DYES AND PIGMENTS

MONICA BETHE

Chapter 8
THE SIGNIFICANCE OF COLOR

The *kosode* in the Nomura Collection are decorated with dyes made from the bark, stems, leaves, flowers, or roots of various plants and with pigments extracted from the soil or made as by-products of the dyes. The dye baths were extracted from the plants by boiling, squeezing, or fermenting, and then the colors were bonded to the fibers with the aid of chemical mordants available in nature. Most of the dyes in the Edo dyer's palette were already known in the Nara period (645–794), though increasingly sophisticated methods of extraction and application evolved through the centuries.

The Japanese tendency to preserve old habits while inventing new techniques brought it about that Edo period (1615–1868) attitudes toward colors and their production incorporated traditions going back to the fifth and sixth centuries. Each *kosode* reflects not only the taste of the time when it was made but also the assumptions of that period when the class to which its wearer belonged dominated society. The imperial court nobility, though powerless and even poor during much of Japan's later history, continued to carry on the elaborate rituals and elegant formalization of its heyday, the Heian period (794–1185). Thus the colors of the Kyoto nobility's layered ceremonial costumes were determined according to rank and season and the dyes produced by traditional methods as of old. The military aristocrats, in their official role of de facto rulers, wore the matched vest and divided skirt over *kosode* that had been their customary attire in the Muromachi period. Their women wore *kosode* dyed purple and scarlet, colors formerly reserved for the highest ranks of the imperial aristocracy and officially prohibited in the Edo period to the commoners. The wealthy merchants, lowest on the social ladder but increasingly powerful during the Edo period, delighted in display but learned to hide flamboyance under sober exteriors when sumptuary laws were enforced. Grays, browns, and blues—the permitted "commoners' colors"—were, during Edo, elevated to the height of fashion and elaborated into a myriad subtle hues and shades. Actors and courtesans, the celebrities of their time, required novelty in their dress, and for these clients dyers worked to develop new shades and techniques of application.

All classes shared a love of color in itself. To this was added a consciousness of the dye sources, an awareness of the intricacies of extraction, and an appreciation of color as a reflection of nature. A color carried associations—literary, historical, social, and economic. It brought to mind a web of human activity, from cultivation to processing, distributing,

and dyeing. Worn on specific occasions, a color could convey defiance or compliance, or courage, or grace, the visual impression enriched by literary inference. Just as the well-preserved garments attest delight in the colors themselves, so Japanese poems, diaries, and novels amply document sensitivity to the connotations of colors.

COLOR SYMBOLISM

For the Japanese, particularly through the Heian period (794–1185), colors had a spritual force independent of the cloth on which they were dyed. Ritual regulated the art of making and using the colors, which were thought to invest the dyed cloth with magic power.[1] A band of black, for example, was protection against evil.[2] Almost all of the dye plants served also as herbal medicines (see Appendix 5 for ailments specific dyes were expected to cure), and to wear the medicine as dyed cloth served as a prevention, if not cure, for disease. Belief in the spiritual power of colors had two sources. The first was the age-old native reverence toward *kami*, the numinous spirits of natural phenomena, including plants. The second and later source was imported Chinese cosmology.

Chinese Influence

In the sixth century the Japanese turned toward the more advanced and sophisticated culture of China as a model for improving and reworking their own culture and institutions. Remodelling their administration along Chinese lines, in 603 they established a system of government ranks based on an all-embracing cosmology controlled by the five agents (C. *wu xing*; J. *go gyō*): fire, water, earth, wood, and metal. These agents were associated with the directions of the compass, the seasons, and the basic virtues, as well as primary and intermediate colors. Their correspondences and interactions formed a complex system considered the key to the proper functioning of government and of nature. From their role in this cosmic order the colors derived their numinous significance. The following chart makes the correspondences clear:[3]

FIVE AGENTS

	FIRE	WATER	EARTH	WOOD	METAL
seasons	summer	winter	—	spring	autumn
directions	south	north	center	east	west
virtues	decorum	wisdom	integrity	excellence	righteousness
colors	red	black	yellow	blue	white

The Chinese held these primary colors in the highest esteem, considering them pure, but the Japanese often preferred intermediate hues, which were also associated with each of the directions. Particularly high in their esteem was purple, which they reserved for imperial use, despite the Chinese dislike for that color.[4] The desirability of purple was probably in direct proportion to the rarity of the dye plant and the difficulty of its dyeing process. Other well-liked intermediate hues were safflower pink and shades of green.[5]

Along with the five agents came the Chinese passion for hierarchical arrangement. The government ranks established in 603 were each identified by the color of ceremonial hat and gown worn by its members on official occasions. The colors, in descending order, were: purple (virtue), blue (human excellence), red (decorum), yellow (integrity), white (righteousness), and black (wisdom). Each rank had an upper and lower grade, denoted respectively by darker and lighter shades of the same color, making in all twelve degress of officialdom. In succeeding centuries the rank colors underwent some change, the number of ranks increasing as the government became more complex, and the order of the colors shifting.[6] Most noticeable is the temporary elevation of white in 701 to the highest color, reserved for the emperor himself, followed by its disappearance from the list altogether. Purple remained consistently high.

The system of five agents was also applied directly to the art of dyeing, for each agent was seen to play a specific part in creating dyes. Wood (i.e., vegetable matter) was a source of dye and acid, earth was food for wood's growth, water was a vehicle for extracting the dye, fire boiled water and also made ash for alkali and mordants, metal was a source of mordants (metallic salts) that helped fix the dye on textile fibers.[7]

Color Names and Their Literary Associations

From the beginning the Japanese showed an acute awareness of the sources of the colors they used. The earliest color names were generally those of their plant sources: purple was *murasaki* (gromwell) (see Appendix 5 for botanical names of dye plants and related information), red was *akane* (madder), blue was *ai* (indigo), scarlet was *benibana* (safflower). These plants and their dyes were familiar to the elite, whose writings are full of metaphors taken from dyeing, and who themselves may have practiced the art of extracting dyes. The eighth-century poetry anthology *Manyōshū* contains dozens of poems in-

corporating observations on dye plants, dyeing processes, and dyed colors into their imagery. Sometimes the dye itself is a symbol: in one poem fugitive safflower scarlet (*beni*) is the color of a courtesan's robe and the metaphor of her fickle affections, while unfading gray, worn by the constant wife, signifies her lasting love.[8] In other poems physical properties of the plant are used as similes for emotions: the petals of the safflower when plucked are yellow, yet they dye red, a color associated with heightened emotion, usually love. Thus one poem bemoans the need to hide true feeling by identifying the would-be lovers with safflower petals:

Yoso nomi ni	Let my love for you
mitsutsu koinamu	Be only from afar—
kurenai no	Even though like the scarlet
suetsumuhana no	Of plucked safflower petals
iro ni idezu to mo.[9]	It does not show on the surface.

Often, however, the reference to a dye is unrelated to the primary meaning of the poem, the two forming separate statements linked by poetic device rather than significance. Some poems establish a tenuous connection between the dye statement and the main meaning. One, for example, associates love yearning with the length of *murasaki* roots (both very long, therefore, by extension, eternal). The implications are developed through a deft use of the homonyms "root" (*ne*) and "sleep" (*ne*).[10]

The abundance of dye references in poetry indicates how deeply embedded in Japanese consciousness dyes and colors were. To this day these poems serve as models for literary composition. Their color images furnish metaphors, similes, and proverbs that enrich popular expression. The complexity of these images has grown by accretion. They mold as well as convey attitudes toward and emotional associations with colors. Today, in addition, these poems supply the dye historian with a major key to reconstructing dyes and techniques used over a thousand years ago.

In the Nara period, as we have seen, dyes were associated primarily with emotions; the Heian nobility related them to the phenomena and seasons of nature as well. New color names were invented, based on the flowers they resembled rather than those they were extracted from. A warm yellow known during Nara as *kuchinashi*, after the gardenia whence the dye was extracted, acquired in Heian times the name *yamabuki*, for the yellow kerria rose whose color it resembled. Heian nobles also developed an elaborate system of color combinations (*kasane iro*) appropriate to each season. These were worn in layers by court ladies. In spring, for instance, when the kerria rose was in bloom, one might wear *yamabuki gasane*, an ochre garment with bright yellow lining. [11]

FROM RANK-COLORS TO FASHION COLORS

Kamakura Period

Although political power shifted decisively at the end of the twelfth century from the imperial court in Kyoto to the military government in Kamakura, Kyoto remained a cultural center and the Heian court's way of life continued, albeit somewhat constricted. There the uppermost stratum of society maintained its preference for clear, pure, transparent tones, gradated shadings, and seasonal color harmonies, and preserved the ritual and class associations of colors. As the military class gained power and status, however, the system of rank-colors began to ease. Blue ceased to be a rank-color and was open to all classes in the twelfth century.

The new military elite's love for the decorative value of color led them to embellish their garments with pattern, of which color was only one element. This contrasts with the Heian period preference for solid colors worn in layered combinations. Although the shift led to a gradual lessening of the numinous associations of colors, it added a symbolism of form and stimulated the development of dye techniques. The military wore armor whose leather and lacings were lavish with color and pattern, typically in bold, robust, dark colors like navy blue, black, dark green, or dark shades of purple and scarlet. Particularly favored was a midnight blue called victory blue (*kachi iro*), achieved by repeated dippings in the indigo vat. On the oldest surviving armor, the *omodaka* armor at Daisenshi Shrine, the lacings are dyed scarlet, moss green, and yellow. [12]

Muromachi Period

Few garments survive from the early Muromachi period (1333–ca. 1500), and other sources, such as portraits and paintings, give only a suggestion of colors. As a result, preferred colors for clothing of the fourteenth and fifteenth centuries remain somewhat conjectural, though browns and yellows seem to have been common. Documents suggest a conflict between a government-supported moralistic sobriety, sporadically enforced by edicts, and a natural love of decoration. [13]

Momoyama Period

Both preferences are more clearly apparent during the Momoyama period (1573–1615), when the influence of the tea masters supported sober hues of brown and gray, while mainstream taste, led by successful warlords like Toyotomi Hideyoshi and Tokugawa Ieyasu, revelled in many-colored garments, favoring above all safflower scarlet (*beni*). So predominant, in fact, was this color in dyed, embroidered, and brocaded clothing that the textile historian Kirihata Ken has proposed *beni* as the representative color of the age. [14]

Early Edo Period

The very beginning of the Edo period saw a tempering of Momoyama brilliance: large areas of black offset the reds of Keichō and Kanbun *kosode*. Dark or black grounds underlie the dense embroideries of tiny flowers popular at this time. Soon, however, white and light colors emerged again, and the development of *yūzen* dyeing in the latter half of the seventeenth century greatly expanded the number of colors that could be combined on one garment.

Mid-Edo Period

By the end of the seventeenth century Kabuki actors and courtesans, increasingly central to the amusements of city dwellers, began to lead fashion. Segregated by law from respectable society, they enjoyed as a result considerable immunity from sumptuary restrictions, and the gorgeousness of their dress was a large ingredient in their fame.

A well-known actor would commission from one of the dye houses a new shade or hue. (New designs were often taken up as well.) His appearance in the new color would create a stir among the theatergoers of Edo and Osaka (where the Kabuki houses were located). *Ukiyo-e* print makers would further popularize the color by their faithful representations of the theatrical idol in costume. With luck, the color would catch on, to become not only the actor's trademark but also a fad among the general public. Fad status assured the color a place in the *hiinagata* design books, and this, of course, would popularize it even further. Young women, particularly of the merchant class, were the most avid imitators of theatrical fashions, including fashions in color, but the military class and imperial court followed their lead. This color consciousness represents a sharp change in custom and attitude from earlier centuries, when the use of color was far more class bound and tradition-directed.

Trends could be created equally well by actors of male or female roles. The brown called *rokō-cha*, fashionable for over seventy years,[15] was first worn by Segawa Kikunojō, who played women, while *masubana iro*, a light blue-green, came to symbolize the "male lead" Ichikawa Danjūrō and his entire theatrical lineage.[16] Just as an actor could popularize a color, the right color could also contribute to theatrical success: when Ichikawa Danjūrō V in 1749 made an outstanding hit as the great lover and dandy Sukeroku, the purple headband he wore in the part became identified with him and with the role.[17]

When even the increasingly powerful and moneyed merchant class became too ostentatious in its dress, the Tokugawa government would attempt to enforce sumptuary restrictions on fabrics and colors in order to maintain class distinctions. Brown, gray, and blue owed their popularity in part to sumptuary edicts that forbade commoners to wear brighter colors like *beni* scarlet and *murasaki* purple. New shades of these humbler colors multiplied; there were forty-four named hues of brown, twenty-two grays, fifteen blues.[18] Restricted upper-class colors could often evade shogunal prohibition by being called brown, blue, or gray: even purple might be worn by commoners if it went by a newly invented name with the suffix *ai* (blue) or *cha* (brown). The dyers glibly defended themselves by saying, "They do the naming, we do the dyeing".[19] Making a virtue of necessity, Edo merchants also brought the permitted colors into the forefront of fashion, propounding an aesthetic of hidden flamboyance. True elegance meant luxury camouflaged under simplicity. Understatement was the mark of sophistication, and the words *iki* (stylish, chic) and *tsu* (connoisseurship) were coined to denote mastery of the art of understatement, principally in dress. Plain-weave cotton outer garments, often striped or checked, hid silk linings dyed in bright, expensive colors. These peeked out only at the cuffs or flashed into view at the hem in a sudden gust of wind. Luxury, officially proscribed, went under cover.

Late Edo Period

Late Edo fashions capitalized on the beauty of the sober colors by turning again to solid grounds, usually dark, decorated with delicate white or light designs on limited areas such as the hem or neckline.

Chapter 9
EARLY DYE MAKING

By the fifth century methods of imparting color to cloth included rubbing earth pigments mixed with *gojiru* (a liquid pressed from presoaked soybeans) into a cloth temporarily pasted to a flat surface.[1] Most common among these pigments was *nitsuchi*, a red mentioned in the *Kojiki* (Japan's earliest extant chronicle, completed in 712).[2] This was followed by the practice of rubbing flower petals (or perhaps their extracted juices) into cloth. The *Manyōshū* mentions iris (*kakitsubata*) and dayflower (or spiderwort) (*aobana*) as flowers "rubbed" (*suritsuke*) into cloth.[3] When a character in the *Kojiki* wades through waist-high water, "his garments rubbed with blue and decorated with a red cord turned to red when the water soaked the red cord".[4] The notion of coloring cloth blue by rubbing it with fresh indigo leaves (*suri ai*) developed naturally out of the practice of rubbing cloth with flower juices.[5]

Making dye by boiling parts of plants—roots, bark, nuts, etc.—was also known in prehistoric (i.e., before about A.D. 500) Japan. Probably the oldest such dye was the strong lemon-yellow produced by boiling the inner bark of *kihada* (philodendron), since cloth dyed in *kihada* requires no more than steeping and drying to be colorfast (i.e., will not run or fade). Since this dye also acted as a pesticide, it was used to preserve important materials, such as the paper on which Buddhist sutras were to be written.[6]

MORDANTS

Most other dyes extracted by boiling require the presence of a metallic salt, or mordant, to complete the chemical bonding between dye molecules and cloth molecules. The mordants known to the Japanese of the Nara period were ash lye (*aku*), iron (*tetsu*), and vinegar made from plums (*umekawa su*) or rice (*yone-zu*).[7]

For ash lye, water was poured through the embers (or ashes) of burned wood, straw, or plant stems, or else the embers were steeped overnight and the clear water at the top of the container drawn off for use. This water would have picked up metallic salts from the plant material and at the same time would have been turned alkaline by the ashes. Iron was found in the waters of certain rivers or ponds and in certain muds. Mud dyeing (*doro-zome*) is still done today in parts of Okinawa and Hokkaidō. Plum vinegar, which had a more limited application than ash lye or iron, was derived from the skins of the Japanese green plum. If the skins were first smoked, the vinegar was called *ubai*.

Since the chemical composition of the mordant affects the color of the dyed cloth, a single dye could produce a number of related hues, depending on the mordant with which it was combined. Although ignorant of chemistry, the craftsmen of premodern Japan were keenly observant pragmatists, who soon learned what mordant would turn a given dye a particular hue. Purple, for instance, was achieved with the aid of the alum-rich camellia-ash lye. While alum turns *murasaki* dye reddish, the alkali in the ashes turns it bluish. Thus the single camellia-ash mordant, containing both alkali and alum, enabled dyers to achieve a true purple. In the following poem from the *Manyōshū* a rather flat romantic image is introduced by this significant, albeit concealed, dye fact, with the word camellia (*tsubaki*) acting as the pivot connecting the two:

Murasaki wa	Camellia is the ash
hai sasu mono zo	For *murasaki* purple.
tsubakichi no	Who is it here
yaso no chimata ni	At the crossroads
aeru ko ya tare.[8]	In Camellia Market?

ORIGINS OF DYESTUFFS

Some of these mordant dyes (dyes requiring mordants to make them colorfast) were native to Japan, others were imported from the Asian continent between the third and sixth century. Of the early native dyes, perhaps the color most prized (for its spiritual potency) was the yellowish red called *akane iro* (madder color) or *ake* or *hi*.[9] It was produced from madder (*akane*) roots and was associated with the sun. The annals of the Chinese kingdom of Wei record in A.D. 243 a gift of *kōseikin* cloth from Japan to the Wei emperor. This has been interpreted by scholars to be silk dyed red with madder and blue with indigo.[10] The *Kojiki* (712) refers to a gown "dyed with the juice of the pounded plant of *atane*", which dye researchers (although not all scholars) interpret as *akane*.[11] Similar references suggest that native Japanese dye plants also included *kuchinashi* (gardenia) and *kariyasu* (*miscanthus*) for yellows and *murasaki* for purple.[12] Since no cloth dating from before the seventh century has survived, we can only guess at the actual colors.

Before the fifth century blue was produced by rubbing leaves of the native indigo, *yama ai*, into the cloth or by dyeing with water in which the fresh leaves had been soaked. *Yama ai* produces a weak greenish blue. Doubtless finding the color unsatisfactory, the Japanese quickly adopted *tade ai* (known as buckwheat, dyer's knotweed, or Chinese or Japanese indigo), which came from China about the fourth or fifth century. Probably taught by Korean artisans who came to Japan with the introduction of Buddhism, the Japanese learned to ferment these new indigo leaves by letting them stand in water over the summer months. With the new method they could produce deep shades of blue (*hanada* or *kon*). Another imported dye plant that arrived during Nara (645–794) or earlier was *benibana* (safflower).[13]

In addition to these plants, which were introduced into Japan and then cultivated there, a number of dyes from subtropical plants were imported in dried form from Southeast Asia and India in the Nara period. Most common among these were *suō* (sappanwood), dyeing crimson, maroon, or purple; *asen*, or *katekyū* (cutch, or acacia catechu), dyeing browns but used in the early period mostly for its medicinal value; and *binrōji* (betel nut, from the areca palm), dyeing browns and black.

SURVIVING SOURCES ON EARLY DYES

Fabrics

The oldest extant dyed fabrics date from 607. They belong to the Buddhist temple Hōryū-ji outside Nara but are presently kept at Tokyo National Museum. These, plus the textiles preserved at the Shōsō-in from 756 onward, constitute the artifacts on which research on ancient dyes is based. In these fabrics all the dyes mentioned so far appear, some in remarkably strong shades despite the lapse of thirteen centuries, though we cannot of course know their original appearance. The various articles of dyed cloth, paper, and yarn preserved from the Asuka (552–645) and Nara (645–794) periods were not all produced in Japan by Japanese craftsmen; many were treasured Chinese imports and others must have been made by foreign artisans resident in Japan. All, however, evince what must have been a Nara period taste for clear colors in intense shades, created by repeated dippings rather than by strong mordants.

Records

From the Nara period we have little or no account of actual dye methods, apart from what can be inferred from chronicles and poems. The first extensive record of fabrics, dyes, and proportions (but not step-by-step recipes) occurs in the *Engi shiki* [Codes of the Engi era], commissioned by the emperor Daigo (885–930) early in the tenth century. Among its fifty volumes of detailed rules about ceremonies, etiquette, costume, and duties, both at court and in provincial government offices, there are several chapters specifically related to colors, their use and production. The fourteenth book in particular deals with the types and amounts of ingredients necessary to dye the rank-colors of ceremonial court dress. It mentions cloths, dye plants, mordants, and other necessities. Book 41 offers detailed information on the colors permitted to the several ranks.[14] The *Engi shiki* was simultaneously a record of existing customs thought to reflect the methods and organization of previous centuries and a code intended to guide future generations. Thus it supplies a general key to dyes used from the eighth to the twelfth century.

Chapter 10
THE BASIC PALETTE

REDS

To the Japanese red represents color itself and is associated with the sun, with life force, and with passion. The phrase "with color" (*iro ari*) refers to garments with red in their design, such as were particularly suitable for young women, though they could also be worn by men. During the Nara and Heian periods madder red (*akane iro*) was one of the highest-ranked colors; during the sixteenth and seventeenth centuries safflower pinks and scarlet (*beni*) were in great favor. Safflower dye provided the background color of many brocade *kosode* of the Muromachi and Momoyama periods. It was also used lavishly in satin *nuihaku*-decorated *kosode*, in *tsujigahana kosode*, and as an integral part of Keichō and Kanbun *kosode* designs. On extant *kosode* from these periods the *beni* has faded to dull tan. We can only imagine how splendid the *kosode* in Colorplates 25 and 35 and the embroidery in Colorplate 12 must have appeared when their now-faded *beni* stood in pristine contrast with the blacks and whites.

The Edo period (1615–1868) knew three main sources of red: madder (*akane*) roots, the much-loved safflower (*benibana*) petals, and sappanwood (*suō*) chips. These three sources produce reds of quite distinctive hues, although they do not differ greatly in chroma. *Beni* red, the purest, has a bright radiance but fades easily. In light shades it appears pink, as it does when dyed on cotton.

Madder red varies according to the type of madder root used. The four-leaved native Japanese madder, *Nihon akane*, gives an orange-brown-tinged red. The six-leaved madder (*mutsuba akane*) gives hues from true red to yellowish red; light shades are salmon.[1] By the Edo period the native variety had gone out of use, probably due to the difficulty of getting rid of the yellow tinge, and the other types were used less extensively than in former centuries.[2] They continued, however, to be used in top-dyeing and as an ingredient in indigo vatting.

Suō (sappanwood) red has slight bluish undertones and varies in hue with the mordant used: crimson with ash lye or alum (Cpl. 23), maroon with copper, purple with iron. If top-dyed on yellow, *suō* approximates *beni* or *akane* reds. Indeed, the dyer and dye historian Yamazaki Seiju comments that Edo period "*akane* dye" recipes generally call for *suō* chips and not *akane* roots. It is likely that the *kosode* in Colorplate 20 was dyed in this way. Partly because *suō* works well when applied by brush in *yūzen* dyeing, and partly in response to sumptuary restrictions on the use of *beni*, *suō* came increasingly to be the basic red dye of the Edo period.

Through skillful top-dyeing and mordanting, *suō* dyes were made to imitate the hues and shades of the other reds so closely that today it is often difficult to tell which dye was used without careful inspection of the fabric itself. It is probably safe to say that seventeenth-century garments whose red remains reddish were dyed with *suō* over yellow (Cpl. 8), not with *benibana* (Cpl. 7). Yamazaki contends that even among sixteenth-century fabrics, those that retain a hint of their former red probably denote top-dyed *suō* and yellow.[3] This would include, most likely, Colorplates 2 and 3, right, of the Nomura Collection. The quality of the red in the darker areas, which may have been protected from light and thereby retained more of their original hue, supports this surmise. The maroon passages in the leaves and pine-bark lozenges of Colorplates 2 and 3, left, and the rust-brown ground patterned with white squares in Colorplate 1, right, were also most likely dyed with *suō*.

The sappan tree whose wood provides *suō* dye grows in subtropical areas, including Southeast Asia and India. In the Nara period (645–794) dried sappanwood chips were being imported for medicinal and dye purposes, but it was not until the sixteenth century that such imported dyes could compete in availability or cost with those locally produced. Active trade with the south, first through the city of Sakai, itself a center of dyeing, and later through the Dutch traders in Deshima, supplied the increasing demand for this dye.

With *suō* from India came another red dye: *enji* (lac), giving a maroon-crimson (Cpl. 36). The piece of *enji*-colored cotton in the Shōsō-in imperial repository was imported during the Nara period, but such imports must have been rare. Its considerable colorfastness made *enji* popular for *yūzen*-dyed *kosode* and for Okinawan *bingata* (paste-resist-dyed garments) in the middle and late Edo periods.[4]

Enji, unlike the other dyes discussed here, has an animal source. It is secreted in resinous form by lac insects, which feed on trees in India and various parts of Southeast Asia. After copulation the female insects are soaked in slightly alkaline water, and the chocolate brown resin they hold releases its color into the water. Cotton cloth immersed in this bath will absorb the red dye. Once dried, this cotton serves as storage medium for the dye. When the dye is needed, reimmersion of the cotton in an alkaline solution releases the color back into the solution, making it available for dyeing.[5] This process works for any dye that is extracted from its source with the aid of an alkali—for example, *beni*. The cloth used as temporary storehouse for the dye must be of vegetable fiber.

PURPLES

Long associated with the highest ranks of nobility, purple also connoted love longing and elegance. During the Edo period the right to wear *murasaki*-dyed silk was an avidly guarded perquisite of the upper classes. Members of the shogunal family sported garments dyed with purple, as did Buddhist clergy of *sōjō* rank, whose position was "no lower than that of a retired lord".[6] The most skilled of the blind court musicians were also allowed to wear it, but it was a privilege for which they had to pay a good deal of money.

The dye houses of the city of Edo produced their own shade of purple, slightly redder than the classical color. This came to be known as *Edo murasaki* and to symbolize the self-approbation of the newer

capital.[7] Since the particular hue was in part related to the chemical composition of the water in which the dyed cloth or yarn was washed, the advantages of dyeing this color in Edo rivers gave rise to numerous proverbs vaunting the superiority of this upstart city and its culture. Taunts like "If you can't complete the job [of dyeing *murasaki*] in the Kamogawa [a river in Kyoto], come to Edo" carried meaning far beyond the world of dyeing.

Although the original and standard source of purple was *murasaki* (gromwell) roots, very similar hues can also be produced with *suō* mordanted with iron or *suō* top-dyed on indigo. Since *suō* is apt to give a slightly redder shade than *murasaki*, it is likely that the Edo dye houses were skilled in manufacturing this "fake purple" (*nise murasaki*). Like the change from *akane* to *suō* for madder red, the change from *murasaki* to *suō* for purple seems to have occured in the early Edo period (1615–88). The dye historian Yamazaki suggests that on sixteenth-century *tsujigahana* fabrics purple was generally dyed with *murasaki* roots but after the beginning of the Edo period many, though by no means all, purple garments were dyed with *suō* and indigo.[8]

BLUES, GREENS AND YELLOWS

The popularity of blue appears to be universal, crossing all boundaries of time, place, and social rank. In Japan it began as a ranked color but was one of the first to be unrestricted. It became a favorite color of the warrior class of the Kamakura period (1185–1333). When cotton fabric became readily obtainable and popular during the Edo period, the affinity of indigo to vegetable fibers, generally difficult to dye, made blue the ubiquitous color of country-made garments and stimulated a phenomenal expansion of indigo production and indigo dyeing. At the same time *chaya-tsuji*, bast-fiber garments with paste-resisted indigo designs (Cpls. 44, 45), became the exclusive prerogative of the highest elite. The *chirimen* silk crepe *kosode* in Colorplate 53, though a luxury garment, was not officially reserved to upper-class use. Its rich background color is a medium indigo blue.

Indigo, in addition to being a popular color in its own right, is also an important ingredient in dyeing other colors. We have already mentioned *nise murasaki*, "fake purple". Green is produced by top-dyeing yellow and indigo, the order depending on the color desired. Indigo is also a frequent component of black.

Green, being a composite of blue and yellow dyes, offers an exercise in skill to the *shibori* dyer. Skillful dyeing can produce many different hues and shades of green. The *tsujigahana kosode* shown in Colorplate 1, right, illustrates such variations in intensity, with scattered dark green leaves against a paler green. The source of the yellows is not always clear; Yamazaki has suggested that *kihada* (philodendron) was the commonest, but that *kariyasu* (*miscanthus*), *kuchinashi* (gardenia), *enju* (*Sophora japonica*), and *ukon* (turmeric) could also have been used.[9]

Yellow was less commonly used alone as a background color, which makes the *kosode* shown in Colorplate 38 unusual. The warmth of the mustard yellow suggests that it may have been dyed with one of the red-yellows such as gardenia.

BLACK

Lowest of the ranked colors, and associated with wisdom, black also carried the more universal connotations of mystery, magic, and fear. In wedding gowns of the Edo period, which were often worn in layers of three, one black, one white, and one red, all decorated with the same design elements, the black stood for propriety and austerity, white for purity and neatness, and red for elegance and sensuality.

Black was an important design element in early Edo *kosode*, which used dark backgrounds to set off the brilliance of embroidery (Cpls. 2 and 3, right, and 12) or areas of black to counterpoint areas of more vivid colors, as in the red, black, and white of the typical Keichō divided-background *kosode* (Cpls. 5, 7, 8, 9, 11). The somewhat brownish black of Keichō and Kanbun style *kosode* was most likely made with indigo as one ingredient, though we do not know which of several dye recipes was in fact used. An old method, described as a source of the black in some Nara period garments, involved top-dyeing indigo and madder, with either dye applied first.[10] The good preservation of these garments is evidence for the use of this method, for indigo acts as a pest repellent and preservative, while iron mordant, another common component of black dyes, can damage fibers and shorten the life of fabrics. One dye historian, however, comments that browning is a common age discoloration of iron mordant and believes that a tannin-containing dye from the betel palm or a mixture of trees was top-dyed with iron mordant on an indigo base.[11] Still another possibility is *sumi* (ink) top-dyed over indigo.[12] Tooth blackener (*ohaguro*, a cosmetic commonly made with ground betel nut and iron) is said to have been used on cheaper fabrics, but an *ohaguro*-dyed *kosode* could only be expected to last about fifteen years

due to the corrosive effect of excessive iron mordant on the fibers.[13]

BROWNS AND GRAYS

Brown and gray, for long the ubiquitous commoners' colors, grew in popularity during the Muromachi period and became preeminent in the mid-Edo period (1688–1781). It was the tea masters who first heightened the popular appreciation of browns and grays, in part by pointing out the beauty of browns in prized scraps of Chinese cloth used to make tea caddy bags. From association with the tea ceremony, in fact, brown acquired its generic name, in use to this day: *cha* (tea). Formerly each hue and shade of brown had borne a distinct name, derived either from its appearance (*kuchiba iro*, "dead leaf color") or from its dye source (*chōji iro*, "clove brown").

One indication of brown's rising status is the amount of space devoted to it in the *Zasshoshū*, an anonymous miscellany of the early Muromachi period containing much information about medieval dyes.[14] The colors mentioned in this work include Chinese brown (*kara cha*), yellow-brown (*ki cha*), dark brown (*koge cha*), and bluish brown (*ao cha*). Many of the plants discussed produce brown dye, and at least two of them—plum and persimmon—were first used as dyes during the Muromachi period.

New shades of gray were also created. The famous and profoundly influential tea master Sen no Rikyū (1522–91) held that gray, with its quality of refined understatement, could express myriad colors. Rikyū developed the shade of olive gray named after him (Rikyū *nezumi*) and encouraged its use along with simple striped patterns.

Both brown and gray can be produced from any number of sources. Their key chemical component is tannin, found in various woods. Tannin will dye gray when mordanted with iron and brown when mordanted with a combination of iron and alkali. Earlier browns, mostly yellowish, had been mordanted with ash lye, but Muromachi dyers learned to use lime, a more potent alkali, which brings out the red tones in brown.[15] They also produced browns by elaborate top-dyeing, using three colors. Browns composed of madder red, yellow, and indigo are found in some *tsujigahana* fabrics.[16]

The popularity of browns and grays surged again in the mid-Edo period, when dye houses vied with each other to produce new shades, using complex methods of mordanting and top-dyeing. Colorplate 47 exemplifies the trend toward brown backgrounds setting off a white design.

Chapter 11
DYE HOUSES AND
DYEING TECHNIQUES

DYE HOUSES

During the Nara and Heian periods, when colors held strong cosmological and social significance, properly dyed garments for the various ranks of the nobility were so important that dyers were incorporated into the government bureaucracy as a department of the Weaving Office (Oribe no tsukasa). By the end of the Heian period (794–1185) the dyers, like the weavers, had begun to produce for private sale. These men established Kyoto as a leading dye center, a position it retains to this day. In addition, dyes and dyed cloth were being made in the provinces, as is attested by the *Engi shiki*, which lists them as taxes in kind.[1] From the thirteenth century, as the balance of wealth and patronage shifted increasingly to the provincial military aristocracy, the dyers' arts were further disseminated.

Beginning in the Muromachi period (1333–1573) two types of dye houses evolved: the descendants of the court dyers specializing in a single dye plant and new houses dyeing a variety of colors. Survivors of the former type can still be found in the back streets of Kyoto, where one might happen on a dye house for black (*kuro-zome ya*) or one for purple (*murasaki-zome ya*). Until quite recently Kyoto contained dye houses specializing in producing the Heian rank-colors for the Imperial Household.[2] Indigo dyeing, being both time-consuming and difficult, was always a specialized art, though in the Edo period the *kon ya* (or *kō ya*, "blue-dye houses"), particularly the rural ones, often produced other colors on the side.

Purple, too, was always a specialized enterprise. Some especially famous *murasaki ya* were situated in Edo along the Tama River, which must have run purple much of the time from the quantities of dyed cloth being rinsed in its waters. Kyoto dye houses specialized—some producing the classical purple and others the new "Edo *murasaki*". The *Jinrin kinmōsui*, an illustrated book about artisans and their crafts published in 1690, mentions the Ishikawaya for standard purple and another Kyoto firm, on Abura-nokōji Street, for Edo purple.[3]

In contrast with these single-color dye houses were those that produced patterned cloth and dyed a spectrum of colors under one roof. These proliferated as multicolored dyed cloth rose in popularity during the medieval period. The Kariganeya in Kyoto and the Sakai workshops that produced *tsujigahana* fabrics during the sixteenth century are typical examples of dye houses working in many colors. Edo period *yūzen* dye houses, specializing in a technique requiring an almost unlimited palette, were their natural outgrowth.

Considering the vast number of hues and shades in which most colors were made, the number of dye sources used by any given dye house (as listed in their manuals) was remarkably limited: one or two sources of tannin for browns, grays, and black; *kariyasu* (*miscanthus*) and perhaps one more plant for yellow; *suō* for reds; and indigo for blues.[4] From these few plants over one hundred separately named colors were produced. All the subtle permutations of color were obtained by exceedingly skillful top-dyeing and mordanting, often with several mordants in succession. The dye houses (like almost all Japanese occupations) were family businesses, and their recipes were strictly guarded family secrets. The intricate blending and resultant complex tonalities of Edo colors stand in sharp contrast with the unmixed clarity of Heian colors.

IMMERSION DYEING AND BRUSH DYEING

Broadly speaking, there are two methods of applying dye to cloth: the cloth can be immersed in a dye bath or vat, or the dye can be brushed onto the cloth. The immersion (or dipping) technique is older and highly effective for dyeing solid colors and *shibori* designs. It allows the dye to be heated, which in many cases increases bonding between dye molecules and fiber molecules. It also keeps the cloth out of contact with oxygen during dyeing, which lessens the chance of sedimentation and makes for more even coloring. In dip dyeing, too, the whole fabric is immersed simultaneously, an advantage with unstable dyes. Brush dyeing, on the other hand, makes for better control of tone and more even application and allows an almost infinite range of colors in one design and great subtlety in shading. All the *shibori*-patterned *kosode* in the Nomura Collection, including the *tsujigahana*, Keichō, and Kanbun designs, are dip dyed, as are the *chaya-zome kosode*. *Yūzen*-dyed garments have been mostly colored by brush.

PROBLEMS OF YŪZEN DYEING

In the development of paste-resist dyeing the principal problem to be overcome was the fragility of the resist paste, which cracks under too much handling, dissolves from prolonged exposure to water, and melts from too much heat. *Yūzen*, therefore, demanded colors that could be brushed on rather than dipped, and this required stable dye baths. It also necessitated colors that adhered well to cloth even at room temperature.

Indigo, *murasaki*, and *beni* do not meet these requirements well. Indigo oxidizes in a matter of minutes when exposed to air, making vatting imperative. *Murasaki*, being imperfectly soluble in water, sediments easily and cannot be kept in bath form for any length of time. *Beni* dye is thinly saturated and requires so many applications as to threaten erosion of the resist paste; it also fades when exposed to intense heat, such as the steaming process that sets the colors in *yūzen* dyeing. Therefore these three dyes are used primarily for solid-colored or *shibori*-dyed *kosode* or as embroidery or pigment decoration. To create *yūzen* designs on indigo or *beni* backgrounds, the background is generally dip dyed first.

YŪZEN TECHNIQUES

Stencilling

Neither resist paste nor *hiki-zome* was newly developed for *yūzen*; both date at least from the Muromachi period (1333–1573). The paste-resist technique grew out of direct stencil dyeing, which may have been employed as early as the Heian period to decorate commoners' clothing. At least illustrated scrolls of the period show costumes with patterns most likely executed with stencils.[5] Direct stencilling was certainly in use during the Muromachi period, from which time garments decorated with ink-stencilled designs survive. In direct stencilling color is applied through the cut stencil; no resist paste is necessary.

Stencilled Paste-Resist Dyeing

Resist paste applied through the stencil before the cloth is dyed creates a reserved design—the opposite of direct stencilling. The technique may have been used first during the Muromachi period to render family crests (*mon*) on outer garments.[6] By the end of the Muromachi period it appears, highly refined, in indigo-dyed *katabira* with small paste-resisted repeat designs (*komon*). Different pastes were developed for different purposes: some adhered better to vegetable fibers and others to silk, some withstood handling better and others melted or dissolved less easily.

Indigo, which requires no mordanting and colors well with repeated brief (five–ten minutes) dippings, does not tend to dissolve resist paste and can therefore be used to dye cloth with paste-resisted designs. Most of the early *komon*-patterned garments were dyed with indigo.

Brush Dyeing

Dyes other than indigo, which take longer to penetrate and require a mordant, call for some method of application other than dipping in order to be usable with resist paste. It has been suggested that brush dyeing was developed during the Muromachi period to dye *komon*-patterned *kosode* in colors other than blue.[7] The number of dye recipes calling for brush dyeing in the early Muromachi miscellany *Zasshoshū* indicate how widespread the technique was by that time.

There are various Japanese terms for brush dyeing, depending on purpose, technique, and type of brush used. For applying background and large design elements, a large, soft, thick brush is used, in back-and-forth or circular strokes. This is known as *hiki-zome*. Small design elements are colored in with a small rounded, pointed, or slanted brush of the type used for painting and calligraphy; this process of filling in an outlined pattern with color is called *iro-sashi*. Both *hiki-zome* and *iro-sashi* involve repeated thin applications of dye alternating with applications of mordant. The outline itself was created by resist paste squeezed onto the fabric freehand from a tube (*tegaki-yūzen*), following faint blue outlines drawn in *aobana* juice.

Pigments

Much of the fine detail in *yūzen* designs was supplied not by dyes but by pigments. These, being insoluble in water, did not bond to the fabric but rested on top of it and had to be fastened to avoid crocking. To fasten the pigments, soybean liquid (*gojiru*) was mixed with the ground pigment and the color applied in several thin layers with plenty of drying time in between. When steamed, the *gojiru* protein would bond to the fibers of the cloth and form a film over the pigment.[8]

Pigments may be organic or inorganic. Inorganic pigments are derived from various minerals. Organic pigments are made from vegetable dyes, generally by adding a mineral salt that precipitates the dye material to form a color lake, sludge, or dye concentrate (see chap. 12). *Beni* (safflower scarlet), *ai* (indigo), and *murasaki* (purple), being unsuitable for brushing in dye form, were among the dyes most commonly made into pigments. In addition, *akane* (madder) and *suō* (sappanwood) could be precipitated by adding alum to the dye bath. The sediment collected by this process would be filtered out and dried. It could be marketed in powdered form, or it might be mixed with a binder such as animal glue (*nikawa*) and then molded into a stick or painted onto a small porcelain plate, like watercolors.

Earth pigments predate dyestuffs as coloring matter for cloth, various reds and yellows having been rubbed into garments in prehistoric times. The practice continued among commoners during Nara and Heian. In the Edo period many of these ancient pigments were used on *yūzen*-dyed and freehand-painted kosode. Among the more common were *bengara*, a reddish brown from hematite; *ōdo*, an ochre made of hydrated iron oxide; and *shu*, a vermilion known as cinnabar, made from mercuric sulfide. The raw materials were collected from mountainsides or riverbeds and the pigments extracted by levigation, then dried and ground to a fine powder.[9] *Gofun* (gesso made from limestone) was used for white highlights; under or mixed with other colors *gofun* rendered opaque pale tints. *Gofun*-painted fabric remains stiff even after steaming.

Most important among the pigments was *sumi* (black ink), used for outlines and freehand drawing (Cpl. 52) as well as for background wash. It was made by combining the soot from lampblack (*yuen*) or pine resin (*shōen*) with animal glue (*nikawa*), then placing this viscous mixture in molds to harden into stick form. To obtain liquid ink, one rubbed the stick with water against a special stone. Large amounts, such as were used for *hiki-zome*, were perhaps marketed in liquid form, having first been processed to emulsify all the coarse bits of soot. A preliminary application of soybean liquid (*gojiru*) ensured that the *sumi* took to the cloth. *Sumi* blurs easily and must be applied with very fast, even strokes for *hiki-zome*. For the sharp outlines and shading on the petals of *tsujigahana* flowers (Cpl. 1, right) a special *sumi* known as *kachin* was used. *Kachin*, made from charred bamboo, had the advantage of running less than other kinds of *sumi*.

Chapter 12
FROM DYE PLANTS TO DYED FABRICS

Almost every plant contains coloring material, if one knows a way to extract and fix it. The particular color is determined by the chemical properties of the plant and is not necessarily the same as the color of the flowers or leaves. *Murasaki* flowers are white but the roots dye purple; *benibana* petals are yellow but dye red as well; indigo leaves are green but dye blue. The most ubiquitous color in nature, green, cannot be extracted from any single plant but must be compounded of blue and yellow dyes.[1] Soaking or boiling in water are the easiest methods of extracting dye color and are reasonably effective for most dyes. Discovering the precise timing and temperature that will obtain the best quality dye from each kind of dye plant transforms the simple processes into a sophisticated art.

The Japanese of the Nara period (645–794) were quick to learn, by experiment and probably from Korean artisans, what procedures best suited each dye source. They knew that *kariyasu* (*miscanthus*) must be harvested just before it blossoms; that indigo leaves, unless fermented, must be used immediately; that several months' maturation in a dark place increases the dye potential of *murasaki* roots and deepens the intensity of *murasaki*-dyed cloth.

They knew that *akane* (madder) red would not be clear unless the first and third boilings were discarded, and that *murasaki* roots yield gray instead of purple if pounded in water that is too hot. Until modern times there were no precise written formulas: the body of dye lore, empirically accumulated, was empirically transmitted from master to apprentice, often from father to son. When synthetic dyes threatened to extinguish the tradition of natural dyeing, certain descendants of the old dye houses systematically went about preserving it, so that the ancient art continues in the present day.[2] The Edo period plantations of indigo and *benibana* and *murasaki* still exist, though reduced in size, due to continuing demand for natural dyestuffs.

Dyeing cloth or yarn with plants involves a number of steps: cultivating and harvesting the plant; processing the harvested plant for either immediate extraction or storage; extracting the dye; preparing the material to be dyed; transferring the dye to the material; setting the color and drying the material; rinsing and redrying it; aging the dyed material to bring the color to full maturity. Each step contains a series of operations, many of which are seasonal. For certain dyes the process is so complex and time-consuming as to require specialization and division of labor. To gain some notion of what traditional dyeing involves, let us briefly consider the making and using of three of the more important and complex Japanese dyes: *murasaki* purple, *beni* scarlet, and indigo.

MURASAKI

The purple dye called *murasaki* comes from the roots of the perennial flowering plant also called *murasaki* by the Japanese. These homonyms have given rise to some botanical confusion: at least four other species whose roots give purple dye have been periodically imported from China to Japan, all under the name *murasaki* or *shikon* ("purple root", the medicinal name).[3]

Growing Murasaki

Murasaki purple comes almost entirely from wild plants, being extremely difficult to cultivate. In Heian (794–1185) literature we find references suggesting that the area of Musashino, around present-day Tokyo, was known for its fields of *murasaki*.[4] During the Edo period (1615–1868) much *murasaki* came from northern Honshū, particularly Iwate Prefecture. The silk was dyed mainly in Kyoto and Edo, using roots brought from the mountains.

The tall plants growing over the mountains and plains produce three or four clusters of tiny white flowers in early summer. Their long roots grow straight and deep the first year and thicken with supplementary rootlets in the third and fourth years, after which they are ready for harvesting. They are collected and cleaned and then dried for storage.

Mordanting

The cloth or yarn to be dyed with *murasaki* must be thoroughly premordanted and allowed to mature for at least a week, preferably months. This is done at the dye house. Lye made from camellia (*tsubaki*) ash, which contains alum, is the traditional alkali for mordanting, but other alum-rich woods are also used.[5] To make the mordant, water is dripped through the freshly burned wood ash, and in this bath the cloth is repeatedly dipped and then air-dried. Alternate steeping and airing is important, for the chemical reaction that occurs in mordanting uses up the oxygen supply in the mordant bath, which must be replenished before reimmersion of the cloth. About thirty immersions (of about twenty minutes each) done over a period of several months prepare yarn or cloth for *murasaki* dyeing.[6] Generally mordanting is done during the summer months, after which the fabric is allowed to mature, the better to take the dye.

Making the Dye and Dyeing

The dyeing itself is best done in cold weather, when the dye bath is less likely to sour or sediment and the distinctive *murasaki* stench impregnates the cloth less strongly. It has been speculated that the Heian fondness for perfumes may have arisen in response to the smell emanating from purple robes.[7] The following rather ironic poem from the *Manyōshū* captures the mixed feelings associated with the smell:

Murasaki no	If I disliked you,
nihoeru imo o	My beauty
	Redolent with *murasaki* purple,
nikuku araba	Would I still love you
hitotsuma yue ni	Although you are
ware koime ya mo.[8]	another man's wife?

To prepare *murasaki* dye, the roots, along with enough water to cover them, are placed in large stone mortars. Since the dye turns grayish at high temperature, the water is kept at about 60° C.[9] After soaking overnight, the roots are pounded to release the color in their inner bark. When sufficient color has been released to turn the water into dye, this dye batch is strained off and the roots are pounded again in fresh warm water to make a second dye batch. The dye batches from successive poundings are not collected and combined (as is done, for example, with *akane*); each dye batch must be used as soon as possible to forestall sedimentation. When no more color can be pounded from the now-pulverized roots, they may be bagged and put through a wringer to extract a final, weaker, bath, with which light shades can be dyed.

The yarn or cloth is immersed in the dye bath, worked, aired, reimmersed, aired again, and then allowed to steep. As in the mordanting process, the repeated airings replenish the oxygen in the dye bath. Finally the bath grows clear, all its color having been absorbed by the cloth or yarn. After an interval for drying and maturing the color, the process is repeated with new dye batches until the desired shade is reached. Many Edo period recipes call for immersing the cloth in vinegar at this point, in order to neutralize the alkaline mordant, which weakens cloth;[10] some modern dyers use methyl alcohol instead. After resting for a week or more, during which the bonding of the dye to the fabric continues, the dyed material is washed in running water, often a nearby river. The long strips of cloth drifting in the currents send quantities of color downstream: Kyoto's rivers proverbially ran purple for much of the winter. After final drying, the cloth is stored for as long as a year to let the color mature and deepen.

The contemporary dyer Yamazaki Seiju suggests that *murasaki* can be adapted for brush dyeing by adding methyl alcohol to the bath, which stabilizes the solution and slows its sedimentation rate.[11] For *yūzen* dyeing during the Edo period, *murasaki* was used in pigment form.

BENIBANA

Benibana is a biennial whose flowers, round like those of the thistle, bloom almost white, turn gold, and redden before withering. Its petals contain a water-soluble yellow dye and an alkali-soluble red dye. Used in dynastic Egypt as a medicine and as a dye in mummifying, *benibana* travelled through India to China and finally reached Japan about the early Nara period.[12] Since then it has been cultivated in Japan, planted in the fall in warmer areas and in spring in colder regions. In the Edo period major plantations grew up in Yamagata Prefecture in northeastern Honshū, and the area around the Mogami River in Yamagata is the one place where *benibana* is still grown commercially.[13]

Growing Benibana

Here the flowers come to bloom in early July. The first few buds appear as single pale yellow pompons, referred to as "midsummer lone blossoms"; soon deeper yellow flowers open in profusion. The flowering, which lasts for about two weeks, is at its height on the tenth day. As in other dye-giving plants, the dye potentiality is greatest before the color is fully developed in the flower, and when a hint of red appears at the base of the petals they are ready for plucking. Harvesting takes place in the early morning, when the dew has softened the plants' piercing thorns. The petals must be plucked without the calyx, a process requiring considerable deftness. A single stem will produce forty-five to fifty petals. Until about the Edo period the petals were set to dry in the sun directly on being harvested; otherwise they would blacken or rot. This made for a precarious crop, since sunshine is essential but July is the end of the rainy season and its weather is unpredictable.

Dye Making and Dyeing

Extracting *beni* dye from loose dried petals is a three-stage process that takes place at the dye houses. First the abundant and persistent yellow dye must be totally removed from the petals. This can be accomplished by putting the petals, enclosed in a porous cloth bag, into running water for two or three days, but it is faster to work and squeeze the petals

in bucket after bucket of fresh water until they give off little or no yellow. This yellow will dye silk, though not vegetable fibers, but for unknown reasons it was not generally used.[14]

Second, the petals (now free of yellow dye) are placed in a cotton or bast-fiber bag and immersed in alkaline solution—traditionally straw-ash or wood-ash lye. Again, the petals may simply be left in this bath for a few days, but the quicker method is to steep the bags for an hour or so and then work and rub them in the liquid and finally squeeze them dry. The result, either way, is a muddy brownish liquid. Only when this muddy alkaline bath is neutralized by the addition of an acid—traditionally *ubai* (vinegar made from smoked green plum skins)—does the dye clarify to a transparent red. This chemical reaction takes only a few minutes.

Silk yarn or cloth for dyeing must be thoroughly washed and air-dried. Any trace of oil from the hands would prevent *beni* dye from adhering at that spot.[15]

As with *murasaki* dyeing, the material immersed in the dye bath, worked, aired, and allowed to steep, will absorb almost all the color from the bath. It is thereupon hung in the shade to dry. The process must be many times repeated in new dye baths to achieve a deep scarlet. A poem in the *Manyōshū* implies eight dye baths, though "eight" may simply connote "many".[16] In any case, records show that at least twelve kilograms of petals were needed to make one scarlet *kosode* by the extraction method described above, which was the basic technique of making *beni* dye during Nara and Heian. The same method is still used today on Chinese *benibana*, which is imported in the form of loose dried petals.

The enormous expense involved in dyeing *beni* is summed up in the adage "A pound of *beni* is worth a pound of gold".[17] Yet its popularity led the Heian government to ease sumptuary restrictions and allow *beni* pink, which took only six hundred grams of petals, to be worn by the lower ranks of the nobility. During the Muromachi period (1333–1573) the court nobility declined steadily in power and importance, and in 1471 the government removed all restrictions on wearing *beni*-dyed clothing. Thus liberated, demand far outran supply, which must have stimulated efforts to use the available dye more efficiently. Whatever its origins, by the Edo period a new method of concentrating the color, speeding the dye-making process, and facilitating transport of the dye source had grown up.

Following the new method, the petals, instead of being dried immediately, are washed and trampled upon. The crushed petals are then placed in a container to ferment for two or three days, during which time they acquire a jam-like consistency and the yellow dye in them disappears, leaving a deep red color. (This eliminates the work of washing out the yellow.) The red "jam" is mashed smooth with mortar and pestle and worked into small balls. These are placed in rows on a straw mat, covered with another straw mat, and stamped into flat cakes (*beni mochi*), which are dried in the sun.[18] All this is done at the *benibana* plantation by the farmers.

At this point middlemen enter the scene. Merchants from towns near the *benibana* plantations check the dried cakes (*beni mochi*) for quality. (If fermentation was insufficient, the cakes will be fluffy; if drying was incomplete due to bad weather, the cakes will have turned blackish.) The cakes are then packed and shipped down the Mogami River to Sakata, the nearest seaport, and thence south over the Japan Sea to the port of Tsuruga. From there they go overland to Lake Biwa, and across Lake Biwa to Ōtsu, just a hillside away from Kyoto. In Kyoto the precious goods are received by special wholesalers (*toi ya*), who pass them on to storage wholesalers, who sell them to the *beni-zome ya*, the dye houses for safflower.

The principals in this lengthy transaction were the wholesalers and the dye houses, who together formed a guild. Not until they took delivery of the *beni mochi*, months after the harvest, were the farmers of the Mogami area paid for all their work.

In 1735 Kyoto boasted at least 147 dye houses specializing in *beni*.[19] A single-page illustration in the consumer's guide *Kyoto no sakigake*, published in 1883, illustrates the activities of a typical *beni* dye house, including the making of ash lye and the elaborate machines for squeezing the *beni mochi* in the lye to make a dye bath.[20] Unlike the loose dried petals, the fermented dye cakes reach the dye houses with the unwanted yellow already eliminated and the red much concentrated by the fermentation. Otherwise the dye-making and dyeing processes remain similar to those described above for use with loose dry petals.

A dye bath that looks clear (i.e., all its color absorbed by the fabric) after dyeing silk would yet contain enough color to dye cotton, which, like other vegetable fibers, has a close affinity with alkaline-base dyes like *beni*. Since these fibers have no affinity with yellow, the color they pick up is a true pink. Repeated dipping deepens and intensifies the color. Even during Edo, when the government was again most anxious to preserve visible distinctions in rank and *beni*-dyed silk was only for the imperial court and the upper samurai class, *beni*-dyed cotton was permitted to the lower orders. Demand increased continually.

The Japanese also make use of the peculiar affinities of vegetable fibers with *beni* to store the color and to create color lakes. Cotton or bast cloth dyed to a deep *beni* scarlet can be dried and stored, away from light, for any length of time. Since the dye works as a pesticide, it also preserves the cloth from insects. When the dye is needed, for example during the summer months, when high humidity is apt to rot *benibana* petals, the red cloth is reimmersed in an alkaline solution, which releases the color back into the solution. This bath, neutralized to a pH of about 7, can be used for brush dyeing (*hiki-zome*) if the pH is kept constant, if the dyed fabric is allowed a long time to dry and mature before final setting and washing, and if steaming, which damages the color, is omitted.[21]

Pigment

The dye thus collected and stored can also be used to make a color lake and create pigment. This is done by adding enough vinegar to turn the bath decidedly acid, thereby inducing sedimentation. After pouring off the water, the thick residue is collected and painted onto small porcelain plates (*beni zara*) for storage.[22] The pigment was used for highlights in *yūzen* dyeing, as a cosmetic, and as a medicine painted on the body to relieve burns and pains and to reduce high blood pressure.[23]

Benibana is used to dye embroidery yarn, weaving yarn, solid-color cloth, *shibori* designs, and *yūzen* designs in various hues and shades of red. Pink in various shades is dyed with *beni* alone. Scarlets are top-dyed over yellow, often from *kuchinashi* (gardenia) or *kihada* (philodendron). Orange requires a stronger under-dye of *kuchinashi*. By simply *not* washing the natural yellow out of the *benibana* petals, one gets salmon pink. Top-dyed over light indigo, *beni* produces lavender; over darker indigo it gives purple. It also serves as a base color for various browns.

When sumptuary law prohibited the wearing of *beni*-decorated *kosode*, the color continued to be used for linings and undergarments. Among these, the undergarments worn by imperial ladies-in-waiting are notable for being dyed with a block-resist technique (*itajime*) used only with this one dye. Elaborate designs, often in imitation of other techniques like *shibori*, were carved in relief into wooden boards, two boards of mirror-image pattern being placed face to face with the cloth carefully sandwiched between them. A stack of several such boards, all provided with holes and ducts for the dye to run through, was clamped tight and the whole was immersed in the dye bath or dye was poured through the ducts. This resulted in repetitive, often geometric, designs reserved in white on a dyed background.[24] A similar but more complex polychrome technique, called *kyōkechi*, had existed during Nara and into the Heian period, but all forms of it except this *beni itajime* had died out by the eleventh century.

INDIGO

The term indigo (*ai*) refers to a number of botanically different plants all of whose leaves contain indican, a colorless substance that turns blue when exposed to oxygen. Bruised spots on the leaves of the growing plant will reveal the hidden color. By the Nara period the imported Chinese *tade ai* (buckwheat) had been domesticated and had supplanted the native *yama ai* as the standard source of Japanese indigo dye. In the nineteenth century, particularly on Okinawa, a variety of indigofera (more common as an indigo source in the West) came under cultivation, and soon became a commercial rival of buckwheat indigo.

Making the Dye

The colorless indican turns blue, that is, turns into indigo, only on oxidation. But indigo blue, being insoluble in water, does not bond to fabric fibers. Unless the indigo molecules can be physically trapped deep in the fabric fibers, the color merely lies on the surface and is easily worn or washed away. Rubbing cloth with indigo leaves is not only the oldest method of dyeing blue but also the most impermanent. To enmesh the indigo molecules among the fabric filaments, the dye must be in a soluble state, i.e., not indigo blue but indican or a soluble, colorless derivative of indigo blue known as indigo white.

Method 1:
Dyeing with Fresh Leaves

The simplest way of achieving this is known as *namaha-zome* (dyeing with fresh leaves). The newly picked leaves are immediately crushed or chopped in water, releasing indican, which readily affixes to animal fibers such as silk or wool. The chopped leaves turn the water and the fabric immersed in it bright green, but once the fabric is removed from the water and exposed to air, the indican molecules trapped in it oxidize. In other words, the colorless indican turns to indigo and the fabric turns brilliant sky blue, the precise intensity of tone being determined by the proportion of leaves to water. Cloth or yarn is immersed only once, for a brief seven minutes. Since any exposure to air converts indican to insoluble

indigo, immediate processing before the leaves begin to wither and immediate dyeing once the juice is extracted are imperative, which greatly limits both the dyeing season and the quantity that can be dyed by this method.[25]

Method 2:
Dyeing with Fermentation
Vat of Fresh Leaves

During the Nara and early Heian periods the Japanese used a fermentation method that made it possible to keep an indigo vat over a period of months and produce more saturated, though less brilliant, shades of blue. The leaves, collected in early July, are placed with water in a deep, covered vat. The mixture is left to stand in the summer heat until the end of August, by which time the leaves have disintegrated and the bacteria in the organic refuse have induced fermentation. This consists of a continual set of slow chemical reactions within the vat: the feeding process of the bacteria robs indigo blue of its oxygen, converting whatever indican has turned to indigo blue into soluble indigo white. The dye is ready for use when purple bubbles form on the surface of the vat. Bacterial action on the leaves makes the bath itself a muddy brown, but materials immersed in it turn pale blue when exposed to air. Repeated dippings produce deeper color, all the way to navy blue.[26]

This method, still used in Okinawa with indigofera, has advantages as well as drawbacks. It permits dyeing over a longer period of the year than the *namaha-zome* method, though the vat can be maintained only as long as the temperature stays warm, into early October. As no alkalis are used in this dye process, textile fibers suffer little damage, even with the repeated or prolonged immersions necessary to produce deep blues. Dyeing times are lengthy because the small percentage of indican in fresh leaves makes for a weak (i.e., relatively unsaturated) vat. Since the leaves must be vatted in water immediately, before they begin to wither, the dyeing sites must be close to the indigo plantations.

By the ninth century the Japanese had discovered that indigo would color bast fibers, such as ramie, if ash lye was added to the fermented fresh-leaf vat.[27] The tenth-century *Engi shiki* mentions dried leaves used with an alkaline solution and distinguishes between this method and the use of fresh-picked leaves (presumably for fermentation, but possibly for *namaha-zome*). It is possible that the dry-leaf method, referred to as "new", involved composting. Certainly by the Muromachi period (1333–1573) the use of dried leaves and alkaline solution had evolved into a double-fermentation process in which the dried leaves are first made into a compost called *sukumo*.[28]

Method 3-A:
Dyeing with Fermentation Vat of Composted Leaves

To make *sukumo*, dried leaves are piled in a drafty storehouse, where they are kept damp but not wet and raked every five days.[29] After about seventy-five days thirty-three hundred pounds of chopped and dried leaves will have shrivelled to a pile approximately one by three by six feet. This pile is covered with a straw mat, weighted with large stones, and left to compost further. The result is a small quantity of highly concentrated indigo blue containing bits of organic material from the leaves.

To be usable as a dye, the concentrate must be dissolved in liquid and the indigo blue reduced to indigo white.[30] Actually, the two processes occur simultaneously. The *sukumo*, together with ash lye, is placed in a vat. There reduction is accomplished by the bacteria in the organic material, whose life processes consume oxygen, reducing the indigo blue to indigo white, which is soluble in the ash lye. This combined process takes several weeks, as opposed to the several months necessary to ferment a dye bath of fresh leaves in water. In effect, the *sukumo* method requires two fermentations: first the leaves are fermented in the storehouse to reduce their bulk and form the *sukumo*, then the *sukumo* is fermented in the vat to form the dye bath.

This method, known as *akudate*, is based on the concentrated dyestuff *sukumo*, which is easy to transport and makes dyeing possible in areas remote from the indigo fields. It also permits a more concentrated dye bath, which gives deeper blues in a shorter time. Light blues could be dyed in old indigo vats from which much of the indigo white had been used up. Still, because the second fermentation requires summer heat, it does not permit year-round dyeing. Some time before the seventeenth century the Japanese overcame the seasonal restriction by sinking the vats in pits heated with smoldering sawdust, usually four vats to one heat source.[31] They also learned to regulate the heat, keeping the vats at the optimum 30° C. Today many dyers, finding the humidity and uncertain weather of summer unfavorable to dyeing, leave off each year at just that time when the work used to begin.

Method 3-B:
Dyeing with Heated Fermentation Vat of Composted Leaves

The method of making dye using *sukumo* and heated vats is known as *shōai-zome*. It was employed throughout the Edo period. First the *sukumo* is soaked and kneaded, a small amount at a time, in ash lye to moisten and soften. Then it is placed in a large pottery vat, to which more lye is gradually added. Often lime is also added to increase alkalinity and thereby speed the dissolving process. To feed the bacteria that reduce the *sukumo* to indigo white, *sake* and rice bran are also put into the vat. The mixture is well stirred and then allowed to rest. The vats require daily tending: every morning and evening their pH is checked by smell, taste, and color. Additional lye might be necessary, or more bran or *sake*. For full and even reduction and dissolution the mixture might need stirring, but too much agitation decreases bacterial action and introduces unwanted oxygen. Every dyer has his own secret variations on the basic technique and proportions.[32] In a well-maintained vat, with an optimum pH of 10.5–11, the bacteria can continue to turn *sukumo* into indigo white over many months of dyeing, or until the dye molecules have all been transferred to cloth or yarn. Should the bacteria begin to die, an "indigo doctor" is called, who may recommend a bit more bran in the vat or a quiet rest for the mixture. When the dye is ready for use, deep purple bubbles called indigo flowers float on the surface of the muddy brown liquid.

Since the making of indigo dye demands much time, space, and sophisticated empirical knowledge, it had become a specialized occupation by the twelfth century. During the Edo period, what with the growing popularity of indigo-dyed cotton, every village had its *kon ya* (blue-dye house), whose main business was making and using indigo dye.[33]

The eighteenth century saw a further refinement on the *sukumo* method, probably developed in response to the rising demand for indigo to dye cottons. The *sukumo* is pounded into powder form and the powder made into cakes or pellets (*ai dama*). The pellets, being more concentrated even than the *sukumo*, are even easier to transport and produce an even more saturated dye bath.[34] Making *ai dama* was heavy work: gangs of workmen wielding large mallets pounded the *sukumo* all day in time to the rhythm of antiphonal work songs.[35] *Ai dama* are little used nowadays, perhaps because the ease and efficiency of modern transport renders such labor-intensive reduction in bulk unnecessary.

Dyeing

Before dyeing can begin, the purple bubbles floating on the surface of the dye bath must be moved to one side, for they are bits of oxidized indigo, which would not adhere to the fabric and would leave undyed spots. Washed and aired cloth or yarn is then immersed in the vat—gently, so as to minimize agitation of the bath, which would aerate it. Ten minutes per dip is sufficient for indigo white to lodge among the fibers. Generally, repeated brief dippings with ample airing after each dip and thorough drying after several dips make the best job, particularly when dyeing a paste-resisted design, for the paste will begin to dissolve if left in the vat too long. Because a *sukumo* dye bath can be more concentrated than one made with fresh-picked leaves, the dyeing time can be reduced. This is advantageous for paste-resist dyeing, but the dye molecules may be less deeply enmeshed in the fabric fibers and therefore more subject to crocking.

In dyeing yarn, permeation is facilitated by immediate and vigorous wringing followed by thorough airing. This is accomplished by whipping and rotating the skeins, which are stretched between two bamboo poles. Since oxidation proceeds quickly, streaks appear where excess liquid prevents the air from reaching the material, making even exposure and good weather necessary for good dyeing.

In order to dye paste-resisted cloth, the Japanese fasten bamboo tensors (*shinshi*) end to end along one selvedge of the cloth, then fold the cloth accordion style before dipping it into the vat. During the short immersion periods the tensors are either hand held or else suspended from a bamboo pole that can be rested across the mouth of the vat. When removed from the dye vat, the cloth is unfolded to dry, held open by the tensors spread out along the bamboo pole. To compensate for the unavoidable buildup of color on the lower edge of fabric hung from tensors, the cloth is turned upside down after every few dips. The same piece may be dipped and dried several times in one day, but then it will be allowed to rest for at least a week to let the color set. To get a good black-blue takes close to twenty dippings over a period of many weeks.

Growing Indigo

By the seventeenth century northeastern Shikoku, centering around present-day Tokushima Prefecture, had become the major indigo-growing area in Japan and the chief exporter of indigo to the major dye centers. Smaller plantations were scattered across the country, concentrated near villages famous for their indigo-dyed cottons with *shibori* or *kasuri* (*ikat*) designs. Many of the new villages which sprang into existence on Shikoku include the character *ai* (indigo) in their names.[36] The Yoshino River, flowing toward the port city of Tokushima, fertilized the fields by its flooding and also provided convenient transport for the harvested leaves fermented into *sukumo*.

Indigo seeds are planted in late February or early March and sprout within about three weeks. Seedlings are thinned and transplanted in May, after which they are carefully guarded against parasites that might bruise the leaves. In early July, before flowers can develop, the stalks are cut a few inches above the ground and the leaves stripped and laid out on mats to dry. A second harvest is taken in September, by which time the plants have more than regained their original stature and have also spread, sending out fresh roots at the nodes of the stalks. In November the plants, which have again grown up, are allowed to come to blossom, with clusters of tiny white, red, or pink flowers along a single stamen shooting up from the central stalk. The seeds are dried and saved for the next planting. The percentage of germinations from these seeds drops heavily if they are stored over the summer, so they are best replanted the first spring after they are gathered.

Growing and Marketing Indigo

Harvested leaves, stripped from the stems and dried, were laid on a mat and pounded into leaf indigo, which was then sold to the indigo processors, whose business it was to ferment the leaves into *sukumo*. *Sukumo* and *ai dama* (indigo pellets), packed in rice-straw bags marked pine, bamboo, plum, cherry, or peach (in descending order of quality), were sent down the Yoshino River to Tokushima City for an annual market on November 15. Here buyers from Osaka and Kyoto gathered. Before the product could be sold, however, it was tested by officials, who smelled it, kneaded the wetted *sukumo* to check elasticity, and pressed the *sukumo* ball against paper to check its color. The very highest quality was then labelled *zui-ichi*. At the dye houses small quantities of *zui-ichi* were often added to less exalted dye baths in order to enhance the desirability and raise the price of the dyed cloth.[37]

Indigo, like *benibana*, created a social network that extended over a large geographical area and included many middlemen. The ever expanding popularity of indigo generated an expanding trade that linked not only major cities but villages all over Japan, each of which specialized in different indigo-dyed designs. The system of interchanges included, in addition to indigo itself, all the tools required for its cultivation, processing, and use. Special rakes and hand-plows were manufactured for planting and tending, and a pronged bamboo instrument for stripping the leaves. The fresh leaves were crushed with sticks and bamboo brooms, and dirt was sifted out with large wicker baskets.[38] Most remarkable of these implements, however, are the large ceramic dye vats, produced from special elastic clay found in Tokushima Prefecture, and known as Odani ware. They are the height of a man, comparatively thin-walled, and tapered downward in order to make stirring easy. To ensure their stability, they are sunk into the ground.

Indigo is a component of many colors. It is used as an under-dye to make green and some purples, like *futa ai* (indigo plus *beni)* and *nise murasaki* (indigo plus *suō*). As a very light over-dye it softens other colors. Combined with *akane* (madder red) or with tannin-containing tree extracts, it can make black. It is highly advantageous to make dark colors with indigo, which acts as a cloth preservative and pesticide.[39]

Pigment

In addition to acting as a dye, oxidized indigo blue could be collected, purified, and used as a pigment. The Japanese did this by skimming the purple bubbles of oxidized indigo from the top of the mature dye bath, then drying and pulverizing them. The resulting powder, mixed with animal glue, was hardened in molds (like *sumi*) to make indigo sticks (*ai bō*). Sometimes *sumi* was added to the indigo powder to darken the shade.[40] Another source of pigment was old indigo-dyed clothes, which were collected and soaked in alkaline solution containing sugar. The indigo dissolved into the alkaline solution, and bacteria, nourished by the sugar, reduced the indigo molecules again to indigo white, which fermented. Purple bubbles of indigo blue formed on the surface of the fermented dye and were skimmed aside in the usual way.[41]

To make liquid pigment for painting, the indigo stick (again like *sumi)* was rubbed with water on an inkstone. If the pigment was intended for painting on cloth, the indigo stick might be rubbed with soybean liquid (*gojiru*) instead of water; if water was used, the cloth was first thoroughly treated with soybean liquid. On *yūzen-* and *chaya-zome kosode* indigo pigment appears as thin outlines or opaque areas of blue (Cpl 45).

The Chinese seem to have made indigo sticks by precipitating the bath, collecting the solid particles of color, and washing them. This creates a purer blue than the Japanese method. The indigo wax imported to Japan from India (*ai rō*), which appears blacker than the Chinese or Japanese pigments, was also probably obtained by precipitation.[42]

This brief essay could only touch on some highlights of the history of Japanese color sensibilities and on selected aspects of the Japanese preparation and use of colors. The Japanese experience of colors is and was both intimate and manifold.

Throughout Japanese history colors themselves have had metaphoric, connotative significance as well as decorative value. What a color signifies is as important to the wearer as how it looks. The emotional significance of colors was enriched by widespread acquaintance with the plants from which they derived and with the actions and instruments by which they were transferred from plant to garment. Equally well known were the proverbs and the literary references that attached to the plants and the processes. Colored, patterned fabrics did not reach consumers as finished products created by remote and anonymous agencies. Such publications as the *hiinagata* books and the consumers' dictionaries (*kaimono tebikigusa*)[43]—which described the best dye houses for each color, the best shops for stencil making and resist dyeing—testify to a continuing close involvement between the wearer of a fabric and its creation.

CHRONOLOGY

Asuka	552–645
Nara	645–794
Heian	794–1185
Kamakura	1185–1333
Muromachi	1333–1573
Momoyama	1573–1615
Keichō	1596–1615
Edo	1615–1868
Early Edo	1615–1688
Kanbun	1661–1673
Mid-Edo	1688–1781
Genroku	1688–1704
Late Edo	1781–1868
Meiji	1868–1912
Taishō	1912–1926

NOTES
In the footnotes and records of previous publication all works appear in abbreviated form. Full citations will be found in the Bibliography.

Japanese terms for techniques, materials, and conventionalized design motifs can be found in the Glossary.

The dimensions of intact *kosode* are given in the following order:
length (*mitake*)—center back seam, excluding neckband;
width (*yuki*)—center back to sleeve opening (this is half the full width);
sleeve width (*sode haba*)—shoulder seam to sleeve opening;
sleeve length (*sode take*)—top of shoulder to lower edge of sleeve.

CATALOGUE

1 SCREEN WITH TWO KOSODE (DETAIL)

LEFT: *Tsujigahana* **design of white flower sprays**
Stitch-resist and capped *shibori*
Purple *nerinuki* **silk**
Momoyama period, second half sixteenth century
All Screens are approximately 175cm × 175cm.

The pattern of flower sprays reserved in white was created wholly by means of *shibori*: the outline of the leaves and the stems of the flowers in simple stitch resist and the solid white blossoms in capped *shibori*. This may have been a man's *kosode*, as suggested by Tōhaku's portrait of Takeda Shingen (1521–73) and by the robe worn by one of the seated male figures in the screen painting *Maple Viewing at Takao*.[1] Representative of the simplest type of *tsujigahana*, in which the pattern is reserved in white against a dyed background, this piece is probably the earliest in the Nomura Collection.

1. The portrait of Shingen, by Hasegawa Tōhaku, is in the Jōkei-in, Wakayama Prefecture. *Maple Viewing at Takao* is in the Tokyo National Museum. They are reproduced in Itō, *Tsujigahana*, pls. 73, 79.

RIGHT: *Tsujigahana* **design of white squares on horizontal brown band, white**
 camellias and wistaria on horizontal green band
Shibori **and black ink**
White *nerinuki* **silk**
Momoyama period, sixteenth century

Two broad bands of *tsujigahana* decorate the white silk ground, the upper band patterned with white squares on rust brown, the lower with camellias and wistaria reserved on a green background. The upper band is continuous with the white background at its upper edge but seamed onto the white silk at its lower edge. The flowered band is seamed to the white background at both top and bottom. The unglossed warp yarns of *nerinuki* silk are fragile and break easily. In particular, the borders between pattern and background areas are weakened by the hemp threads pulled tight during the *shibori* process. In this fragment some of the hemp threads used in the resist stitching were accidentally left in the fabric. Probably this *kosode* had disintegrated along the lines of *shibori* stitching and the pieces were later sewn together, perhaps when they were mounted on the screen. These seams suggest that the present composition may differ from the original composition of the *kosode*.

In the lower band capped *shibori* renders the camellia and wistaria blossoms and leaves, with stitch resist defining some of their outlines and stems. Occasional dark yellow leaves appear to be pinch dyed rather than brushed in. Dewdrops and insect holes, the fine details of the camellia blossoms, and the shading of leaves and flowers are painted in black ink in the *hakubyō* style. Although the *shibori* techniques employed appear simple, the addition of delicate ink painting makes this a fine example of the lightness that characterizes *tsujigahana* designs. There are many extant examples of this typical mode.[1]

1. See Itō, *Tsujigahana*, pls. 68–69, 72, 74–78, 81, 83–84, 86–88, 90–92.

PUBLISHED: Imanaga, *Kosode I*, pl. 12.
 Itō, *Tsujigahana*, pl. 82 (left only).
 Minnich, *Japanese Costume*, pl. 46.
 Nomura, *Hiinagata byōbu*, pl. 6.
 Royal Academy of Arts, *Great Japan Exhibition*, no. 339. (In the first printing of this
 catalogue the left-hand fragment was mistakenly identified as "*nuihaku* with *Tsujigahana*".)
 Senshoku no bi 1, pls. 1, 11.
 Tokyo National Museum, *Nihon no senshoku*, nos. 118, 119.

LEFT: *Tsujigahana* design of grapevines, grape leaves, and lozenges
Shibori and black ink
White *nerinuki* silk
Momoyama period, sixteenth century

Stitch resist combined with another *shibori* method, perhaps tub resist, has reserved the entire background of this plain-weave silk in white. Only the purple, yellow-ochre, and yellow-green grape leaves and lozenges have been allowed to absorb the dye. Against the white silk fruiting grapevines, grape leaves, and lozenges have been executed in a variety of techniques. The vines, grapes, and leaves are delicately painted in black ink and lightly colored with pale blue. Small pine trees painted in ink are enclosed in pale blue lozenges, as if seen through diamond-shaped windows. Veins in the leaves are rendered in ink or in lines of white dots reserved by stitch resist. Insect holes or dewdrops on the purple leaves are similarly reserved in white. Purple lozenges paved with *kanoko* dots are centered with reserved water chestnut bulbs; the deep yellow lozenges are solid colored, with five-petalled purple blossoms in their centers. (In another fragment of the same *kosode*, preserved in a private collection, olive green lozenges appear as well.)[1]

This fragment may be close in date to garments owned by Toyotomi Hideyoshi and Tokugawa Ieyasu and made probably in the late sixteenth century.[2] Such a date is suggested by its graphic simplicity of design and by technical similarities to those garments, particularly the use of *shibori* to define dyed motifs on a white background and to depict insect holes. The free execution and high quality of the ink painting, related more closely to Chinese style ink painting than to the stiffer *hakubyō* style, are rare in the art of *tsujigahana kosode* decoration. A superb formal balance is maintained among the painted pictorial areas, *shibori* areas, and white background. Although only a fragment, this is one of the masterpieces of the Nomura Collection.

1. This fragment has been published in Itō, *Tsujigahana*, pl. 67, and in *Senshoku no bi* 1, pl. 42.
2. Itō, *Tsujigahana*, p. 30 and pls. 2–4, 55.

RIGHT: Keichō black-background style with mountain peaks, waves, pine-bark
    lozenges, and snow roundels
Shibori, embroidery, and gold leaf
Black figured satin: 1/4 weft-faced figure of key fret on 4/1 warp-faced ground
Early Edo period, early seventeenth century

Capped *shibori* reserves snow-covered mountain peaks that merge with cresting waves across the left sleeve, the shoulder, the neckband, and the lower part of the skirt. The black background encroaches upon the lower borders of these forms, creating pine-bark lozenges. Large *kanoko shibori* roundels with irregular outlines suggest the crenellated snow disks popular during early Edo. Fan papers are irregularly disposed across these roundels and the background; some are rendered in *kanoko*, others in black against *kanoko*, yet others in white capped *shibori*.

By comparison with the *shibori* motifs, the embroidered motifs are minute in scale. They include flowing white streams; chrysanthemums, pinks, and pines in red and two shades of green; latticed fan papers and lozenges, both filled with squared spirals; and, just below the central roundel, two miniature cranes. Traces of gold leaf remain, but its pattern is indistinguishable.

Snow-capped mountains, surging waves, pines, and snow roundels constitute an illusion to a poem from the *Kokinwakashū* by Fujiwara no Okikaze (see above, pp. 48). This new interest in allusive pictorial representation is skillfully combined with the textural richness characteristic of Keichō *kosode*, a union rare in *kosode* design of the early seventeenth century.

PUBLISHED: Nomura, *Hiinagata byōbu*, pl. 4.
          Royal Academy of Arts, *Great Japan Exhibition*, no. 340.
          Senshoku no bi 19, pl. 22 (right only).
          Tokyo National Museum, *Nihon no senshoku*, nos. 122, 123.

3 DETAIL OF COLORPLATE 2

In this detail we see clearly the contrast between the plain-weave *nerinuki* silk of the earlier, *tsujigahana*, fragment (left) and the figured satin of the later Keichō example (right). The *shibori* techniques that reserved the entire background of the *tsujigahana* textile while dyeing limited pattern areas are more complicated than those needed to reserve pattern areas on the Keichō cloth.

LEFT: *Tsujigahana* design of bellflowers and camellias on divided background
Shibori
Brown and white *nerinuki* silk
Momoyama period, late sixteenth century

Alternating horizontal bands of chestnut brown and white have undulant outlines
defined by stitch-resist *shibori*. Six narrow strips of deep red within the brown areas
probably reveal their original, unfaded, color, which may have been dyed with
sappanwood. Within the brown bands are Chinese bellflowers reserved in capped
shibori, their fine stems executed in stitch resist. Red camellias with light and dark
green leaves stand out against the white areas. Stitch-resist *shibori* outlines the petals
and delineates the leaf veins; petal markings and dewdrops on the leaves have been
reserved in capped *shibori*. An occasional petal is patterned with *kanoko shibori*,
adding a curious three-dimensional effect to the otherwise flat design.

   Where the overlap joins the left front the motifs do not match, suggesting that the
present arrangement of fragments on the screen is not the original composition.
Comparison with other *tsujigahana* garments containing strong horizontal elements
shows that in most cases an effort was made to match the design at the seams.[1]
Further evidence that the original *kosode* may have differed in composition is
provided by a temple banner, made from what is clearly the same *kosode*, in the
Kyoto National Museum, and an additional fragment in the Tōyama Kinenkan,
Saitama Prefecture.[2] The fragments on the Nomura screen may have been taken from
similar banners. If so, the deep red strips would have been protected from the light,
and therefore from fading, by the horizontal struts of the banners, while on the
unprotected areas the fragile red dye faded to brown.

   Unfortunately neither the banner nor the Nomura piece is dated, but the boldness
of the design and compositional and technical similarities between the fragment and
garments said to have been owned by Toyotomi Hideyoshi and Tokugawa Ieyasu
suggest a late sixteenth-century date.[3] The combination of reserved pattern on dyed
ground with dyed pattern on reserved ground implies advanced skill and further
links the Nomura fragment and Kyoto banner to this group of garments.

   Plain-weave *nerinuki* silk was the material used most frequently for *tsujigahana*
decoration. No woven pattern obscures the subtleties of fine *shibori* or ink painting,
and the slightly crisp fabric displays perfectly, as here, the flat, graphic quality of
tsujigahana design.

---

1. Itō, *Tsujigahana*, pls. 2, 6, 38, 48–50, 55.
2. Imanaga, *Kosode I*, pl. 33.
3. Itō, *Tsujigahana*, pls. 2, 6, 55.

RIGHT: Allover design of flowers and clouds
Shibori, embroidery, and gold leaf
Plain-weave black glossed silk
Early Edo period, early seventeenth century

On a black background of plain-weave glossed silk, clusters of chrysanthemums,
pinks, plum blossoms, and pines are embroidered in red and two shades of green.
Clouds executed in *kanoko shibori* drift among these motifs, which resemble
mountains in their groupings. Only traces now remain of the mist, overlapping

circles, and other gold-leaf diaper patterns that once completely covered the background, making this an example of *ji-nashi* (without background) *kosode*. The brownish black color is typical of what are known as Keichō *kosode*, but there is disagreement about what dye or dyes were used to produce it.

PUBLISHED: Itō, *Tsujigahana*, pl. 33.
Minnich, *Japanese Costume*, pl. 47 (left only).
Nomura, *Hiinagata byōbu*, pl. 1.
Senshoku no bi 1, pl. 12 (left only).
Tokyo National Museum, *Nihon no senshoku*, nos. 120, 121.

5 KOSODE SCREEN IN DIVIDED-BACKGROUND STYLE WITH ALLOVER DESIGN OF FLOWERS AND GRASSES OF THE FOUR SEASONS

Shibori with embroidery and gold leaf
Red, black, white, and light blue figured satin: 1/4 weft-faced figure of key fret,
 plum blossoms, and bamboo grass on 4/1 warp-faced ground
Momoyama period, early seventeenth century

In a typical example of the Keichō style the surface of this figured-satin *kosode* was divided into large overlapping and juxtaposed abstract forms by means of stitch-resist *shibori*. Although the *kosode* is predominantly red, the areas of black, white, and pale blue also serve as backgrounds for embroidery and gold leaf; thus it is referred to as a divided-background *kosode*. These color areas, though abstract, at the same time resemble specific natural forms: the black areas, mountains; the white, clouds or rocks; the blue, clouds or crenellated snow roundels; the red, earth, clouds, or snow roundels.

Flowers and plants of the four seasons, including cherry blossoms, wistaria, hydrangea, scouring rush, pampas grass, pinks, bush clover, chrysanthemums, and pines, are embroidered on the red and white grounds in blue, white, red, and dark and light green. Gold leaf has been applied to the black areas in the mist pattern. Overlapping circles of gold leaf, only traces of which now remain, extend across the back at shoulder level from the center to the left shoulder and down the left side. Where four circles intersect, diamond shapes, slightly concave, are embroidered in dark green, yellow-green, and white. *Kanoko shibori* appears only in narrow, parallel bands just to the left of the right sleeve. Some of the larger forms, including clouds and snow roundels, are crudely outlined in ink; at the left shoulder, a rough lattice has been painted between the white clouds.

Although the red color is considerably faded and much of the gold leaf has been lost, this *kosode* is a fine example of the mature Keichō style. A *kosode* comparable in style and date belongs to the Kanebo Collection, Osaka.[1] The Kanebo *kosode*, however, contains silver embroidery, while the Nomura piece has applied gold leaf but no metallic embroidery. This *kosode* proved too fragile to include in the exhibition at Japan House Gallery.

---

1. Imanaga, *Kosode I*, no. 48.
PUBLISHED: Nomura: *Hiinagata byōbu*, pl. 2.
 Tokyo National Museum, *Nihon no senshoku*, no. 141.

Pattern crams the surface of the figured satin so that the background seems to disappear: *ji-nashi* (without background) is clearly an appropriate appellation. The woven figure, consisting of key fret, plum blossoms, and bamboo grass, is larger in scale and more prominent than on comparable examples in the Nomura Collection.

KOSODE SCREEN IN DIVIDED-BACKGROUND STYLE WITH FLORAL MOTIFS AND AUSPICIOUS SYMBOLS ON ABSTRACT SHAPES

Shibori, embroidery and touches of gold leaf
Red, black, and white figured satin: 1/4 weft-faced figure of key fret and flowers on
    4/1 warp-faced ground
Early Edo period, first half seventeenth century

On a ground divided into large, abstract shapes of red, black, and white a pine bough, pendent paulownia blossoms, and floral sprays are depicted in *kanoko shibori*. The pine bough is composed of rows of hexagons, a conventionalized form of tortoise-shell diaper pattern. Black and white forms to its left resemble giant chrysanthemum leaves. Beneath the pine bough are embroidered a smaller pine bough and paulownia flowers with chevron-patterned leaves outlined in gold couching. Pinks, *ominaeshi*, chrysanthemums, and vine scrolls sprouting cherry blossoms are embroidered in blue, white, light and dark green, purple, red, and couched gold. In the open central area hover two embroidered cranes. They are miniaturized, like the two embroidered gold tortoises below them to the left, incongruously floating above tiny pines. Cherry-blossom scrolls and blue wave patterns (*seigaiha*, a pattern resembling overlapping fish scales) are embroidered in narrow vertical bands faintly outlined in gold leaf on the white chrysanthemum-leaf shape at the left.

Pines, cranes, and tortoises, all auspicious motifs derived from Chinese art, symbolize longevity and endurance. From the early Edo period onward such auspicious themes become increasingly popular in *kosode* design. Here they are freshly and freely interpreted, but in nineteenth-century *kosode* they become highly formalized and predictable and thus less interesting. Early Edo style is seen in the use of *kanoko shibori* to represent concrete forms such as the large pine bough and paulownia blossoms and in the increase in open space in the composition; Keichō style remains apparent in coloration and technique.

PUBLISHED: Nomura, *Hiinagata byōbu*, pl. 9.
    Tokyo National Museum, *Nihon no senshoku*, no. 147.

**KOSODE SCREEN IN DIVIDED-BACKGROUND STYLE WITH CHRYSAN-
THEMUM LEAVES, FANS, AND ABSTRACT SHAPES**

Shibori, embroidery, and gold leaf
Red, black, and white figured satin: 1/4 weft-faced figure of key fret and chrysanthe-
   mums on 4/1 warp-faced ground
Early Edo period, early seventeenth century

Plume-like chrysanthemum leaves, fans, and bold abstract forms in red, black, white,
and pale blue have been created by means of stitch-resist and capped *shibori*.
Kanoko shibori partially fills a number of fan papers and one leaf form. Bamboo,
bamboo shoots, floral medallions, and mandarin orange trees are embroidered on the
red area only in blue, white, light and dark green, purple, and couched gold.
Delicate gold leaf completely fills the black areas with various diaper patterns, some
with superimposed pines and cranes. Some of the white areas, including the fan at
the upper left and the leaf at the lower end of the neckband, are painted in pigments
with a treasure sack, a pomegranate, and pines. Although the combination of motifs is
suggestive, it has no evident significance.

   Typically (although not universally) in Keichō *kosode*, metallic leaf is confined to
the black areas and embroidery to the red and white. The forceful curve of the
composition from sleeve to hem, the increased use of gold embroidery, and the
magnification of individual elements suggest an early seventeenth-century date.

PUBLISHED: Imanaga, *Kosode I*, pl. 55.
   Nomura, *Hiinagata byōbu*, pl. 13.
   Tokyo National Museum, *Nihon no senshoku*, no. 151.

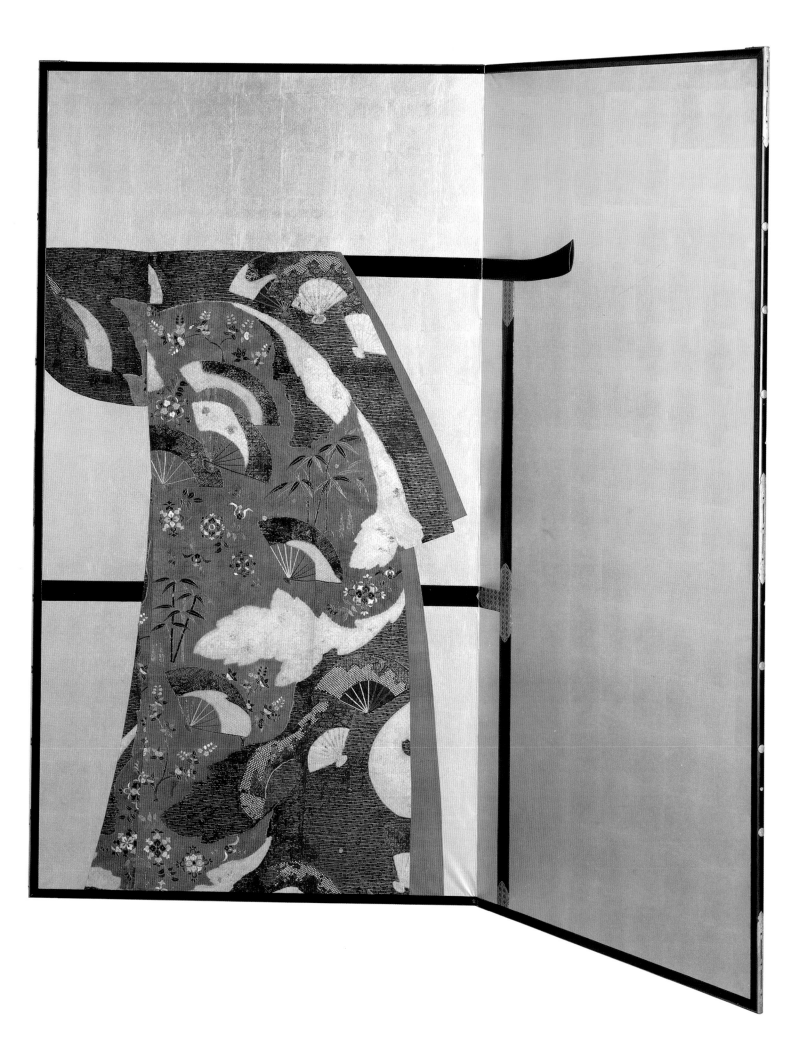

9 KOSODE SCREEN IN DIVIDED-BACKGROUND STYLE WITH FLORAL MOTIFS, FENCE, AND ABSTRACT SHAPES

Shibori with embroidery, gold leaf, and ink painting
Red, black, and white figured silk twill: 1/4 weft-faced figure of key fret and
   chrysanthemums on 4/1 warp-faced ground
Early Edo period, first half seventeenth century

The bold abstract shapes of red, black, and white, created by means of stitch-resist *shibori*, can also be interpreted pictorially as leaves, flowers, rocks, a wave, open space. At lower right a rustic fence is juxtaposed with oversized flowers, both depicted in *kanoko shibori*; the flower motif, again in *kanoko*, is repeated above the waist. A white cresting wave, which might also be read as a pond, threatens to engulf the fence. Pine trees and bamboo grass are dwarfed by chrysanthemums, pinks, and pampas grass, all embroidered in red, white, dark and light green, and brown (originally probably purple, now faded). Gold-leaf mist pattern once covered the black areas, and traces remain also on the red area between fence and wave, as well as on the little cloud freely outlined in black ink at the upper left.

This *kosode*, like the one in Colorplate 7, which it resembles, is typical of the late Keichō style.

PUBLISHED: Imanaga, *Kosode I*, pl. 58.
      Nomura, *Hiinagata byōbu*, pl. 31.
      Senshoku no bi 19, pl. 62.
      Tokyo National Museum, *Nihon no senshoku*, no. 149.

10 KOSODE SCREEN IN DIVIDED-BACKGROUND STYLE WITH WISTARIA VINES, AUSPICIOUS SYMBOLS, AND ABSTRACT SHAPES

Stitch-resist *shibori* with embroidery and gold leaf
Black and white figured silk twill: 1/3 weft-faced twill figure of key fret and
 chrysanthemums on 3/1 warp-faced ground
Early Edo period, first half seventeenth century

This stunning *kosode* is divided into black and white areas by stitch-resist *shibori*, sparingly decorated with embroidery, and enriched with gold leaf. Although at first glance purely abstract, the black and white forms resolve themselves into tree trunk and boughs or, alternatively, into an expanse of dark water against a white shoreline, with smaller islands of white on the sleeve and hem.

From the massive yet graceful black tree form hang flowering wistaria and other vines embroidered in light and dark green, blue, white, and red, with silver couching. If we interpret the black as water, then the embroidered blossoming cherry trees and pines with cranes perched in their branches line a white shore. Pines and cranes both symbolize longevity, as do tortoises. Although no tortoise is depicted here, this auspicious motif is present in the tortoise-shell lozenges embroidered at center left. The black areas are closely textured with gold leaf in the familiar mist pattern, on which are superimposed crenellated snow roundels figured in gold leaf with various diaper patterns, phoenixes, and foliage. Some of the roundels contain embroidered motifs as well. The extensive use of metallic leaf, unusual in combination with couched embroidery in gold or silver leaf-wrapped thread, gradually disappears from *kosode* decoration after this period. Compositionally, this *kosode* represents a transition between the Keichō and Kanbun styles.

The "sandy beach" (*suhama*) motif, freely interpreted here, dates from the Heian period, when miniature landscapes of rocks, trees, birds, and various auspicious objects were constructed in footed trays for use as decorations on festive occasions such as the New Year. The motif was also used on robes and is mentioned in the narrative literature of the period. It derives from the theme of the sacred Mt. Hōrai, associated in Chinese legend with the island where the Immortals dwell. A Chinese bronze mirror dating to the Tang dynasty (618–907) is decorated with variations of the sandy beach and Mt. Hōrai motifs.[1]

From the Muromachi period comes a beautiful example of the sandy shore motif in costume design: the drawing of a pine-fringed shore, reeds, and ducks on the divided skirt (*hitoe-bakama*) dedicated to the Hayatama Taisha Shrine at Kumano in 1390.[2] Another example in the Nomura Collection dates from the eighteenth century (Cpl. 37).

---

1. *Treasures of the Shōsō-in*, pl. 56 and p. 64.
2. *Senshoku no bi* 23, pl. 30.
PUBLISHED: Nomura, *Hiinagata byōbu*, pl. 7.
 Tokyo National Museum, *Nihon no senshoku*, no. 150.

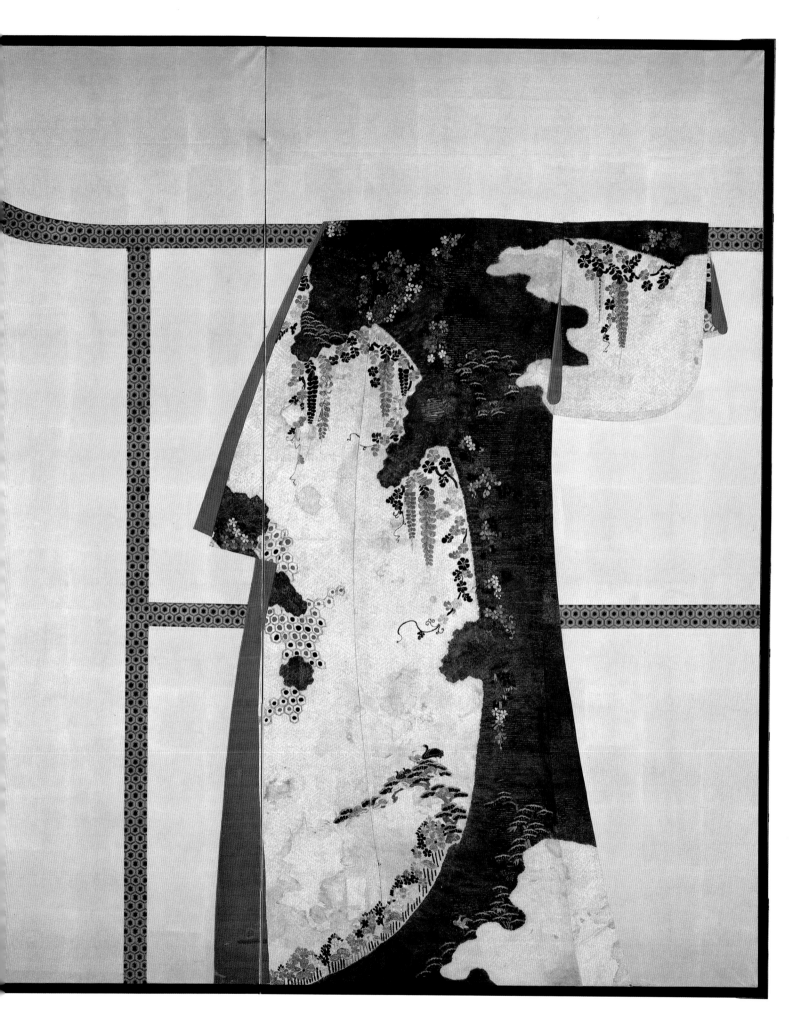

KOSODE SCREEN IN DIVIDED-BACKGROUND STYLE WITH TREE
PEONIES, PINES, AND CRANE ROUNDELS ON VERTICAL STRIPES

Stitch-resist *shibori* with embroidery and gold leaf
Red, black, and white figured satin: 1/4 weft-faced satin figure of key fret, orchids,
and plum blossoms on 4/1 warp-faced ground
Early Edo period, first half seventeenth century

Broad vertical stripes of red, black, and white, their sawtooth edges defined by
means of stitch-resist *shibori*, contrast sharply with the pictorial representation of
tree peonies, pines, and crane roundels embroidered in red, white, dark green,
yellow-green, and blue. (The crane roundels are probably decorative elements rather
than family crests.) The embroidered motifs are larger than in earlier Keichō textiles,
permitting the depiction of such details as the bark and moss on tree trunks. Traces of
gold leaf remain on the black areas, but the original pattern is indistinguishable.
Vertical stripes are unusual in seventeenth-century *kosode* design, but the coloration,
the *shibori*-divided background, and the presence of gold leaf point to a late
development of the Keichō style.

Most of the fabric is quite darkened with soil, against which cleaner horizontal
strips stand out clearly, especially in the white areas. This suggests that the material
was once folded into pleats whose inner folds were protected from discoloration. This
kosode may have been dedicated to a Buddhist temple on the death of its owner, to
ensure recitation of prayers for her soul—a common practice in the Edo period.
Often these *kosode* were made into altar cloths or cut up and pieced into priests'
stoles, the patchwork signifying clerical poverty. It was not uncommon, however, to
simulate such patchwork by pleating the cloth, thus preserving the integrity of a
valuable fabric. This *kosode* may well have been pleated into such a stole, then
painstakingly reassembled by Nomura Shōjirō for his collection.

PUBLISHED: Imanaga, *Kosode I*, no. 56.
Nomura, *Hiinagata byōbu*, pl. 11.
Tokyo National Museum, *Nihon no senshoku*, no. 153.

Shibori, embroidery, and traces of gold leaf
Black figured satin: 1/4 weft-faced figure of key fret and plum blossoms on 4/1
 warp-faced ground
Early Edo period, first half seventeenth century

Interlocking sections of bamboo fence reserved in capped *shibori* and *kanoko* against
the black background establish the basic diagonal composition of this design. It is
emphasized by diagonal bands of embroidered motifs stretching from upper right to
lower left: pines, cherry blossoms, pinks, chrysanthemums, crane roundels, and
geometric figures such as tortoise-shell diaper, interlocking circles, and a vertical
zigzag pattern (known as mountain path) are depicted in red, white, and two shades
of green. Scattered maple leaves in *kanoko shibori* soften the rigidity of the
diagonals. The entire black background was originally covered with gold leaf, but only
faint traces remain, primarily in the mist pattern. The diagonal rows of what appear
to be undecorated circles were originally filled with gold leaf in a pattern now
indistinguishable.

 The well-ordered surface of this *kosode* establishes it firmly within the context of
the early Edo period.

PUBLISHED: Nomura, *Hiinagata byōbu*, pl. 5.
 Senshoku no bi 21, pl. 2.

13 KOSODE SCREEN IN BLACK-BACKGROUND STYLE WITH SCATTERED BLOSSOMS, PINES, AND SNOW ROUNDELS

Shibori, embroidery, and gold leaf
Black figured satin: 1/4 weft-faced figure of key fret and interlocking circles on 4/1 warp-faced ground
Early Edo period, first half seventeenth century

White snowflake roundels reserved in capped *shibori* and *kanoko* overlap with embroidered roundels of chrysanthemums, pinks, hydrangea, and pines in red and two shades of green. Tiny embroidered cherry blossoms, chrysanthemums, and vine scrolls in the same colors form vertical streamers. The entire ground was originally covered with gold leaf; remaining traces are primarily in the mist pattern, but there are areas of key fret and chrysanthemums, possibly pieced in from another part of the *kosode*.

Although the *shibori* is somewhat crudely executed and the decoration is, overall, weak, this *kosode* is interesting as an obvious link between the Keichō and Kanbun styles, showing the coloring and small-scale design motifs of the former along with the asymmetric composition of the latter.

PUBLISHED: Nomura, *Hiinagata byōbu*, pl. 8.
Tokyo National Museum, *Nihon no senshoku*, no. 154.

14 KOSODE IN BLACK-BACKGROUND STYLE WITH GIANT GRASS BLADES

Kanoko shibori, embroidery, and gold leaf
Black figured satin: 1/4 weft-faced figure of key fret, orchids, and peonies on 4/1
    warp-faced ground
L. 150   W. 63.5   S.W. 30.5   S.L. 56 cm.
Early Edo period, first half seventeenth century

Four blades of grass or perhaps bamboo leaves, magnified to fill the entire back of this *kosode* (the front is similar) are depicted in *kanoko shibori*. Three of them are further embellished with flowering clematis vines and paulownia blossoms embroidered in red, white, dark green, yellow-green, and couched gold. The black background is completely covered with gold leaf in the mist pattern. The small embroidered floral motifs, the decorative techniques, and the colors are typical Keichō features, but the dramatically asymmetrical composition prefigures the Kanbun style.

Certain peculiarities suggest that this garment may have been recut some time after its completion, possibly for use as a Nō costume. The body has been widened at the shoulder seam; the sleeves are long for a normal *kosode* and may originally have been open under the arm in the *furisode* (hanging sleeve) style. Both front overlaps have oblique rather than right-angled corners, a characteristic of Nō robes. The simple, stark design, softened by restrained embroidery and enriched by the copious use of gold leaf, reflects a taste associated with the military elite and with the Nō, of which they were enthusiastic patrons.

PUBLISHED: Imanaga, *Kosode I*, pl. 60.
        Nomura, *Zoku kosode*, pl. 4.
        Royal Academy of Arts, *Great Japan Exhibition*, no. 344.
        Senshoku no bi 21, pl. 3.

Kanoko shibori, embroidery, and gold leaf
Black figured satin: 1/4 weft-faced figure of key fret and flowers on 4/1 warp-faced ground
Early Edo period, first half seventeenth century

On the black figured-satin surface cascading waterfalls are executed in areas of closely spaced *kanoko shibori* and parallel rows of *kanoko* dots. The curve of the falling water is emphasized by chrysanthemums, clematis, five-petalled flowers, and vine scrolls embroidered in red, white, dark and light green, and couched gold on bands of black. Gold leaf outlines the *kanoko* areas and also appears in blue wave and key-fret patterns as part of the streaming waterfall. Above the falls cluster embroidered chrysanthemums and vine scrolls. The unifying composition and bold design closely link this *kosode* to the Kanbun style.

Chrysanthemums with flowing water or waterfalls compose a recurrent theme in *kosode* design, particularly during the early Edo period. Chinese legends associate the dew that collects in chrysanthemum blossoms with immortality or longevity; to drink of this dew or of the stream into which it drops ensures long life. In one of these legends the chrysanthemums grow on a cliff above the current, and from this may have arisen the waterfall motif. A number of Nō plays treat this theme, including *Kiku jidō* and *Shōjō*.[1] The association with Nō and the connotation of longevity (both of particular concern to the military aristocracy) made chrysanthemums and flowing water especially appropriate to the decoration of *kosode* for the military class, but we cannot assume that a theme so common in the seventeenth century and so widely represented in the Nomura Collection was confined to that class.

The imagery of chrysanthemums and flowing water is central to the celebration known as *chōyō*, or *chōyō no sekku*, which takes place on the ninth day of the ninth month of the lunar calendar. The festivities include a "chrysanthemum banquet" (*kiku no en*), at which the guests admire and compare the chrysanthemum blossoms, exchange *sake* cups, and compose poems appropriate to the occasion. Other *kosode* in the Nomura Collection that display this theme are Colorplates 16, 22, 24, 26, and 33.

---

1. Imanaga and Kirihata, *Nō, kyōgen, kabuki*, pp. 253–54.

PUBLISHED: Imanaga, *Kosode I*, pl. 80.
         Nomura, *Hiinagata byōbu*, pl. 41
         Senshoku no bi 21, pl. 1.
         Tokyo National Museum, *Nihon no senshoku*, no. 157.

Shibori, ink painting, embroidery, and gold leaf
White figured satin: 1/4 weft-faced figure of key fret and orchids on 4/1 warp-faced
    ground
L. 153.5   W. 60.5   S.W. 27   S.L. 45 cm.
Early Edo period, seventeenth century

From a black crag a golden waterfall plunges to a black footed tray. The white
background has been reserved in some type of stitch-resist *shibori*, possibly tub
resist. The streams of water and splashes of foam are delicately drawn in black ink;
the rocky crag and the tray are detailed in *kanoko shibori*; four-petalled white flowers
clinging to the rocks are reserved in capped *shibori*. Embroidery in red, purple, light
blue, and light green renders sprays of chrysanthemums. On the right front of the
garment a bold design of plum blossoms and bamboo stump appears in *kanoko* on
black, outlined with gold leaf. The entire white background was originally covered
with gold leaf in a large fish-net pattern, still visible on the right sleeve.

    This *kosode* is unusual for its incorporation of the flower-arrangement tray into the
theme of chrysanthemums and flowing water. It retains elements of *tsujigahana*
decoration in the use of *shibori* and finely detailed ink painting, while the asymmetric,
if rather stiff, composition suggests an early phase of the Kanbun style. But the
tightly packed embroidery, whose outlines do not quite match the underdrawings of
the petals, was probably added at a later date. The mismatched wave crests at the left
shoulder seam and the comparatively new sleeve facings suggest that the sleeves may
have been recut at some point, possibly from *furisode* sleeves.

    A striking example of the imaginative powers of the early Edo *kosode* designer, the
"golden waterfall" *kosode* is also an important link between the late phases of
tsujigahana decoration and succeeding styles.

PUBLISHED: Imanaga, *Kosode I*, pl. 79.
             Minnich, *Japanese Costume*, pl. 100.
             Nomura, *Kosode to furisode*, pl. 1.
             Senshoku no bi 21, pl. 11.

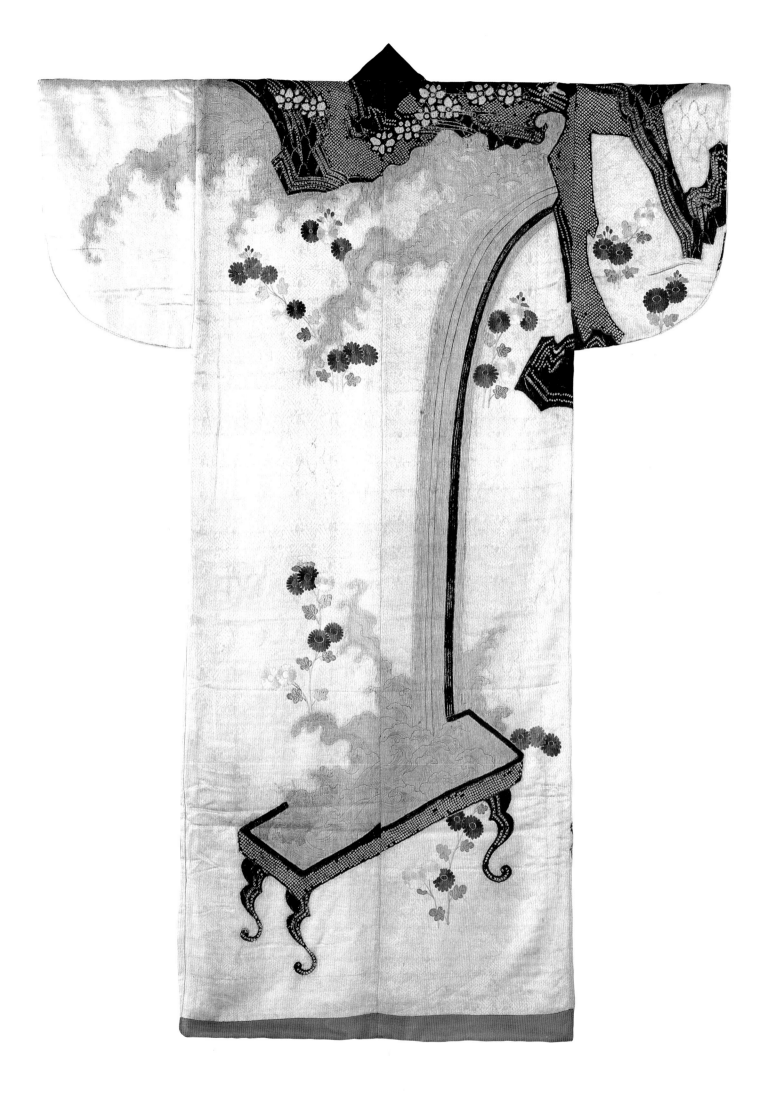

Shibori and embroidery
White figured satin: 1/4 weft-faced figure of key fret and peonies on 4/1 warp-faced
   ground
Early Edo period, third quarter seventeenth century

On this starkly handsome *kosode* a broad plank bridge sweeps across the shoulders
and down to waist level at the right, while waves break around the bases of its pilings.
Against the white background reserved with some form of stitch-resist *shibori*,
possibly pinch dyeing or tub dyeing, bridge and waves appear in *kanoko shibori* on
black and blue. Faintly visible disks, whiter than the background color, appear to left
and right of the wave crests; these may originally have been covered with gold leaf,
but no traces of it remain. These circles may, as in Kanō school paintings, represent
droplets of water (see also Cpl. 20). The bridge has been treated in a highly
decorative manner: broad bands of tortoise-shell lozenges in *kanoko* on blue are
separated from the black-background *kanoko* areas by bands of peony vine scrolls
embroidered in red, dark green, and yellow-green.
   All areas of stitch-resist *shibori* have been precisely outlined in purple embroidery.
This technique, known as *fuchi-dori* (taking away the edges), was not used in the
Momoyama period and is characteristic of the taste for clear-cut forms and hard
outlines typical of Edo period decoration, a preference further developed in the crisp
white outlines of eighteenth-century *yūzen* dyeing.
   Uji Bridge with the Uji River swirling around its base is a recurrent theme in the
arts of the Edo period. Its dramatic and strongly asymmetrical treatment here
epitomizes the style of the Kanbun era.

PUBLISHED: Imanaga, *Kosode I*, pl. 73.
            Kawakami, "Edo jidai zenki no kosode", fig. 7.
            Nomura, *Hiinagata byōbu*, pl. 21.
            Senshoku no bi 1, pl. 16.
            Tokyo National Museum, *Nihon no senshoku*, no. 180.

Shibori, embroidery, and gold leaf
White warp-faced satin
Early Edo period, third quarter seventeenth century

Large-brimmed hats filled with chrysanthemums are depicted in *kanoko* on black, blue, and red (now faded) against a white ground reserved by means of *shibori*. Gold leaf outlines the petals and centers of the blue and black flowers. The remaining flowers are embroidered in red with gold centers, and the embroidered red leaves are veined in green. Braided cords couched in gold tie the hats loosely together. To create the scalloped edges of the flowers by means of *shibori* dyeing is an especially difficult feat, here most skillfully achieved. The *kanoko* has been restored, probably with stencilled *kanoko*, on the black hat at the upper left and on the sleeve. The *kosode* from which this fragment came may have been made into an altar cloth or priest's stole.[1]

Five or six hats, somewhat smaller than normal size and tied together with cord, are used as a prop in Kabuki dance. From the seventeenth century on, not only the Nō drama but popular entertainments as well influenced fashion and supplied themes for *kosode* design.

Only if the entire *kosode* back were visible could the asymmetric composition characteristic of Kanbun style be seen to full effect, but even in this fragment the use of unfilled space and the compositional weight on one shoulder are consistent with that style.

---

1. See Minnich, *Japanese Costume*, pl. 73.

PUBLISHED: Minnich, *Japanese Costume*, pls. 72, 73.
Nomura, *Hiinagata byōbu*, pl. 23.
Senshoku no bi 21, pl. 18.
Tokyo National Museum, *Nihon no senshoku*, no. 178.

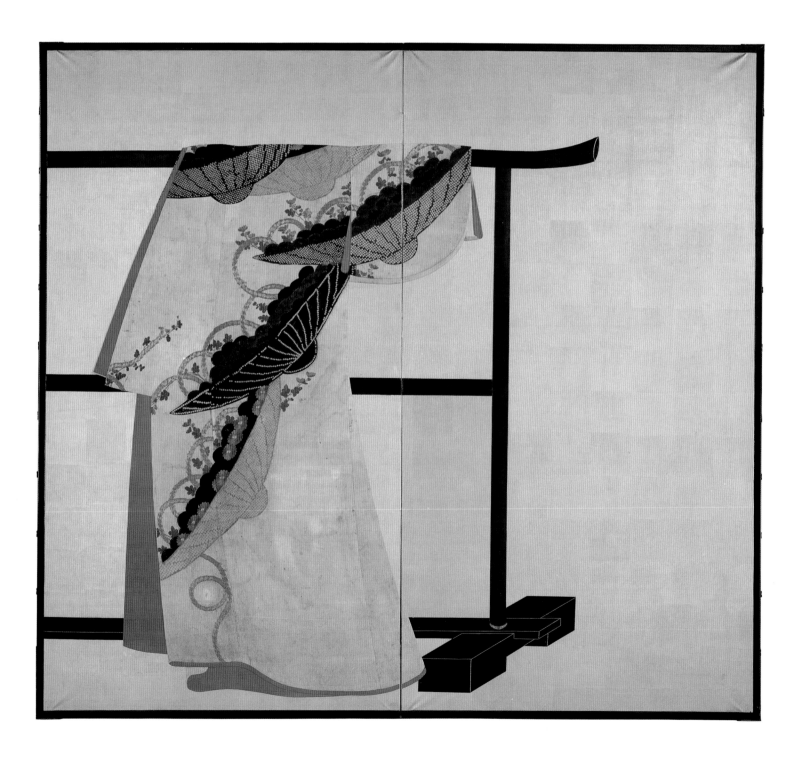

19 KOSODE SCREEN WITH DIAGONAL BANDS, CHRYSANTHEMUMS, AND NARCISSUS

Shibori, embroidery, and gold leaf
Golden-beige 4/1 warp-faced silk twill
Mid-Edo period, late seventeenth–early eighteenth century

Diagonal blue and black bands and a black roundel are dyed on a beige background reserved by means of stitch-resist *shibori*. The two stiffly diagonal bands are filled with closely spaced *kanoko shibori* and flanked by striking chrysanthemum flowers and delicate blossoming narcissus, both embroidered in red, white, dark green, light green, and couched gold. On the black roundel chrysanthemums and vine scrolls are depicted in *kanoko*. Narrow lines of gold leaf define the boundaries of the *kanoko* areas.

The embroidered chrysanthemums appear half submerged in the wavy black *kanoko* band, suggesting the familiar theme of chrysanthemums and flowing water, symbolic of longevity and associated with the celebration of *chōyō* on the ninth day of the ninth month of the lunar calendar (see Cpl. 15). The inclusion of narcissus is puzzlingly inconsistent with this autumnal theme.

Stylistically, the *kosode* is inconsistent with a date earlier than the Kanbun era (1661–73). The delicacy and emphasis of the embroidered detail, the tightness of the embroidery, the stiffness of the design as a whole, and the compositional weight just above the waist level suggest a date even later, perhaps, than Kanbun.

PUBLISHED: Nomura, *Hiinagata byōbu*, pl. 18.
Tokyo National Museum, *Nihon no senshoku*, no. 174.

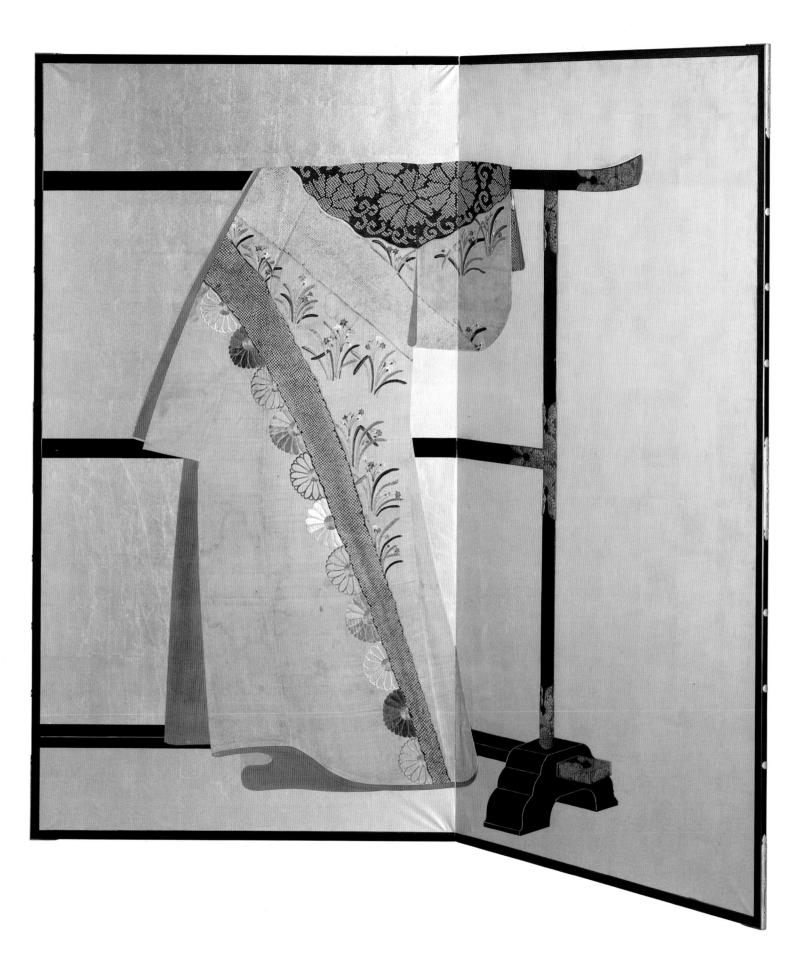

20 KOSODE SCREEN WITH WAVES AND FISH NETS

Kanoko shibori and gold embroidery
Red 4/1 warp-faced satin
Mid-Edo period, late seventeenth century
Illustrated on cover

Foaming white waves are abstractly represented in *kanoko shibori*, with their crests graphically depicted in gold couching. Fish nets, also couched in gold thread, assume the shape of waves as well. Just above the point of the lower net appear four faded yellow circles. These, like the pale circles in Colorplate 17, may have been intended as bubbles or splashing drops of water, but as such their placement is unusual. The yellow undertones in safflower red become more prominent with age, but it is not clear how these circles were executed. Dark spots visible in the *kanoko* areas, especially at the upper right, indicate *kanoko* circles that were retouched with white face powder (*oshiroi*), which due to its lead content has turned silvery black with age.

The dramatic Kanbun style persists in this splendidly simple *kosode*, but the fine detail in the couched gold fish nets and wave crests, and the sweep of the curved forms into the lower half of the garment, suggest a mid-Edo date.

PUBLISHED: Imanaga, *Kosode I*, pl. 99.
Nomura, *Hiinagata byōbu*, pl. 42.
Senshoku no bi 21, pl. 26.
Tokyo National Museum, *Nihon no senshoku*, no. 175.

21 KOSODE SCREEN IN BLACK-BACKGROUND STYLE WITH ABALONE STRIPS, CHRYSANTHEMUMS, AND MYRIAD TREASURES

Shibori and embroidery
Black figured satin: 1/4 weft-faced figure of key fret, orchids, and chrysanthemums on 4/1 warp-faced ground
Mid-Edo period, late seventeenth century

Strips of dried abalone were served with *sake* on ceremonial occasions. Because their length suggested continuance or perpetuation, abalone strips came to be used also as auspicious gift decorations. Eventually they were replaced in this latter function by paper streamers. Along with chrysanthemums, abalone strips are associated with the celebration of *chōyō* (see Cpl. 19) on the ninth day of the ninth month of the lunar calendar. During the Edo period great daimyo, samurai, and commoners alike went to Edo on that day, bearing gifts for the shogun of silks, rice cakes, and abalone strips attached to sprays of chrysanthemums.[1]

Here the streamers are depicted in *kanoko* on black and red. Embroidered red and white chrysanthemums, tightly clustered, likewise form streamers, as do the embroidered "myriad treasures", all symbols of wealth and good fortune.[2] Smaller chrysanthemums, embroidered in red, white, green, and couched gold, emphasize the nervous outlines of the *kanoko* streamers. Probably the yellow *kanoko* dots on the red areas are due to discoloration. The black background is figured in one of the most common figured-satin patterns—key fret with orchids and chrysanthemums.

Although the asymmetry of the design and large expanse of open background reflect the Kanbun style, the minute embroidered detail and mannered treatment of the fluttering streamers indicate a somewhat later development. A similar design illustrated in a 1692 *hiinagata bon* (design book) suggests that the Nomura *kosode* may be a conscious revival of an earlier style; *hiinagata bon* were sometimes reissued thirty years or so after their original publication, indicating an interest in stylistic revivals.

1. Nishitsunoi Masayoshi, *Nenjū gyōji jiten* (Tokyo: Tōkyōdō, 1958), p. 489.
2. The myriad treasures (*takara zukushi*) comprise the magic hat that confers invisibility on its wearer; cloves (symbolizing wealth); the wish-fulfilling mallet of the god of plenty, Daikoku; and the Seven Precious Things of the Buddhist scriptures (gold, silver, lapis, crystal, coral, agate, and pearl). The motif occurs frequently on heavily embroidered *koshimaki* of the eighteenth century (Cpl. 49).

PUBLISHED: Nomura, *Hiinagata byōbu*, pl. 17.
Tokyo National Museum, *Nihon no senshoku*, no. 156.

Stitch-resist *shibori* with *kanoko shibori*, embroidery, and gold leaf
Black figured satin: 1/4 weft-faced figure of key fret, orchids, and chrysanthemums
  on 4/1 warp-faced ground
L. 149   W. 63   S.W. 30   S.L. 39 cm.
Early Edo period, seventeenth century

Giant chrysanthemum blossoms depicted in *kanoko shibori* on red are half submerged in waves composed of curving ribbons of solid blue and blue-ground *kanoko*. Stitch-resist *shibori* was used to separate the red and blue areas from the black background. Wave crests embroidered in gold couching hold the flowers afloat, and gold leaf outlines the *kanoko* areas. Smaller chrysanthemums are embroidered in white, red, light green, and silver-gray. Dark spots in the red and blue *kanoko* indicate retouching with white powder containing lead.

The use of gold leaf and the boldness of the composition suggest a mid-seventeenth-century date. The original design may have reflected the sparser Kanbun style; gray and white chrysanthemums on the back of the left sleeve and extending across the back at waist level appear to be later additions. The sleeves have been shortened and widened approximately two centimeters, and the thickly padded hem (*fuki*) revealing the red lining is not a seventeenth-century feature and was also probably added later. On the right front the overlap has been replaced with undecorated black figured satin.

The familiar chrysanthemums and water theme, symbolizing longevity, is represented here in a strong and simple design whose striking asymmetry is carried through on the front of the garment as well.

PUBLISHED: Minnich, *Japanese Costume*, pl. 82.
  Nomura, *Kosode to furisode*, pl. 3.

Shibori and embroidery
**Purple figured satin: 1/4 weft-faced figure of key fret, orchids, and chrysanthemums
    on 4/1 warp-faced ground**
L. 148   W. 63.5   S.W. 32.5   S.L. 42.5 cm.
Mid-Edo period, late seventeenth century

Blossoming plum trees reserved in stitch-resist *shibori* spread across the back of this purple *kosode*, their blossoms and branches embroidered in light green with silver couching or detailed in black ink. Additional plum blossoms are executed in *kanoko shibori*, as are the tree trunks and magnified snow roundels.

The trunks of the plum trees are jointed like bamboo, and the crenellated snow roundels resemble pine boughs such as the one seen in Colorplate 7. Thus, allusions to bamboo and pine are concealed within the images of blossoming plum and snow. The combination of pine, bamboo, and plum (*shōchikubai*), particularly amid snow, was a metaphor for steadfast endurance and loyalty in adversity. Derived originally from Chinese painting, it appears frequently in *kosode* design of the Edo period (see Cpl. 30) and by the nineteenth century becomes the most common decorative theme for *kosode* to be worn at New Year's or wedding festivities.

The fabric of this *kosode* is somewhat coarsely woven and the execution of the *kanoko shibori* is somewhat rough, but the exuberance of the design is extremely effective. In the forceful asymmetric sweep of the composition the Kanbun style is preserved, but the spread of the design across the center back and lower skirt is characteristic of early Genroku (1688–1704).

PUBLISHED: Nomura, *Zoku kosode*, pl. 11.

Shibori, stencilled *kanoko*, paste resist, and embroidery
White figured satin: 1/4 weft-faced figure of key fret and flowers on 4/1 warp-faced
 ground
L. 154 cm.
Mid-Edo period, late seventeenth century

Giant chrysanthemum leaves in *kanoko shibori* with blossoms embroidered in red
and green and couched in gold extend across the shoulders and diagonally down the
back of this *kosode*. Beneath them, waterfalls are schematically represented in stripes
of *kanoko shibori*, stencilled *kanoko* (on black), and solid dark blue. The blue stripes
are uneven in shade but sharp in outline, revealing that they were outlined with
resist paste and brushed on rather than dipped. From left to right across the
shoulders in stencilled *kanoko* are the three characters *fukai* (deep), *tsuya* (luster),
and *koi* (dark). The theme is clearly chrysanthemums and waterfalls, already familiar
from Colorplates 15, 16, 19, and 22, but the significance of the characters and their
relation to this theme remain unclear.

 The profusion, strength, and vitality of this design, its sweeping curve typical of
the Kanbun style, and its use of characters point to a date in the last quarter of the
seventeenth century.

PUBLISHED: Imanaga, *Kosode I*, pl. 98.
  Nomura, *Zoku kosode*, pl. 18.
  Senshoku no bi 21, pl. 41.

Shibori with stencilled *kanoko* and embroidery
Red figured satin: 1/4 weft-faced figure of chevrons and cloud roundels on 4/1
    warp-faced ground
Mid-Edo period, late seventeenth century

Cart wheels partly submerged in cresting waves are executed in various techniques: some have rims of *kanoko* with couched gold detailing on red or blue backgrounds, and spokes couched in gold against white centers; others have rims outlined in brown embroidery (perhaps originally purple) against white, with spokes of light blue or light blue and brown against green centers. Alternate bands of solid white and *kanoko* on red and blue compose the waves. Wave crests are rendered in *kanoko* or in gold couching. The uniformity of the *kanoko* circles and the regularity of their central protrusions in the red-background areas suggest that they were stencilled rather than tied. Stitch-resist *shibori* reserved the white and blue areas when the red background was dyed.

The asymmetrical and energetic design of this *kosode*, in which the weight of the composition has shifted downward and across the lower skirt, represents an early phase of the florid exuberance of Genroku (1688–1704).

Cart wheels half submerged in waves have been a popular theme in Japanese decorative arts, especially lacquer and textiles, since the Heian period.[1] These wooden wheels belonged to the ox carts in which nobility travelled. To prevent their drying out and cracking, the wheels required periodic soaking in shallow streams or inundated rice fields, and from this practice the decorative motif is said to derive. Cart wheels alone, without flowing water, form the motif known as Genji wheels (Genji *guruma*), named after the hero of the *Tale of Genji*.

---

1. The lacquer toiletries box dating from the Late Heian period and now in the Tokyo National Museum is an early example of this theme. See Mizoguchi Saburo, *Design Motifs*, Arts of Japan, no. 1 (New York and Tokyo: Weatherhill/Shibundo, 1973), pl. 62.

PUBLISHED: Minnich, *Japanese Costume*, pl. 104.
        Nomura, *Hiinagata byōbu*, pl. 62.
        Senshoku no bi 21, pl. 15.
        Tokyo National Museum, *Nihon no senshoku*, no. 173.

26 KOSODE SCREEN WITH FANS, *SAKE* CUPS ENCLOSING CHARACTERS, AND FLOWERING VINE SCROLLS

Kanoko shibori with embroidery
White warp-faced satin
Mid-Edo period, late seventeenth–early eighteenth century

Broad bands of gold couching form the ribs of giant folding fans and outline abstract zones of white background and red and blue *kanoko shibori*. Gold couching also defines some of the roundels representing *sake* cups, as well as the Chinese characters enclosed within them. Other roundels and the characters they enclose are embroidered in white or purple. The black fans are closely embroidered with flowering vine scrolls in red, white, and two shades of green.

Literature was an increasingly important source of themes for *kosode* decoration in the early and mid-Edo periods, and the inclusion of written characters in designs was especially popular during the second half of the seventeenth century. The characters within these *sake*-cup roundels form a couplet from an eight-line poem by the Chinese poet Bo Juyi (772–846), in which cranes, signifying longevity or immortality, are linked with *sake* cups:

> Sound: Above my pillow alights the thousand-year crane.
> Shadow: Into my *sake* cup falls the peak of Wu-lao.

The couplet is included in the *Wakan rōeishū* [Collection of Japanese and Chinese poems for recitation].[1] This anthology, compiled about 1013, was exceedingly popular from the Muromachi period onward and is one of the main sources of poetic allusion in Nō plays and in the decorative arts.

In the vitality of this design the Kanbun style remains apparent, but a Genroku (1688–1704) date is suggested by the rich profusion of decorative detail over most of the robe's surface and by the shift in design emphasis from shoulder to waist level.

---

1. The Chinese characters of the poem are read in Japanese as follows:
   Koe wa makura no ue ni kitaru sennen no tsuru
   Kage wa sakazuki no uchi ni otsu Gorō no Mine.
   See Kawaguchi Hisao and Shida Nobuyoshi, ed., *Wakan rōeishū ryōjin hishō*, Nihon koten bungaku taikei, no. 73 (Tokyo: Iwanami Shoten, 1965), p. 163.

PUBLISHED: Imanaga, *Kosode I*, pl. 93.
   Kyoto National Museum, ed., *Kōgei ni miru koten bungaku ishō* (Kyoto: Shikōsha, 1980), fig. 6.
   Nomura, *Hiinagata byōbu*, pl. 27.
   Senshoku no bi 21, pl. 27.
   Tokyo National Museum, *Nihon no senshoku*, no. 160.

Shibori and embroidery
Beige 4/1 warp-faced satin
Mid-Edo period, early eighteenth century

Large snow roundels in red- and blue-background *kanoko shibori* enclose cranes, pines, and tortoises in green, blue, white, red, yellow, black, purple, and couched gold. Bits of poems are embroidered in couched gold on solid black snow roundels. The roundels are distributed against horizontal bands outlined by gold couching and enclosing embroidered paulownia leaves and flowers. Crane, pine, and tortoise, all symbolizing longevity, were standard motifs for festive *kosode* in the mid- and late Edo periods. The paulownia with which they are combined here may have been the wearer's family crest; more likely, however, they were employed simply for decorative effect.

The Chinese and Japanese characters couched in gold on the black roundels are auspicious syllables and words from two poems on winter themes. On the upper roundel:

Ike mizu no	Because your reign
taezu sumu beki	Will always be clear
miyo nareba	Like the waters of the lake.
matsu no chitose mo	I shall behold you, my lord, forever,
towani aimimu.	Like the thousand years of the pine.[1]

On the lower roundel:

Hisakata no	Doesn't it look
sora ni tsumoru to	As if it's piling up
miyuru ka na	In the sky itself—
kodakaki mine no	White snow on the pines
matsu no shirayuki.	On the tree-covered peak.[2]

A number of characters from unidentified poems are also included. The verses themselves are thoroughly conventional, but their meaning and imagery reinforce the auspiciousness of the design and associate it with winter. And the gold embroidery on black enhances the sheer gorgeousness of the garment.

Compared with Colorplates 15–26, the composition of this *furisode* is notably static. The slight diagonal movement of the snow roundels above the waist is anchored by the horizontal placement of those near the hem and further stabilized by the straight-edged, evenly spaced, horizontal ribbons of paulownia. This static quality, and the division of the composition into two centers of emphasis (one above the waist, the other near the hem), suggest an early eighteenth-century date.

---

1. By Fujiwara no Tameie (1198–1275), in *Zokushūi wakashū*, Bk. 10, no. 729.
2. By Fujiwara no Tameyo (1251–1338), in *Shin senzai wakashū*, Bk. 6, no. 694.

PUBLISHED: Imanaga, *Kosode I*, pl. 95.
   Kyoto National Museum, ed., *Kōgei ni miru koten bungaku ishō (Kyoto: Shikōsha, 1980)*, pl. 60.
   Nomura, Hiinagata byōbu, pl. 15.
   Senshoku no bi 21, pl. 38.
   Tokyo National Museum, *Nihon no senshoku*, no. 188.

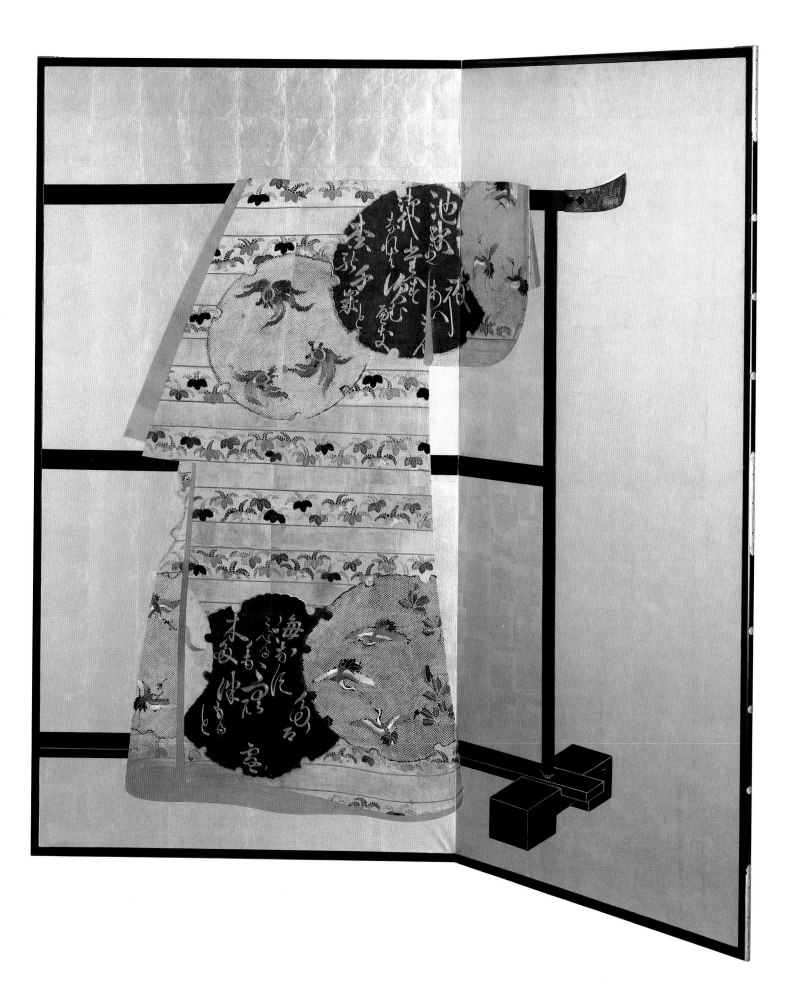

Shibori and embroidery
Black figured satin: 4/1 weft-faced figures on 4/1 warp-faced ground
Mid-Edo period, eighteenth century

Diagonal bands of alternating blue- and red-background *kanoko* are embroidered
with chrysanthemums in purple, red, white, and couched gold. These are crossed
by opposing diagonal stripes of black-background *kanoko* alternating with bands
of auspicious motifs, including chrysanthemums, plum blossoms, bamboo,
camellias, pines, tortoises, cranes, bamboo shoots, and the myriad treasures (see
Cpl. 21), closely embroidered in red, white, light green, dark, green, purple, and
couched gold.

In its coloration and its balance of *kanoko* with small embroidered motifs this robe
recalls the "Temmon" *kosode*, which is dated to the early seventeenth century. But
the rigidity of the composition, tightness of the embroidery, and proliferation of
highly detailed motifs in this *uchikake* (formal outer garment) suggest an eighteenth-
century date. Both the densely packed, tight stitches that make up the lustrous
chrysanthemum, plum, and camellia petals, and the highly twisted yarns that outline
the large red and white chrysanthemums are more consistent with the later date.

Nomura believed this garment to have belonged to Tōfukumon-in, consort of
Emperor Go-Mizunoo, but no documents or inscriptions substantiate this claim.
Since her daughter Akiko was born in 1627, Tōfukumon-in was probably about sixty
years old at the time of her death in 1678. She is not likely to have worn so gay a robe
after the age of thirty (Nomura, in fact, dated the robe to 1624), but garments made in
the first half of the seventeenth century reveal an organic and dynamic composition
completely different in feeling and style from the compartmentalized rigidity of this
design. So few dated garments or genre paintings depicting costumes survive from
Tōfukumon-in's lifetime, however, that we cannot rule out the possibility that this
uchikake was indeed hers.

PUBLISHED: Imanaga, *Kosode I*, pl. 96.
Nomura, *Hiinagata byōbu*, pl. 16.
Senshoku no bi 21, pl. 39.
Tokyo National Museum, *Nihon no senshoku*, no. 159.

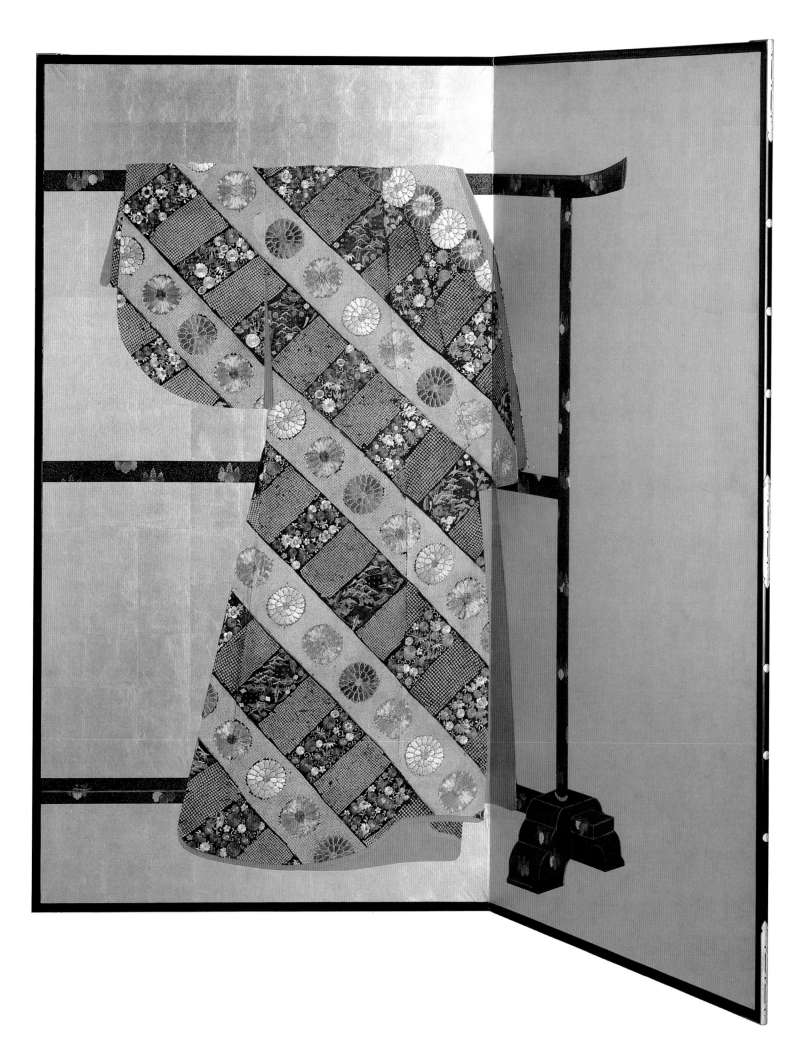

Shibori and embroidery
Black figured satin: 1/4 weft-faced figure of key fret and peonies on 4/1 warp-faced
  ground
Mid-Edo period, late seventeenth-early eighteenth century

Hills rendered in *kanoko shibori* on red and blue slope down from right to left against a black backgound. Between the hills grow blossoming cherry trees embroidered in red, green, purple, and couched gold. The trees themselves, overshadowed by their giant blossoms, are shown in minute detail, including gnarled roots and growths of lichen (often depicted in polychrome screen paintings of the Momoyama and Edo periods but not usually represented in *kosode* design).

In many places the red and blue wedge-shaped *kanoko* hills have been stitched onto the black background, but a sufficient number are continuous with it to establish that the integrity of the original design has not been lost. The stitching lines of stitch-resist *shibori* exert considerable stress on such delicate fabrics as figured satin. The seamed boundaries between black, red, and blue zones in this *kosode* probably represent repairs where the fabric tore along the *shibori* lines. Similar damage can be seen in the *tsujigahana* fragment on the right in Colorplate 1. Dark spots on the *kanoko* areas indicate retouching with white powder containing lead.

These parallel ranges of wedge-shaped hills lined with flowering cherry trees have their counterparts in Japanese and Chinese landscape paintings. Their composition recalls the mountain road overgrown with ivy on a pair of six-fold screens by Tawaraya Sōtatsu (act. early seventeenth century) and is even closer to a pair of screens by Watanabe Shikō (1683–1755) depicting the wild cherry trees in blossom in the Yoshino hills.[1]

---

1. Royal Academy of Arts, *Great Japan Exhibition*, nos. 19, 34.
PUBLISHED: Nomura, *Hiinagata byōbu*, pl. 49.

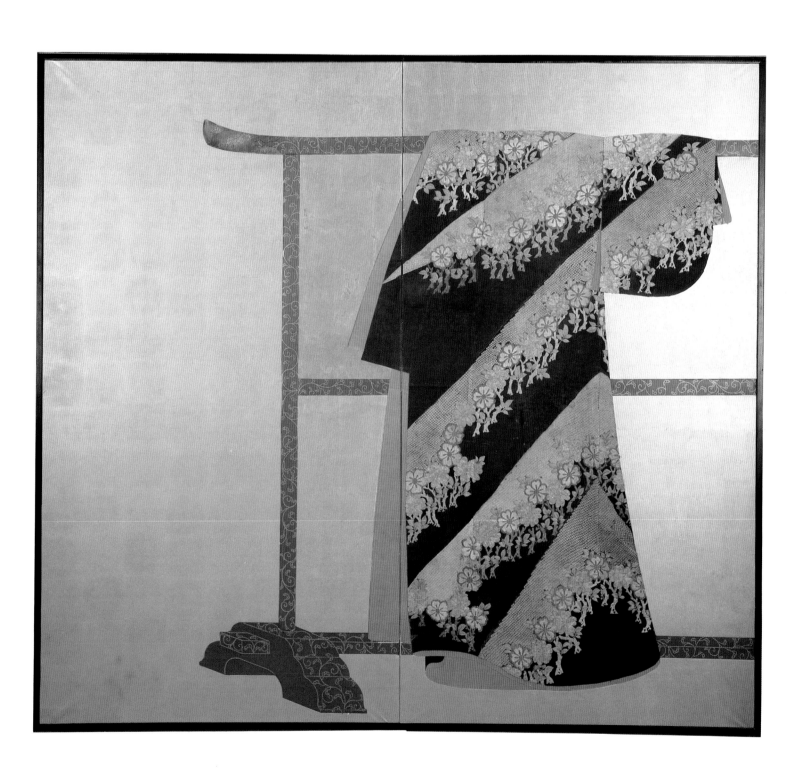

Paste resist with embroidery, *shibori*, and traces of gold leaf
Black figured satin: 1/4 weft-faced figure of key fret, orchids, and chrysanthemums
on 4/1 warp-faced ground
Mid-Edo period, early eighteenth century

Plum blossoms, some embroidered in red, green, purple, and couched gold and others reserved in white and detailed with gold leaf, cluster along bent branches. The hard outlines of the white forms, as well as the absence of stitch marks, indicate that they were reserved with resist paste rather than with capped *shibori*. The *kanoko shibori* plum branches on black and blue backgrounds bear traces of gold leaf outlines. Red-ground *kanoko* renders both a long, thin crescent representing a single bamboo leaf and the character *shō* (also read *matsu*, pine) below the neckband. After the *kanoko* areas forming the leaf, the character, and the blue plum branch had been dipped and dried, their outlines were sharpened with black dye. Although this *kosode* was probably dip dyed rather then brushed, the preference it displays for sharp rather than soft outlines (achieved by paste resist rather than *shibori*) presages the overwhelming popularity of *yūzen* dyeing from the Genroku era (1688–1704) onward.

The richly embroidered plum blossoms, the character of "pine," and the single bamboo leaf constitute a rebus for the familiar combination of auspicious motifs known as *shōchikubai* (pine, bamboo, plum). We have seen characters used as decoration on other *kosode* of this period (Cpls. 26, 27), but those *kosode* bore quotations from Japanese and Chinese poetry, suggesting educated patrons and probably reflecting the taste of the military aristocracy. The *shōchikubai* attests a broader, less specific notion of auspicious themes and a more playful, punning disposition, which permeated the new urban culture of the townsman (*chōnin*) class.

The reduced size of the individual design elements, the more even distribution of these elements over the surface, and what appears to be a compositional emphasis on the lower half of the garment (difficult to determine because of the fragmentary state of the *kosode*) suggest an early eighteenth-century date. The use of gold leaf, although somewhat unusual, is not unknown in this period.

PUBLISHED: Minnich, *Japanese Costume*, pl. 104.
Nomura, *Hiinagata byōbu*, pl. 68.

31 KOSODE SCREEN WITH FANS, PINES, REEDS, SAIL, AND THE CHARACTER *URA* (INLET)

Embroidery, gold leaf, and black ink
White figured satin: 1/4 weft-faced figure of peony vine scrolls on 4/1 warp-faced ground
Mid-Edo period, early eighteenth century

On the upper half of this *kosode* fans decorated with plovers and waves, a tortoise and a crane, myriad treasures, and paulownia partly cover the spreading branches of a pine tree. All this is embroidered in red, white, dark and light green, light blue, purple, and couched gold. Some of the pine boughs and paulownia leaves are delicately outlined in black ink and covered with gold leaf.

On the lower half of the garment, which forms a discrete decorative unit, a curtain screen (*kichō*, a frame hung with strips of silk) is disposed among reeds so as to resemble the sail of a small boat. The screen-sail is patterned with chrysanthemum vine scrolls and the myriad treasures. All this is embroidered in two shades of green, light brown, red, and white. Superimposed on the screen-sail is the character *ura* (inlet, bay) in gold leaf.

The upper design seems to be merely a pleasing arrangement of auspicious motifs, but the lower one probably alludes to a poem by Tsumori Kunisuke:

Omohi nomi	A boat on the bay of Waka no Ura,
michiyuku oki no	Always impeded by reeds offshore
ashiwake ni	Where the tide flows in,
sawari mo hatenu	Never reaching the port.
Waka no Ura bune.[1]	I am filled only with longing.

Waka no Ura, a famous scenic spot in the city of Wakayama, Wakayama Prefecture, was a frequent subject of classical poetry, often in conjunction with reeds. In this poem the imagery of the boat making its way through a thick growth of reeds, unable to reach its destination, is a metaphor for the poet unable to meet with his beloved. The *kosode* design, however, ignores the poem's sorrowful meaning and incorporates only its concrete imagery: the boat, adorned with auspicious motifs, the reeds, and the identifying character *ura*. Pines, crane, and tortoise on the upper half of the *kosode* confirm the auspicious intention of the design.

Except for the large scale of some of the motifs, all vestiges of the Kanbun style have vanished. In place of bold forms sweeping from shoulder to hem in a single unified composition, we have here two designs, with the area around the waist, which would be covered by the obi, left undecorated. This is a restrained and delicate *kosode*, in which the subdued glow of gold leaf (unusual for this period) replaces the commoner and more flamboyant couched gold embroidery. Its refinement, as well as the classical literary allusion, suggests a patron from the court or military aristocracy rather than the townsman (*chōnin*) class.

---

1. *Shin gosen wakashū*, Bk. 18, no. 1385.
PUBLISHED: Nomura, *Hiinagata byōbu*, pl. 33.

Paste resist, embroidery, and *kanoko shibori*
Black figured satin: 1/4 weft-faced figure of key fret, orchids, and chrysanthemums
Mid-Edo period, late seventeenth century

Arching ribbons of blue and white, reserved against the black background with resist paste, form waterfalls. Over these cascade a profusion of drumheads embroidered with plum blossoms in purple, red, and couched gold, their green stems heavily rimmed with gold couching or purple embroidery. Some of the drumheads are filled in with *kanoko shibori*. Fancifully looped cords, used to fasten the drumheads (removed when not in use) to the wooden drum bodies, are embroidered in red. Wave crests are schematically represented in couched gold.

This combination of motifs alludes to a Nō play, the text of which is now lost, entitled *Tsutsumi no taki* [The Waterfall of Drums]. At the Waterfall of Drums a traveller encounters an old woodcutter with whom he converses about poetry. The old man reveals himself to be the deity of the place and performs a dance. The theme occurs frequently, according to Kirihata, on *kosode* made for women of the military elite.[1]

In this strong and rich design the asymmetry of the Kanbun style is still evident. But its austerity has given way to an exuberant decorative profusion that fills almost the entire back of the *kosode*. The allusion to Nō suggests that this *kosode* may have been made for a member of the military elite.

---

1. Kirihata, "Kinsei senshoku ni okeru bungei ishō", p. 279.
PUBLISHED: Nomura, *Hiinagata byōbu*, pl. 57.

33 KATABIRA SCREEN WITH CHERRY BLOSSOMS, WATERFALL, HUTS, AND THE CHARACTERS *NO* (FIELD) AND *SAWA* (MARSH)

Paste resist with embroidery and *kanoko shibori*
Black plain-weave ramie with occasional twisted warps
Mid-Edo period, late seventeenth century

Double cherry blossoms, leaves, a ribboned waterfall, and an area representing a pond or cloud are reserved in white by means of resist paste. Other blossoms, wave crests, and the two characters appear in *kanoko* on red (now faded) and blue (the blue-background *kanoko* may be stencilled). Blossoms, leaves, and half-open buds are heavily embroidered in red, purple, green, and row upon row of couched gold. The thatched roofs of the huts are dyed blue, and their structural members are embroidered in red and gold. The black background may have been dip-dyed in ink. Because color was applied by brush only to limited areas (such as the roofs and stencilled *kanoko* characters and flowers), this *katabira* (unlined summer *kosode*) cannot be considered an example of *yūzen* dyeing, even though resist paste was used extensively in the creation of the design. Like the figured-satin *kosode* in Colorplate 32, this *katabira* is a paradigm of the flamboyance and energy of early Genroku (1688–1704).

The theme of this splendid piece is not at first glance identifiable: its combination of motifs is uncommon. Moreover, past misidentification of the flowers as chrysanthemums compounded the difficulty. The pictorial images alone, however, pertain to depictions of Mt. Yoshino, a remote spot in Nara Prefecture famous for its cherry blossoms. A lacquered bookstand in the Tokyo National Museum, thought to represent Mt. Yoshino, is decorated with flowering cherry trees, flowing water, and thatched huts.[1] The design of the Nomura *katabira*, however, refers more specifically to the waterfall of Mt. Yoshino as it figures in a poem from the *Shinzoku kokinwakashū*:

Yoshino yama	Mt. Yoshino:
taki no shiroito	White ribbons of waterfalls.
kurikaeshi	No matter how often I look
mite mo akanu	I never tire of them:
hana no iro ka na.[2]	The color of the blossoms.

The word *nozawa* (*no* + *sawa*: marshes) occurs frequently in classical poetry; it is usually associated with very early spring, when the first herbs are gathered, as in the following poem:

Taga tame no	Although there is no one
wakana naranedo	For whom I gather these young herbs,
wa ga shimeshi	My sleeves grow damp
nozawa no mizu	From the waters of the marshes
sode wa nuretsutsu.[3]	That belong to me.

A pictorial representation of the marshes may have decorated the front of the garment.

The combination of images—early spring, cool water, a remote mountain grove in bloom—must have been chosen to lend a sense of coolness and freshness to a garment intended for city wear during the hottest days of summer.

---

1. Kirihata, "Kinsei senshoku ni okeru bungei ishō", pl. 74.
2. Gidō Sanshi, in *Shinzoku kokinwakashū*, Bk. 2, no. 132.
3. Emperor Tsuchimikado (r. 1198–1210), in *Shoku kokinwakashū*, Bk. 1, no. 23.

PUBLISHED: Nomura, *Hiinagata byōbu*, pl. 64.
 Tokyo National Museum, *Nihon no senshoku*, no. 193.

LEFT: Divided-background style with fence, pine flowers, and the characters *sen zai* (thousand years)
Shibori with embroidery and appliqué
Green and white figured satin: 1/4 weft-faced figure of key fret and peonies on 4/1 warp-faced ground
Appliqué of 3/1 warp-faced silk twill patterned with weft floats of gold-wrapped threads
Mid-Edo period, late seventeenth century

The *kosode* background is divided vertically into white and green areas by means of stitch-resist *shibori*. This division is emphasized by the placement of two immense characters, *sen zai* (also read *chitose*, one thousand years), appliquéd in gold-brocaded green twill. The green background is crisscrossed by a white fence, also reserved by stitch-resist *shibori* and outlined with narrow blue lines, probably indigo in pigment form. Pine flowers—distinguished from chrysanthemums by the three circles at the center of each blossom—are solidly embroidered, some in white and some in couched gold, which also outlines the appliquéd characters.

The word *chitose* (one thousand years) is usually associated with a wish for longevity or a pledge of fidelity, as in an anonymous poem from the *Kokinwakashū*:

Watatsu umi no	Counting the fine sands
hama no masago o	On the shore of the wide sea:
kazoetsutsu	The lifetime of my lord
kimi ga chitose no	Will reach one thousand years.
arikazu ni semu.[1]	

These characters echo and emphasize the symbolism of the pine, which also represents longevity and fidelity.

———————————

1. *Kokinwakashū*, Bk. 7, no. 344.

RIGHT: Divided-background style with bamboo fence and the characters *waka take* (young bamboo)
Shibori with paste resist and stencilled *kanoko* (*kata-kanoko*)
Red and ivory *chirimen* silk crepe
Mid-Edo period, late seventeenth–early eighteenth century

The background of this *kosode* is divided vertically by means of stitch-resist *shibori* into areas of red and ivory, and the division is accentuated by the two immense characters *waka take* (young bamboo). *Waka* appears in *kanoko shibori* on red, *take* in blue stencilled *kanoko*. The blue, dark green, and white bamboo fence on the ivory background has been outlined with resist paste for sharp definition, and the colors applied by brush.

The characters refer to a poem in the "Butterflies" chapter of the *Tale of Genji*:

Imasara ni	Why should the young bamboo
ika naramu yo ka	At this late date
waka take no	Go forth in search
ohihajimekemu	Of roots it has left behind?
ne o ba tazunemu.[1]	

This passage, in which Prince Genji alludes to his not-entirely-honorable love for his stepdaughter Tamakazura, may have held some private meaning for the wearer. Or the characters *waka take* may have been employed simply for their associations with youth and spring.

Both these fragments hark back to Kanbun style in their boldness and strong verticality of design and in their use of characters. But resist-paste dyeing, the use of *chirimen* crepe instead of figured satin for the red and ivory robe, and the profusion of design in the green and white all suggest a somewhat later date. The almost crude vitality and brazen assertiveness of these two designs reflect a taste more readily associated with the *chōnin* (townsman) class, or even with the courtesans who played such an important role in Edo culture, than with the court nobility or the military aristocracy.

----

1. Murasaki Shikibu, *Genji monogatari* 1128; Seidensticker, trans., *Tale of Genji*, vol. 1, p. 426.

PUBLISHED: Imanaga, *Kosode I*, pl. 119.
　　　　　Nomura, *Hiinagata byōbu*, pl. 91.
　　　　　Senshoku no bi 21, pls. 32, 33.
　　　　　Tokyo National Museum, *Nihon no senshoku*, nos. 194, 195.

Yūzen dyeing and embroidery
Yellow ochre *chirimen* silk crepe
Mid-Edo period, first half eighteenth century

A cherry tree laden with double blossoms is brush dyed with pigments and dyes in shades of brown, pink, and blue. Fine white lines defining petals, leaves, and bark texture were reserved with resist paste before the colors were applied. Among the branches of the tree bamboo poles brush dyed blue are hung with poem slips reserved in white or brushed red or purple. When this much of the design was completed, the design areas were thickly covered with resist paste and the whole background was brush dyed, in a hue probably redder than it is now. The cords tying the poem slips to the poles, the outlines of the slips, and the poems on them were then embroidered in red, green, purple, black, and couched gold. Of the black embroidery floss only traces remain, because the iron mordant used in the black dye weakened the fibers so that they disintegrated. Otherwise the *kosode* is in excellent condition.

Eight poems (five seven-character Chinese couplets and three Japanese *waka*), all taken from the anthology *Wakan rōeishū* (see Cpl. 26) have been identified by Kirihata.[1] All of these come from the *Haru* (Spring) section of the anthology. Two specifically mention cherry blossoms and one speaks of plum blossoms, although the tree on the *kosode* is clearly a cherry tree.

In materials, design, and craftsmanship this robe is typical of the best *yūzen kosode* of the first half of the eighteenth century. In scale and conception it retains the generosity of the Kanbun and Genroku styles, which give way to a profusion of small details and technical virtuosity later in the century.

---

1. Kirihata, "Kinsei senshoku ni okeru bungei ishō", pl. 11, p. 241.
PUBLISHED: Kirihata, "Kinsei senshoku ni okeru bungei ishō", pl. 11.
        Kirihata, *Kosode II*, pl. 26.
        Nomura, *Hiinagata byōbu*, pl. 87.
        Senshoku no bi 3, pl. 16.
        Tokyo National Museum, *Nihon no senshoku*, no. 220.

Yūzen dyeing with *shibori* and embroidery
Beige *chirimen* silk crepe
L. 146   W. 62   S.W. 31.5   S.L. 41 cm.
Mid-Edo period, second half eighteenth century

A woven fence of live maple branches covers both front and back of this fine *yūzen kosode*. Black branches sprout leaves in dark green and shaded tones of rose, blue, and yellow. In the apertures of the fence large spots of purple and light blue shade softly into the ground color. The leaf colors, primarily pigments rather than dyes, were applied by brush. The shaded spots resembling ink blots were probably produced by a kind of *shibori* in which portions of the cloth, not tied or wrapped, were dipped by hand into the dye bath. In the purple areas we see the radiating streaks characteristic of *shibori*, but the pale blue spots blend more evenly into the beige. The latter were probably dyed onto wet silk. Scattered small plum blossoms are embroidered in red, green, and couched gold.

Highly contrasting colors, fine white lines (*shiro-age*), and shaded dyes and pigments (*bokashi*) are common characteristics of many mid-Edo period *yūzen kosode*. The undecorated area on the left side indicates the position of the obi, which grew to great width during this period.

PUBLISHED: Kirihata, *Kosode II*, pl. 9.
            Nomura, *Kosode to furisode*, pl. 14.
            Senshoku no bi 3, pl. 3.

37 KATABIRA IN DIVIDED-BACKGROUND STYLE WITH SEA, PINE-FRINGED ISLANDS, AND BRIDGES

Shibori, painted pigments, stencilled *kanoko*, and embroidery
Black plain-weave ramie
L. 136   W. 60   S.W. 31.5   S.L. 42 cm.
Mid-Edo period, eighteenth century

Stitch-resist *shibori* divides this *katabira* into large black and white background areas. Waves executed in *kanoko shibori* turn the black backgrounds into ocean; a fringe of pine trees tells us that the white represents land; and bridges imply that the land areas are islands. Some of the pines are embroidered in brown, green, and couched gold, others are depicted in stencilled *kanoko* on blue and brown pigments (the outlines of these may have been stencilled as well, or sharply defined with resist paste). The center of each tiny stencilled *kanoko* spot has been pushed out (*uchidashi kanoko*) to give the textured effect of tied *kanoko*. The plank bridges are painted in ink, with their wood grain carefully indicated in brown pigment. Parallel rows of gold couching represent the bridge railings.

The sandy shoreline motif, often associated with pine trees, dates from the Heian period and derives from Chinese legend (see Cpl. 10).

Although the design is perfectly continuous across the back seam, at the shoulder seams it is abruptly broken and it is upside down on the front of the sleeves. This suggests that the *katabira* was originally a *furisode* that sustained damage to one of its long flowing sleeves, and that two shorter sleeves were made from the remaining intact sleeve.

PUBLISHED: Nomura, *Kosode to furisode*, pl. 20.

Shibori and paste resist
Yellow *saya* silk: 4/1 warp-faced twill figure of key fret, orchids, and plum blossoms
    on plain-weave ground
L. 164   W. 61.5   S.W. 32   S.L. 42 cm.
Late Edo period, late eighteenth–early nineteenth century

Disposed in horizontal ranks against a vivid yellow background are purple, red, and white chrysanthemums. The blossoms were executed in stitch-resist and capped *shibori*, then leaves and stems were detailed in resist paste and their blue and green brushed on. The blossoms are wholly undetailed and have the softness typical of *shibori* dyeing; their contrast with the forms crisply delineated by means of resist paste results in a *kosode* of unusual delicacy. At the same time the strong horizontality established by the bands of chrysanthemums gives the design a vigor often lacking in garments of the later eighteenth century.

PUBLISHED: Nomura, *Zoku kosode*, pl. 22.

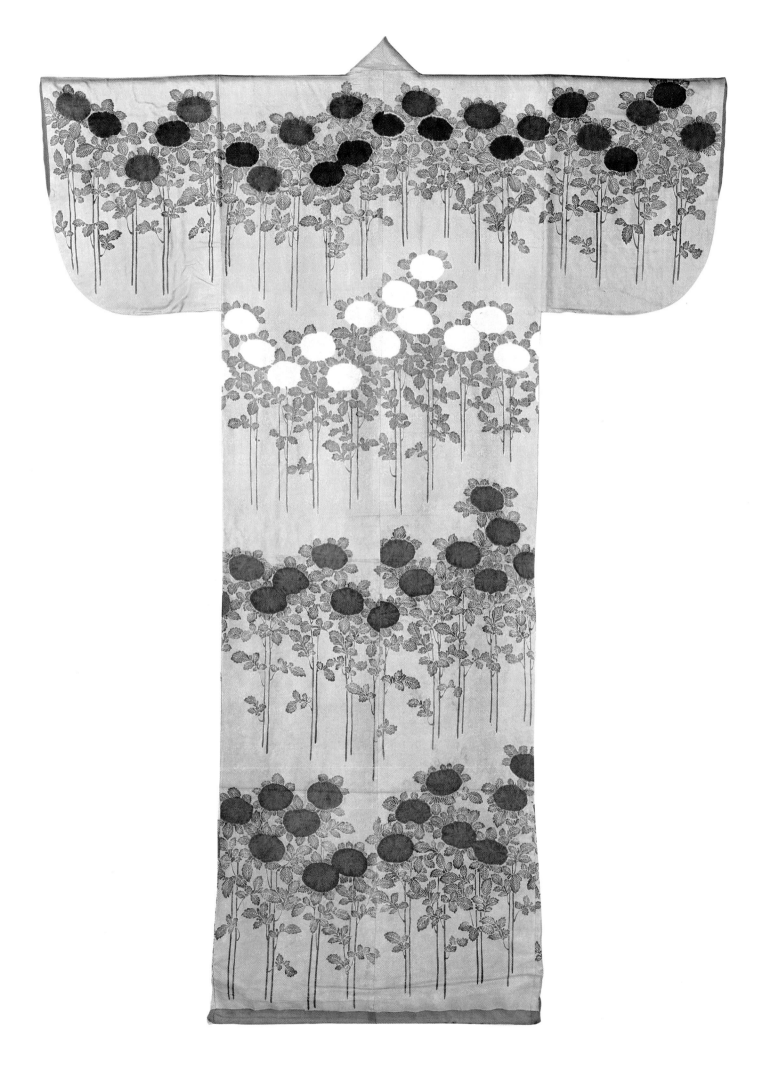

Shibori, paste resist, and painting in black ink and pigments
Red, yellow, and purple sheer silk crepe: 1/2 weft-faced twill figure of pine-bark
   lozenges and mandarin oranges on plain-weave ground
Mid–late Edo period, second half eighteenth century–early nineteenth century

Undulating bands of pale yellow, red, and purple divide the ground into horizontal zones defined by stitch-resist *shibori*. Alternating with these are various types of weirs and gabions, depicted in techniques common to *yūzen* dyeing. Since the background is dip dyed rather than brush dyed, however, this is not, strictly speaking, an example of *yūzen* dyeing. Wooden pilings are drawn freehand in black ink, and resist paste reserved the fine white lines that detail the straw mats used as water barriers, the barrels used to reinforce riverbanks, the wood grain of the blue pilings, and the waves at the hem. Gabions were painted in brown pigment and pigmentized indigo.

The contrast between delicacy of detail and boldness of conception is supported by the careful balance of *shibori*, *yūzen* techniques, and freehand painting, resulting in a superb example of late Edo design. Although the *kosode* is now lined with red silk, it was probably originally an unlined *hitoe* for summer wear.

PUBLISHED: Nomura, *Hiinagata byōbu*, pl. 86.

40 KOSODE WITH VIEWS OF KYOTO AND FLOWERS AND PLANTS OF THE FOUR SEASONS

Stitch-resist *shibori*, *yūzen* dyeing, and embroidery
White *chirimen* silk crepe
L. 148 W. 64 S.W. 32 S.L. 51 cm.
Mid-Edo period, second half eighteenth century

Golden tan clouds defined by stitch-resist *shibori* separate views of famous sites in Kyoto. The clouds were dip dyed, but details of buildings, figures, and landscape were painted in pigments and pigmentized indigo, with the fine white lines characteristic of *yūzen* dyeing reserved by means of resist paste. Plum blossoms, bamboo, pines, paulownia, cherry blossoms, dandelions, chrysanthemums, and reeds were depicted in pigments and in red, green, and couched gold embroidery.

Clearly this *kosode* was modelled after the *rakuchū-rakugai* (sights in and around Kyoto) folding screens so popular in the Edo period, in which clouds painted in gold frame the individual landmarks and indicate distance between them.[1] Kiyomizu Temple and Otowa Falls occupy the center back and right sleeve. Below stands the five-storey Yasaka Pagoda of Hōkan-ji (Hōkan Temple), and on the skirt is the Gojō Bridge over the Kamo River. Most of the places illustrated are in the eastern part of the city.[2] The left overlap and lower part of the left neckband are later replacements.

Human figures in landscape or urban settings were among the design innovations associated with *yūzen* dyeing, which permitted a much wider range of pictorial expression than dip dyeing or even embroidery. During the eighteenth century the representation of specific places, usually famed for scenic beauty, became a common theme of *kosode* design. This and the *kosode* in Colorplates 41 and 42 are fine examples of the liveliness imparted to human activities and familiar places by *yūzen* dyers.

---

1. Metropolitan Museum of Art, *Momoyama*, pl. 28.
2. Kirihata, *Kosode II*, p. 256.
PUBLISHED: Kirihata, *Kosode II*, pl. 22.
     Minnich, *Japanese Costume*, pls. 125, 126.
     Nomura, *Zoku kosode*, pl. 27.
     Senshoku no bi 3, pl. 25.

41 KOSODE SCREEN WITH FOLDING SCREENS SHOWING THE FIFTY-THREE STAGES OF THE TŌKAIDŌ

Yūzen dyeing
Blue-gray *chirimen* silk crepe
Late Edo period, first half nineteenth century

Sections of three folding screens angle across the front of this splendid *kosode*, the boldness of the allover design balanced by its delicacy of depiction, which employed resist paste and hand painting in pigments and dyes.

The fifty-three stages of the Tōkaidō (the main highway linking Kyoto and Edo) were established in 1601 as official stopping-places where food and lodging were available. They were depicted in numerous series of woodblock prints by the *ukiyo-e* artist Ichiryūsai Hiroshige (1797–1858). Famous places were especially popular as subjects of *yūzen* design during the Bunka-Bunsei eras (1804–30). Though fascinating in their detail, these *kosode* scenes lack the sense of life so evident in Hiroshige's prints.

On this *kosode* the two uppermost screens depict and label places from Kameyama to Kyoto, including Kameyama, Tsuchiyama, Mizoguchi, Ishibe (mislabelled "Ishiba"), Kusatsu, and Sanjō Bridge in Kyoto. The lower screen represents stages from Fujieda, west of Shizuoka, to Kuwana in the province of Ise, including Fujieda, Shirosuga, Futagawa, Hoshida, Akasaka, Fujikawa, Okazaki, Imamura (not one of the fifty-three stages but on the Tōkaidō), Chiryū, Narumi, Miya, and Kuwana (the last two linked by the ferry we can see at lower right).

PUBLISHED: Kirihata, *Kosode II*, pl. 27.
Nomura, *Hiinagata byōbu*, pl. 82.
Senshoku no bi 3, pl. 23.
Tokyo National Museum, *Nihon no senshoku*, no. 216.

Ishibe (below right) and the Sanjō Bridge in Kyoto, the western terminus of the Tōkaidō, are illustrated on the left sleeve of this *kosode*. The border of the folding screen imitates a woven key-fret and plum-blossom pattern. This is a typical element in *yūzen* design. Also typical are the careful shading of the pigments in the stones and in the roofs of the buildings and the fine white lines, reserved by means of resist paste, that delineate details and separate one color area from another. The blue-gray background color was brushed on, another characteristic of the *yūzen* process.

RIGHT: Divided-background style with plovers and autumn flowers
Shibori, yūzen **dyeing, and painted pigments**
Putty, white, and purple *chirimen* **silk crepe**
Mid-Edo period, first half eighteenth century

Purple triangles have been divided from areas of putty beige by means of stitch-resist *shibori*. Within the putty-colored areas white triangles have been reserved with resist paste. Autumn flowers and grasses, including chrysanthemums, bush clover, Chinese bellflowers, pampas grass, and pinks, span the putty and white areas. These were brushed on in black and in shaded pigments of blue, green, and gray. Plovers, reserved in white by means of capped *shibori*, are restricted to the purple triangles. Between the plovers and the autumn grasses there is no apparent thematic association. The flattened style of the chrysanthemums closely resembles the so-called Kōrin designs popular during the eighteenth century.

Pasted onto the back of the screen is an inscription on silk, probably from the original lining of the *kosode* or the lining of the altar cloth or priest's stole into which the *kosode* was made. It states that the *kosode* was dedicated by one Kimura Yoshibei in the fifth year of Genbun (1740). This date is consistent with the stylistic and technical properties of the garment.[1]

---

1. See Kirihata, *Kosode II*, p. 257, and *Senshoku no bi* 3, pl. 12.
PUBLISHED: Kirihata, *Kosode II*, pl. 28.
        Minnich, *Japanese Costume*, pl. 95.
        Nomura, *Hiinagata byōbu*, pl. 97.
        Senshoku no bi 3, pl. 12.
        Tokyo National Museum, *Nihon no senshoku*, no. 226.

Chaya-zome with embroidery and supplementary pigments
White plain-weave ramie
L. 165   W. 64.5   S.W. 32.5   S.L. 102 cm.
Mid-Edo period, second half eighteenth century

The white background of this *katabira* was covered with resist paste front and back and the garment dipped repeatedly in the indigo vat to attain the lighter of the two shades of blue. Then these light blue design elements were covered with resist paste and the garment dipped again till the darker shade was reached. The ivory (or pale yellow) dye was probably applied by brush. Yellow pigment was brushed on to accentuate the pine boughs, and fine blue lines were drawn with a stick of pigmentized indigo.

The decoration is typical of *chaya-zome* robes: thatch-roofed huts appropriate for the tea ceremony are set among ponds, flowing streams, bridges, and brushwood fences—a scene invitingly cool in midsummer, when this *katabira* would have been worn. Plum blossoms, irises, narcissi, peonies, mallows, bush clover, pinks, chrysanthemums, maple leaves, pines, and bamboo grass are rendered in indigo and sparsely embroidered in red, dark green, yellow-green, purple, and couched gold. The restrained touches of embroidery perfectly complement the crisp flatness of the fabric and cool, linear quality of the design.

Being extremely arduous to create (and therefore expensive), *chaya-zome* robes were worn only by the highest strata of society. Ladies of the shogunal court found their understated elegance particularly suitable. It is said that some types of *chaya-zome* were restricted by law to women of the most important branches of the Tokugawa house, but this is difficult to substantiate.

No chronology for extant *chaya-zome* pieces has been established. Although stylistically this *katabira* is consistent with mid-Edo taste, the extreme length of the *furisode*-style sleeves suggests, if not demands, a late Edo date.[1]

---

1. Kirihata, "Furisode-kō—sode take no hensen o chūshin ni—", *Senshoku no bi* 15: 72.
PUBLISHED: Nomura: *Kosode to furisode*, pl. 42.
    Tokyo National Museum, *Nihon no senshoku*, no. 280.

One of the most impressive features of *chaya-zome* is the apparent tonal variety
achieved with two shades of vat-dyed indigo and indigo pigment. Up to thirty
dippings were required to produce the darker blue. Pigmentized indigo in stick form
was applied like a crayon to draw the fine blue lines that make up the fish nets, the
dew- or snow-dappled hummocks, bridge planking, eaves, and the texture of rocks.

RIGHT (DETAIL): Design of morning glories on bamboo fence
Shibori and pigment
Red *chirimen* silk crepe
Late Edo period, nineteenth century

Blue and white morning glories climb a fence merely suggested by occasional segments of bamboo. Stitch-resist *shibori* reserved the morning-glory blossoms against the dipped red background; the blue flowers were then brushed on with indigo. Color on color created the vine stems and leaves and the bamboo: indigo brushed over yellow ochre made the dark green leaves and stems, and for the dry, woody texture of the bamboo red-brown pigment (probably *bengara*) was applied over all.

Unlike the white blossoms, around which the holes left by stitch resist are clearly visible, the yellow and green forms display no traces of *shibori* methods, although the soft blending of shape into background at first glance suggests *shibori*. The dyer must have used a technique similar to modern discharge dyeing (*bassen*), in which color is removed from portions of a dyed fabric by controlled application of bleach. For the morning-glory *kosode*, after the areas to be reserved in white had been stitched, capped, and bound, the crepe was dyed first yellow, then red (possibly with madder). While the red dye was still wet, it must have been removed from stems, leaves, and bamboo sections by brushing them with water. This would have to be done quickly, for if the red dye were allowed to dry the outlines of the water-brushed areas would be crisper. Several dyers may have had to work simultaneously in order to achieve the effect of yellow melting into red with no outline.[1]

Only the lower two-thirds of the garment and sleeve are covered with morning glories, leaving the upper part unpatterned. *Kosode* designs employing this kind of composition were created in the eighteenth century and became increasingly common in the nineteenth, along with even more restrained designs in which the pattern was confined entirely to the skirt and lower sleeves or to the hem area alone. The realistically textured bamboo also suggests a nineteenth-century date.

The representation of the morning glories is reminiscent of paintings by Sakai Hōitsu (1761–1828). Many late Edo (1781–1868) robes are either restrained to the point of dullness or garishly flamboyant, but in this *kosode* bold color combines with gently refined pattern to express the best design qualities of the period.

---

1. I am indebted to Monica Bethe for this hypothesis.

PUBLISHED: Minnich, *Japanese Costume*, pl. 94.
             Nomura, *Hiinagata byōbu*, pl. 81.
             Senshoku no bi 21, pl. 47.

Shibori and embroidery
Purple *chirimen* silk crepe
L. 157.5   W. 62   S.W. 31.5   S.L. 41 cm.
Mid-Edo period, mid-eighteenth century

Pliant orchid leaves, depicted in *kanoko shibori* and couched gold embroidery, bend under the weight of fresh snow reserved in capped *shibori*. Loose flecks of snow are embroidered in white, fragile orchid blossoms in red and couched gold with touches of green, and orchid stems in green.

While *yūzen* dyeing was reaching the height of its development during the early eighteenth century, the more luxurious tradition of *kosode* decorated with *shibori* and embroidery persisted, particularly in garments for festive occasions. In this composition, however, the weighty gorgeousness of seventeenth-century *shibori*-and-embroidery *kosode* is absent, and the profusion of fussy detail that commonly mars *kosode* design after the mid-eighteenth century has not yet descended. Its airy lightness is well suited to convey the delicacy of snow-laden orchids.

PUBLISHED: Minnich, *Japanese Costume*, pl. 129.
        Nomura, *Zoku kosode*, pl. 31.

Shibori, embroidery, and brushed pigments
White figured satin: 1/4 weft-faced figure of orchids and chrysanthemums on 4/1
   warp-faced ground
L. 159.5   W. 62   S.W. 32   S.L. 42.5 cm.
Mid–late Edo period, second half eighteenth century

A meandering blue stream winds its way through a field of bush clover. The
background has been reserved in white by means of *shibori*, possibly tub resist, and
the larger leaves of the bush clover were textured and dyed by a combination of
kanoko shibori and pinch dyeing in red, purple, and blue. *Kanoko shibori* patterns
the flow of the stream as well. Resist paste was used to reserve the leaves and stems,
to which dyes and pigments were applied by brush in black and shades of rose,
green, blue, yellow, and ochre. The blossoms are embroidered in pink and white;
here and there leaves are picked out in green and couched gold embroidery. The
pattern of bush clover and stream continues on the thickly padded scarlet hem,
embroidered in green, white, light blue, and couched gold. Padded embroidered
hems became popular in the nineteenth century, especially among the townsman
(*chōnin*) class, and it is likely that this hem was added at that time.

   Rimpa influence is evident in the dramatic curve and asymmetric placement of the
stream. Two garments of similar design but probably somewhat later date, one with
bush clover and one with irises, belong to the Kanebo Collection, Osaka.[1]

---

1. Japan House Gallery, *Tagasode*, Cpls. 29, 30.

PUBLISHED: Kirihata, *Kosode II*, pl. 39.
         Nomura, *Zoku kosode*, pl. 42.
         Royal Academy of Arts, *Great Japan Exhibition*, no. 367.
         Tokyo National Museum, *Nihon no senshoku*, no. 326.

KOSHIMAKI SCREEN WITH MYRIAD TREASURES AND OTHER AUSPICIOUS MOTIFS (DETAIL)

Embroidery
Brown *nerinuki* silk
Mid-Edo period, second half eighteenth century

The golden-brown background, probably faded from blackish brown, is entirely covered with auspicious motifs: tortoise and crane, pines with cranes nesting in their branches, bamboo and bamboo shoots, scattered paulownia crests (more likely a decorative element than the family insignia of the wearer) and the myriad treasures (see Cpl. 21). These are tightly embroidered in yellow-green, dark green, white, couched gold, and touches of purple. The limited palette, particularly the absence of red, gives this robe a quiet elegance lacking in other *koshimaki*.

By the early eighteenth century the heavily embroidered, dark-colored *koshimaki* over a sheer *katabira* was standard summer dress for ladies of the military aristocracy. Although it was worn slipped off the shoulders and held at the waist by a separate obi, it seems inappropriate to Japan's hot and humid summers. Perhaps the role of the *koshimaki* was, at least in part, to emphasize by contrast the cool crispness of the ramie *katabira* (cf. Cpls. 44, 45).

PUBLISHED: Nomura, *Hiinagata byōbu*, pl. 70.
Tokyo National Museum, *Nihon no senshoku*, pl. 278.

Embroidery, brushed pigment, and stencilled *kanoko*
White figured satin: 1/4 weft-faced figure of key fret, orchids, and chrysanthemums
on 4/1 warp-faced ground
L. 158   W. 61   S.W. 30.5   S.L. 42.5 cm.
Mid-Edo period, second half eighteenth century

Long-stemmed lilies are depicted in red, green, yellow-green, and gold embroidery, in black pigment, and in *kanoko* stencilled with a red-brown pigment (probably *bengara*, iron oxide or hematite). Six *Gion mamori* (guardian of Gion) crests are scattered across the shoulder area, embroidered in red and couched gold, and traces of two others remain, probably originally black but now deteriorated by the iron mordant frequently used with black dyes.

The *Gion mamori* crest combines the form of an amulet from the Gion (Shinto) Shrine in Kyoto with the St. Andrew's cross. It was used by worshippers at the shrine—and also by Christians as a covert protestation of faith during the anti-Christian proscriptions that lasted from the early seventeenth century into the Meiji period.[1] As early as the sixteenth century fervent Japanese Christians were adopting the *Gion mamori* as their family crest.

The lily too, of course, has Christian associations—as an emblem of the Virgin Mary, as part of the iconography of the Annunciation, and as a symbol of Easter. It is unlikely that this combination of motifs, both so closely linked with Christianity, is coincidental. Since, however, Christians were subject to official persecution until well into the nineteenth century and the Christian faith continued proscribed even after the fall of the Tokugawa shogunate, the design of this garment must have been based on an old prototype whose Christian symbolism had been forgotten. It is improbable that anyone would have deliberately flaunted emblems whose wearing might bring arrest, torture, and death.

---

1. Imanaga, *Kosode I*, pp. 266–67.
PUBLISHED: Imanaga, *Kosode I*, pl. 120.
        Nomura, *Kosode to furisode*, pl. 38.
        Senshoku no bi 21, pl. 45.

Matsumura Goshun (1752–1811)
Freehand painting in ink and colors
White plain-weave silk with 3-ply warps and single-ply wefts
L. 165.5   W. 61   S.W. 32   S.L. 43 cm.
Mid-Edo period, third quarter eighteenth century

A sparsely populated mountain landscape is depicted in dry brushstrokes and wet dots of ink, colored with washes of blue, green, pale orange, and yellow in the *nanga* style. The foreground begins at lower left, where a traveller approaches a gate; slightly beyond him two scholars pause in conversation as they cross a tiny bridge. A sense of depth is carefully built up: on the upper back and sleeves mountains in ink dots and color washes form the distant background.

This *kosode* bears the seal and signature ("*Goshun utsusu*") of Matsumura Goshun, and the garment's authenticity and unaltered condition are unquestioned. Early in his career Goshun painted in the *nanga* style, as seen here. After meeting the painter Maruyama Ōkyo (1733–95), he adopted the more realistic manner of the Shijō school. Another *kosode* painted by Goshun with spear flowers in snow seems to reflect a later phase of his career.[1]

Kosode painted by well-known artists were popular from the second half of the seventeenth century onward.[2] In *The Life of an Amorous Man* the novelist Ihara Saikaku (1642–93) remarks on the white satin *kosode* painted with a scene of autumn fields for a courtesan named Kaoru by Kanō Yukinobu (1643–82), daughter of the famous painter Kusumi Morikage.[3] Courtesans were often the leaders in fashion, and presumably the Nomura Collection includes *kosode* made for them as well as for the aristocracy, the military elite, and the wealthy townsmen.

---

1. In the collection of the Rakutō Ihōkan, Kyoto. See Kirihata, *Kosode II*, pl. 94.
2. Nagasaki Iwao, "Edo no kosode", *Senshoku no bi* 21: 84.
3. Ihara Saikaku, *The Life of an Amorous Man*, trans. Kengi Hamada (Rutland, Vt. and Tokyo: Tuttle, 1964), p. 185.

PUBLISHED: Imanaga, *Kosode I*, pl. 135.
　　　　　　Senshoku no bi 21, pl. 73.

Sakai Hōitsu (1761–1828)
Freehand painting in ink and pigments
White 4/1 warp-faced satin
L. 149   W. 57.5   S.W. 32   S.L. 43.5 cm.
Late Edo period, early nineteenth century

This magnificent spreading plum tree displays the accomplished mature brushwork of Sakai Hōitsu, a late follower of the *rimpa* school.[1] Rich tones of ink, which may have been mixed with sulfur-tarnished silver pigment, were blended into each other in the puddling technique called *tarashikomi*.[2] This technique had been developed by the painter Tawaraya Sōtatsu, one of the founders of the *rimpa* school. The blossoms were painted in vermilion pigment with delicate gold veins, and at the foot of the tree are dandelions and violets in yellow, blue, and green, also detailed with gold pigment. The right overlap bears Hōitsu's seal.

   This splendid garment may have been worn as an *uchikake*, unbelted over a *kosode*, as the wide obi popular at the time would have intruded on Hōitsu's design.

1. A satin *kosode* painted with autumn flowers and grasses by Ogata Kōrin (1658–1716), one of the founders of the *rimpa* school, belongs to the Tokyo National Museum. See *Senshoku no bi* 21, pl. 71.
2. Grilli, *Art of the Japanese Screen*, p. 66.
PUBLISHED: Imanaga, *Kosode I*, pl. 134.
            Minnich, *Japanese Costume*, pl. 112.
            Nomura, *Kosode to furisode*, pl. 55.
            Royal Academy of Arts, *Great Japan Exhibition*, no. 350.
            Senshoku no bi 21, pl. 72.
            Tokyo National Museum, *Nihon no senshoku*, no. 237.

Yūzen dyeing and embroidery
Blue *chirimen* silk crepe
L. 145   W. 64   S.W. 32   S.L. 43.5 cm.
Mid-Edo period, second half eighteenth century

Deep blue ground intersected by diagonally placed golden-brown shoji suggests a night sky and a lighted room seen from without. White wistaria vines silhouetted against the upper background heighten our impression that this is sky; fallen white pine needles lying on the lower area of blue imply the unseen pine tree around which the wistaria twines and simultaneously inform us that this passage of blue represents the ground. Pines hung with wistaria are a familiar motif in the decorative arts (Cpls. 5, 6, 7, 10).

The wistaria across the shoulders, the shoji, and the pine needles have been reserved with resist paste. *Uchidashi*, a technique usually used to give texture to stencilled *kanoko*, was here applied for the same purpose to the wistaria blossoms. The wistaria leaves have been painted with dark olive green pigment and the shoji with dyes. Additional wistaria are embroidered across the shoji in light blue, gold, and green.

White design motifs without painted detail, reserved by means of paste resist (*shiro-age*, or *shiro-agari*), were popular from the first half of the eighteenth century, especially in the Bunka-Bunsei eras (1804–30).[1] The technique was used most commonly for the *kosode* designs known as *Gosho-doki* (robe designs of the imperial palace), composed of motifs reminiscent of the Heian court and often based on specific incidents from the *Tale of Genji*. Employed for the wistaria and pine needles on this *kosode*, its avoidance of rich decorative effects and flashy coloring creates a sense of depth and mystery. Despite the use of resist paste the blue ground may have been vat dyed, for blue of this depth and evenness is difficult to obtain with indigo applied by brush. Vatting would account for the hazy outlines of the paste-resisted forms. This imperfection notwithstanding, the design is effectively dramatic, yet subtle.

---

1. Nagasaki Iwao, "Edo no kosode", *Senshoku no bi* 21: 86–88.
PUBLISHED: Nomura, *Zoku kosode*, pl. 19.

Embroidery and ink painting
White figured satin: 1/4 weft-faced figure of key fret and flowers on 4/1 warp-faced
    ground
Late Edo period, second half nineteenth century

Three cycad palms, embroidered in shades of blue, green, and brown, spread their fronds two-thirds of the way up this white figured-satin *kosode*, leaving the upper third of the garment unpatterned. Each leaf and each scale of the tree bark is individually represented. A low horizontal counterbalance to the upward thrust of the cycads is provided by the arching earthen bridge, reinforced by the gentle hill covered with bamboo grass at the hemline. Black ink strokes and various tones of brown embroidery silk, in long stitches sparse enough to let the white ground show through, give the earthen surface of the bridge a realistic texture. The bamboo poles that apparently support it, however, are too spindly to bear its weight.

Although a large tree covering most of the back of a garment, as if growing up from the hem, is a common motif of eighteenth-century *kosode* design (see Cpl. 35), here the detailed treatment of tree bark and bridge, suggesting a painted prototype, reflects a nineteenth-century realism. A composition of this scale and theatricality, unless clearly intended for a wedding garment, could have been worn, in the late Edo period, only by a courtesan. The strongly unified composition suggests that it may have been worn unbelted as an *uchikake*.

PUBLISHED: Imanaga, *Kosode I*, pl. 121.
    Nomura, *Hiinagata byōbu*, pl. 50.

Appliqué, *kanoko shibori*, embroidery, and *yūzen* dyeing
White figured satin: 1/4 weft-faced figure of birds in roundels on 4/1 warp-faced
**   ground**
L. 174   W. 62.5   S.W. 32.5   S.L. 105 cm.
Late Edo period, second half nineteenth century

The half-raised bamboo blind, fluttering silk panels of the standing screen, and cypress-slat fans dropped carelessly on the ground imply the inner recesses of a court lady's quarters, into which she or the man pursuing her has hastily slipped. Both meanings of *luxury* are present here—the rich surroundings portrayed, the eroticism implied. This undercurrent of courtly eroticism may seem to us an odd theme for a wedding garment, but perhaps the nineteenth-century Japanese eye admitted only the courtly associations.

The unrestrained profusion of decorative methods employed seems appropriate to the abandon of the subject matter. Visible behind the brush-dyed olive green blind, whose black and red cords are thickly embroidered in a braided pattern, are the red, blue, and white silk streamers of the standing screen. The red and blue panels are formed of pieces of plain-weave silk appliquéd to the white ground. The streamers are decorated with various *yūsoku* patterns (textile patterns first used at Heian court) in *kanoko shibori*; with embroidered phoenixes and paulownia, dragons in clouds, and tortoises in waves; and with background diaper patterns and landscape details in *yūzen* dyeing. Each streamer is bordered in parallel rows of gold couching. The cypress-slat fans with silken cords, a part of formal court dress since the Heian period, bear embroidered chrysanthemums, pines, flowering plums, and other auspicious motifs.

An identical garment but of red rather than white figured satin also belongs to the Nomura Collection.[1] These are probably two of a set of three worn during the wedding festivities; the innermost layer would have been black for solemnity, the middle layer red for gorgeousness, and the outer one white for purity and neatness.[2]

Although it may with reason be said that this *furisode* represents the best of nineteenth-century bad taste, we must remember that by the end of the Edo period everyday dress had become extremely subdued in both color and design, even when such restraint was not imposed by sumptuary laws. It is no wonder that *kosode* designs for the most festive occasions exploded into this kind of exuberance.

---

1. *Senshoku no bi* 15, pl. 32 (left).
2. *Senshoku no bi* 15: 34.
PUBLISHED: *Senshoku no bi* 15, pl. 32 (right).

Embroidery: silk floss on outside of *juban*, couched gold on lining
Gray plain-weave cotton; 7/1 warp-faced yellow satin lining
L. 135.5   W. 62   S.W. 32   S.L. 53 cm.
Late Edo period, nineteenth century

The *juban* (or *jiban*) was the undergarment, often elaborately decorated, worn under the *kosode* by both sexes. This is the only garment in the Nomura Collection that was unquestionably worn by a man.

Embroidered in black, white, and shades of brown, green, and blue, scenes of Edo occupy its entire surface. Moving downward from the right sleeve front we see Mt. Fuji, Edo Castle, a daimyo procession, and, just where the black neckband ends, the bridge at Nihonbashi. On the left front, directly across from Nihonbashi, is the Echigoya, later to become the famous Mitsukoshi department store. Below that is Ryōgoku Bridge. On the lower end of the right overlap the embroiderer's seal is stitched in tan silk; the top character, *nui*, means "embroidery", but the lower character, which would identify the embroiderer's shop, is illegible. On the back are depicted the Asakusa Kannon Temple and the shops along the Nakamise Road leading to it.

The lining is of brilliant yellow satin. Waves breaking on rocks are embroidered in gold couching along the skirt, and across the upper back are couched gold crests in the form of iris roundels. These may have been the wearer's family crest, or they may have been *date mon*, "dandy crests", purely decorative motifs adapted to crest form. The hem and facings of blue silk are probably later replacements; originally the *juban* was completely reversible.

Although the wearing of silk was nominally forbidden and the outer *kosode* may have been an elegant but simple striped cotton, this minutely embroidered and gorgeously lined undergarment would have enabled its wearer to feel himself the pinnacle of fashion and luxury.

PUBLISHED: Minnich, *Japanese Costume*, pls. 119, 120.

Appendix 1
LINING INSCRIPTIONS

A remarkable discovery was made in 1982 while research-ing *Kosode: 16th–19th Century Textiles from the Nomura Collection*. A box containing inscriptions evidently cut from the linings of *kosode* was found among the Nomura family's property. These fragments of tattered silk record in near-illegible script the provenance of certain textiles in the collection. Nomura, in the process of reassembling the robes and mounting them on screens, had saved the inscriptions but, oddly enough, never published them.

With careful study, the Nomura inscriptions could be extremely valuable for scholars of the collection in particu-lar and Edo period textile history in general. This writer's research was limited to the photographs reproduced here: the original inscriptions are for the time being inaccessible. All of us await the day when the inscriptions themselves can be studied and published in full.

The writings are dedicatory inscriptions from Buddhist temples. Traditionally in Japan, when a great lady died, her finest robes would be donated to a family temple. There they might be kept intact as a commemoration, or else carefully taken apart and made into *kesa* (Buddhist priests' vestments), altar cloths, and the like. Sometimes the family would present the valuable textiles already in *kesa* form: the making of a *kesa* was an act of merit.

At the temple brief explanatory dedications were writ-ten on the silk linings. These inscriptions, brushed in ink, indicated in more or less detail the posthumous name and titles of the deceased, the date of her death, the name of the temple and its location, and the names of those dedicating the robe, usually retainers of the lady's family.

The custom of writing dedicatory inscriptions or mak-ing lists of donations to Buddhist temples is an ancient one. Among the most important documents in Japanese history—a treasure for its calligraphy alone—is the *Tōdai-ji Kenmotsu-chō* of the Shōsō-in in Nara. Dated to A.D. 758, this work is a catalogue of donations made by nobles and members of the Imperial family to Tōdai-ji (Tōdai Temple) in Nara. It attests to the Japanese passion for keeping records and inventories of collections.

Inscriptions on Buddhist works of art abound through-out later ages. In Kyoto's Sanjūsangendō, built in 1266 and housing 1,001 images of the Thousand-Armed Kannon, the statues were found to bear inscriptions on their bases stating the name of the carver and the date of carving. By the Edo period the custom of attaching writ-ings had spread from religious to secular works of art. Utensils for the tea ceremony, Nō masks, paintings, and fine calligraphy accumulated documents and inscribed wrappings and boxes. These writings range in content from simple statements of the owner's name and date of acquisition to correspondence with former owners; testi-monials and encomiums by famous tea masters, Zen priests, or imperial princes; and poetic dedications.

It is no surprise, then, that the robes of high-born ladies are accompanied by such writings. Certain robes were prized for their artistry even by the Edo period: quite a few of the Nomura inscriptions designate the tex-tile as "treasure".

What is surprising, in fact, is that we have so few of these dedicatory inscriptions. There are several possible reasons for this. Not all the robes in the Nomura Collec-tion came from Buddhist temples, and robes in the pos-session of their original families would probably *not* be inscribed. Furthermore, it is likely that even in temples only the more exalted robes would be inscribed. This theory is supported by the fact that at least four of the inscriptions found in Nomura's box may be identified as referring to ladies of noble rank. Finally, since the in-scriptions were detached when the textiles were relined or mounted on screens, some may have been lost. We can only guess whether other boxes of inscriptions existed, and why Mr. Nomura chose to preserve this one.

On some of the inscriptions are scrawled notes identi-fying the colors and patterns of the textile. These were probably added at the time the linings were removed from the robes. In a corner of one inscription, for example, are the words "*tanzaku* and *shikishi* papers with cherry"; another notes "grapes on a black background". These notes may help us to link certain inscriptions with the *kosode* from which they were taken. They are of great value, for a dated inscription that can be assigned to a particular robe can provide useful information toward a chronology of these textiles. The job of examining the entire collec-tion and identifying each inscription with its *kosode* is daunting.

1. 松平出羽守直政

2. 什物

爲娟光院殿玉泡春影大童女成三菩提也

命日元祿十四幸巳年三月十一日同十七甲申年三月二日寄附焉

右者雲刕之城主松平出羽守殿御息女也於武刕江戸逝去

御施主同御家中女儀　取次同御家中綿貫彌惣殿

高野山　　[　]安院谷　　[菩][賣]院什物住持　覺眞

INSCRIPTION 1

Inscription 1 reads:

In memory of Kenkōin-dono gyoku Honshun'ei Daidōjō Seisan Bodai. Date of death: 11 March, 1701. Donated 2 March, 1704. The above (robe belonged to) the daughter of Lord Matsudaira, daimyo of Dewa, master of the castle at Unshū. She passed away in Edo in the province of Musashi. Donors: ladies of her household, in commemoration. By the agency of Watanuki Yaso, likewise of her household. Kōyasan, [　]in, Tani[　]in. To be kept as a treasure. Kakushin.

The opening words, "Kenkōin-dono gyoku Honshun'ei Daidōjō Seisan Bodai", are the lady's Buddhist posthumous name. Such names are usually unrelated to the actual name of the deceased and therefore of little use in identifying provenance. The place name Unshū refers to Izumo, on the Japan Sea coast.

The father of the lady in question may be identified as Matsudaira Naomasa.[1] His full title is Matsudaira Dewa-no-kami Naomasa (Dewa-no-kami does not translate as "lord of the northern province of Dewa" but is an honorary office). In 1638 this man was transferred from Matsumoto in Shinano to Matsue on the Japan Sea coast, where he became lord of Matsue, one of the domains in the province of Izumo. His branch of the Matsudaira clan, the so-called Echizen Matsudaira, was related to Ieyasu, founder of the Tokugawa shogunal line. His date of birth is unknown, but he died in 1666. After his death his sons were granted two additional important domains in the Izumo area, the Mori and the Hirose *han*. The family, by virtue of its relationship to the shogun and its great landholdings, was most illustrious. Although we know nothing else concerning the lady this robe commemorates, we can be sure that she represented the highest stratum of society. Hence the word "treasure"[2] concluding the dedicatory inscription.

Kōyasan, mentioned in the inscription, refers to the monastic complex of the Buddhist Shingon sect on Mt. Kōya in Wakayama Prefecture. The names of the sub-temples [　]in and Tani[　]in of Kōyasan, to which this robe was donated, have been scratched out. These smudges of erasure suggest more than they conceal. Probably this robe, once thought to be a treasure, was subsequently sold and either the temple or the new owners tried to cover up their responsibility in the matter. This deaccessioning almost surely took place during or after the Meiji Restoration, when the government encouraged a radical downgrading of Buddhism, which resulted in the sale or destruction of quantities of Buddhist art. The anti-Buddhist phase, though short-lived, had permanent effects. Important art treasures continued to be sold into the 1930s, thus augmenting some of the great collections in Japan.

The last words of the dedicatory inscription, "To be kept as a treasure", mark this robe as one of eminent importance for both material value and noble provenance. Kakushin is the name of the monk at Kōyasan who wrote the inscription upon receipt of the robe.

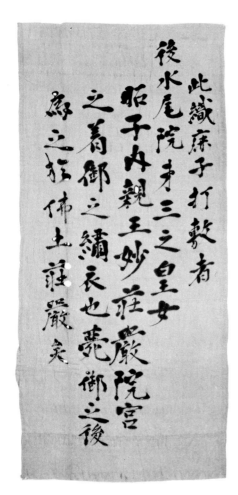

此織麻子打敷者

後水尾院第三之皇女

昭子内親王妙莊嚴院宮

之着御之繡衣也薨御之後

爲之於佛土莊嚴矣

3. 昭子

4. 近衛尚嗣北政所

5. 顯子

INSCRIPTION 2

Inscription 2 reads:

> This woven *asa* altar cloth was [made from] an embroidered robe worn by Imperial Princess Akiko, Myō-Sōgen-in no Miya, third daughter of Emperor Go-Mizunoo. After her decease she is known as Sōgen in the Land of the Buddha.

The inscription has no date, which makes it of limited value. Furthermore, it is in error concerning Akiko's rank and precedence among the imperial daughters, repeating a long-standing confusion concerning Akiko that historians are still unravelling.

There was an Imperial Princess Akiko[3](1629–75), but she was the *fourth* daughter of Emperor Go-Mizunoo. Go-Mizunoo's third daughter (whose name is a matter of dispute) married the regent Konoe Shoshi, and was known as Konoe Shoshi Kita no Mandokoro[4] (Kita no Mandokoro, "The Northern Office", is a title, not a name). This third daughter was never granted the rank of imperial princess. Because Akiko's name was sometimes written with a variant character,[5] some people thought that there were two princesses named Akiko. But there was only one, namely Go-Mizunoo's fourth daughter.

Several elements suggest that this inscription is not contemporary with the donation of the robe. First, it bears no date. Second, its calligraphy differs markedly in style from that of the other inscriptions. Third, other inscriptions typically state the entire posthumous name, not merely a shortened version such as Sōgen. Fourth, the inscription is unclear about Akiko's order of birth. In short, it reads like an explanation rather than a commemoration.

194

此折敷一表者

近衞太閤[様][御]姫　一位君様[御]

養岳本光[□]　心覺慈仙大[御]

御傍出勤[□]　拝領之異　[□]

□□□莊嚴　□　□

INSCRIPTION 3

A curious older inscription, Number 3, may shed some light on the problem. This inscription is in very bad condition, but can be partially read as follows:

> This altar cloth [was worn by] the Princess of First Rank [wife of] the Regent Konoe ... [posthumous title]: Yōka-kuhon Kō-[   ]-shin Kakuji Sendai ... [laboring at the side of ... a humble gift] ... Sōgen".

Could this inscription refer to the third daughter, the one who married Regent Konoe? The partly obliterated "Kō-[   ]-shin" may be Kōmyōshin,[6] the third daughter's posthumous name. But if this is true, why do we find "Sōgen", the fourth daughter's posthumous name, at the end of the inscription? There are many possible answers: a missing segment of the inscription may have mentioned Princess Konoe's sister Akiko, posthumously known as Sōgen; or Princess Konoe may already have been confused with Akiko; or *sōgen*, whose context is here obliterated, may not be part of a name but simply the word "august". Maybe modern-day historians have not solved every twist of this puzzle.

If Inscription 3 were already partially illegible within a century or so of the lady's death, Inscription 2 could have resulted from a compounding of errors in the attempt to interpret Inscription 3. An unwary reader, having mistakenly identified Konoe's wife as Akiko, would naturally have read the word *sōgen* as Akiko's posthumous name, thus merging the identities of the third and fourth princesses. Having made this compound error, such a reader might have written Inscription 2 as an attempted explanation of Inscription 3.

It is likely, then, that we are not dealing with a robe that belonged to Princess Akiko. The real possessor of the robe was Akiko's sister, the wife of the regent Konoe. In Inscription 3 this lady is called *hime*, a general term for highborn ladies, including princesses, but quite distinct from *naishinnō*, the term used in Inscription 2, which denotes an imperial princess.

Nomura, in his publication *Jidai kosode hiinagata byōbu*, did identify one robe (Cpl. 18) as Akiko's, possibly on the strength of this inscription. But this poses yet further questions. For one, Inscriptions 2 and 3 describe the piece as an altar cloth, and Inscription 3 affirms it is of *asa*. But the robe in Colorplate 18 is neither of *asa* nor an altar cloth. Indeed, scholars of the collection are not sure where this *asa* altar cloth is, though many conjecture that it was reassembled as a *kosode* and mounted on a screen.

We know that Nomura believed one of his *kosode* —whether whole or partial—had belonged to Akiko. Yet he did not present these inscriptions as evidence, perhaps because he was aware of the problems they posed. Neither, however, did he discard them. Such inscriptions, as collectors and connoisseurs know, exude an almost mantic power. In them lies justification. These inscriptions, gathered and laid away by Nomura, reappeared providentially with the writing of this catalogue, a last gift to his collection from the dedicated collector.

6. 光明心

195

Appendix 2
WEAVE STRUCTURES AND WOVEN PATTERNS

Fig. 2-1

Plain weave (*hira-ori*).

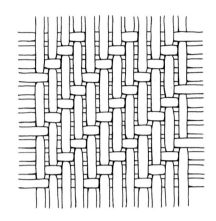

Fig. 2-2

Twill weave (*aya-ori*); example of 3/1 warp-faced twill structure.

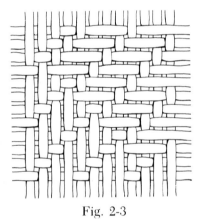

Fig. 2-3

Figured twill (*mon aya-ori*); example of a 1/3 weft-faced twill figure on 3/1 warp-faced twill ground.

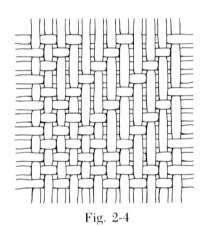

Fig. 2-4

Damasee (*saya-ori*); example of a 3/1 warp-faced twill figure on plain-weave ground.

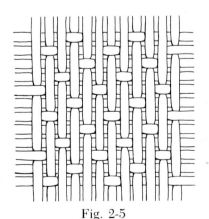

Fig. 2-5

Satin weave (*shusu-ori*); example of a five-harness warp-faced satin structure.

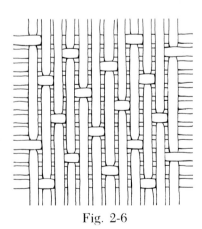

Fig. 2-6

Satin weave (*shusu-ori*); example of an eight-harness satin structure.

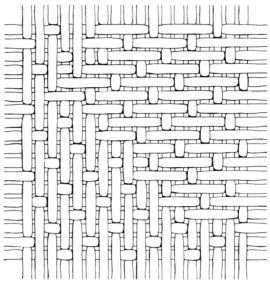

Fig. 2-7
Figured satin (*rinzu-ori*); example of a five-harness weft-faced satin figure on five-harness warp-faced satin ground.

Fig. 2-8
Woven pattern of key fret with orchids and chrysanthemums (*sayagata rangiku*).

Appendix 3
CHANGES IN KOSODE DIMENSIONS

Changes in dimensions of men's *kosode*, late Muromachi period to the present.

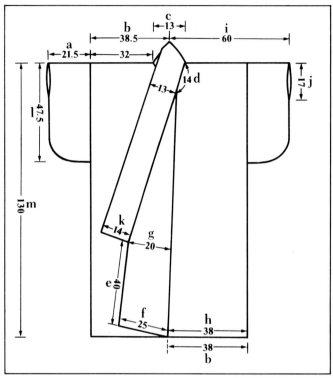

Fig. 3-1.

1566. *Tsujigahana kosode* inscribed Eiroku 9. See also Fig. 4-1.

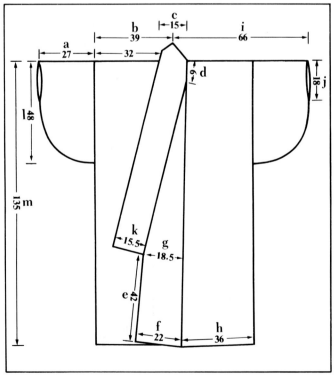

Fig. 3-2.

Ca. 1600–1640. Black satin *kosode* handed down in the Katakura family.

Kosode pieces:

a) sleeve width (*sode haba*)
b) back half-width at hem (*ushiro haba*, center back seam to side seam)
c) neck opening (*eri-kata aki*)
d) top of overlap to shoulder (*okumi-sagari*)
e) lower edge of neckband to lower edge of overlap (*tatezuma*)
f) overlap width at hem (*okumi haba*)
g) overlap width at lower edge of neckband (*aizuma haba*)
h) front half-width at hem (*mae haba*)
i) center back to sleeve opening (*yuki*)
j) sleeve opening (*sode guchi*)
k) neckband width (*eri haba*)
l) sleeve length (*sode take*, shoulder fold to lower edge of sleeve)
m) length, at center back, from lower edge of neckband to hem (*mitake*)

—Excerpted from Kamiya Eiko, ed., *Kosode*, Nihon no bijutsu, no. 67 (Tokyo: Shibundô, 1971), p. 33.

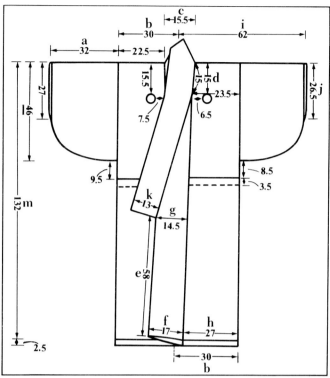

Fig. 3-3.

Ca. 1700. *Komon kosode* reportedly worn by Asakura Hanzô.

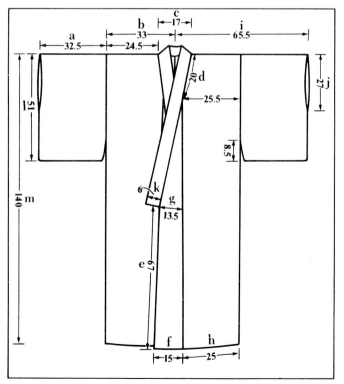

Fig. 3-4.

1970. Standard kimono for man 167 cm. in height. See also Fig. 4-2.

Appendix 4
MEASUREMENTS AND CUTTING LAYOUTS*

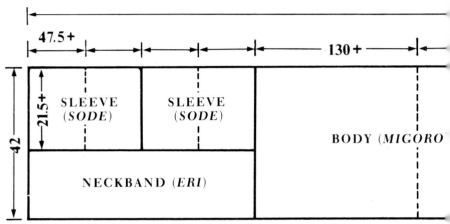

Fig. 4-1.

Measurements and reconstruction of cutting layout for *kosode* dated Eiroku 9 (1566). Woven width of fabric 42 cm.; overall length of fabric approx. 860 cm.

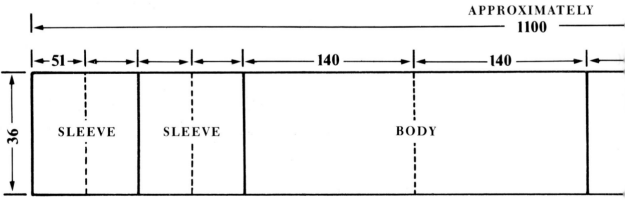

Fig. 4-2.

Measurements and cutting layout for contemporary man's kimono. Woven width of cloth 36 cm.; overall length of fabric approx. 1,100 cm.

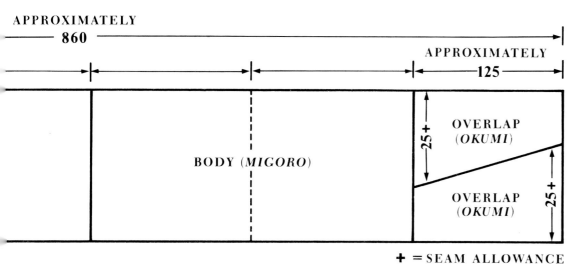

APPROXIMATELY
860

APPROXIMATELY
125

BODY (*MIGORO*)

OVERLAP
(*OKUMI*)

25+

OVERLAP
(*OKUMI*)

25+

+ = SEAM ALLOWANCE

—From Kamiya Eiko, ed., *Kosode*, Nihon no bijutsu, no. 67 (Tokyo: Shibundō, 1971), p. 34.

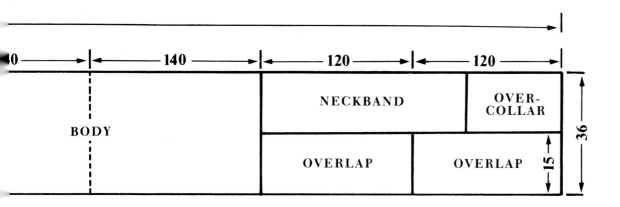

140

140

120

120

BODY

NECKBAND

OVER-
COLLAR

OVERLAP

OVERLAP

36

15

*Not drawn to scale.

Appendix 5
DYES AND COLORS

BLUE

Jap.:	*tade ai*
Bot.:	*Polygonum tinctorium Lour.*
Eng.:	Japanese indigo

Annual. 50–60 cm.
Grows throughout Japan, especially Shikoku.
Leaves, containing indigotin, harvested in July, Sept., and Nov., just before flowering, and used fresh, fermented, or dried and composted

Jap.:	*yama ai*
Bot.:	*Mercurialis leiocarpa Sieb. et Zucc.*
Eng.:	mountain indigo

Perennial. 30–40 cm.
Grows near cedar forests in mountains of central and southern Japan.
Leaves harvested in summer and early fall, used fresh

Jap.:	*aobana*
Bot.:	*Commelina communis L.*
Eng.:	dayflower or spiderwort

Annual. 5–7 cm.
Grows throughout Japan.
Juice of fresh petals contains delphinidin and can be extracted with the morning dew in May and June

BROWN and BLACK: *See* tan. Also made by top-dyeing indigo with tannin source and/or *akane*

GREEN: Made by top-dyeing indigo and yellow

Extraction Method and Mordants	Colors	Characteristics	Comments
1. (Earliest): chop freshly harvested leaves in water	Pale to bright blue, depending on proportion of leaves to water	Light-sensitive	*Tade ai* imported from China before Nara.
2. (Nara–Heian): ferment freshly harvested leaves in water	light to dark blue	Some crocking	Rank-color until Late Heian, later permitted to commoners.
3. (Edo): ferment composted leaves in vat of lye water and other ingredients		Crocking; slight graying in sun; running	Dark tones prized during Kamakura. Composting probably begun in Late Heian, sunken heated vats during Muromachi.
		Washing brightens the blue	Mid-Edo expansion of indigo industry caused by popularity of cotton, on which indigo dyes well.
1 dip	light blue (*mizu iro*)		
3 dips	bright blue (*tsuyugusa iro*)		Leaves, flowers, juice used to treat stomach disorders, fever, snakebite.
5 dips	medium blue (*hanada*)		
10 dips	dark blue (*kon*)		
17 dips	dark blue (*kachi*)		
with yellow top-dye	green (*midori*) grass green (*moegi*) chartreuse (*hiwa iro*)		Dye acts as pesticide. Pigment used as textile paint (*ai bō*)
with *beni* top-dye	lavender (*futa ai*)		
with *suō* top-dye	fake purple (*nise murasaki*)		
with tannin top-dye	black (*kuro*)		
light top-dye of yellow or *akane* decreases purple overtones.			
Rub fabric with leaves or juice from leaves	*Suri ai* ("rubbed blue," light green-blue)	Crocking; running	In use primarily during prehistoric and Nara periods; references continue into Edo period. Color dull due to low percentage of indigo and presence of impurities
1. (Nara): rub fabric with petals	Pale blue	Washes out easily; fugitive	Rubbed color not used after Nara
2. Saturate paper with petal juice, immerse paper in water to re-extract juice			During Edo, liquid used to outline *yūzen* designs for dyeing, outline washed out after dyeing

		Dye Source	**Plant Information**

RED

Jap.: *Nihon akane*
Bot.: *Rubia cordifolia* L.,
     var. *Mungista Miq*.
Eng.: Japanese madder

Perennial vine, leaves
  grouped in fours.
Grows on Honshū and south.
Roots contain purpurin and
  alizarin (anthraquinone).
Roots of plants between 2 and
  7 years old harvested in
  October and dried for
  storage

Jap.: *rokuba akane*
Bot.: *Rubia tinctorum L.*
    and *Rubia cordifolia*
    Linn.
Eng.: madder

Perennial. Vine with stalks
  50–80 cm. and leaves
  growing in sixes.
Found in warmer parts of
  Japan, S.E. Asia, and
  Europe.
Roots of plants between 3 and
  6 years old, containing
  purpurin and alizarin, are
  dried after harvesting in Oct.
Storage brings out purpurin

Jap.: *benibana*
Bot.: *Carthamus tinctorius*
    L.
Eng.: safflower

Thistle. Over 100 cm.
Grows throughout Japan,
  esp. Yamagata Pref.
Petals, containing carthamin,
  harvested in July and either
  dried or fermented and
  made into *beni mochi*

Jap.: *suō*
Bot.: *Caesalpinia sappan L*.
Eng.: sappanwood

Small, prickly tree grown in
  India, S.E. Asia.
Woody tissue, containing
  brasileia, dried and stored
  as chips

Jap.: *enji*
Zool: *Lakshadia chinensis*
Eng.: lac

Colored resin secreted by
  insects feeding on trees in
  India and S.E. Asia.
In fall, insect-encrusted twigs
  washed in a light alkali bath
  to extract color, which is
  dyed onto cotton for storage

RED-BROWN

Jap.: *katekyū*
Bot.: *Acacia catechu Wild*.
Eng.: cutch, catechu

A leguminous plant grown in
  S.E. Asia.
Stems and leaves, containing
  catechin, are dried, or the
  juice is extracted and stored
  in cake form

Extraction Method and Mordants	Colors	Characteristics	Comments
Soak and pound roots in warm water (presoaking in rice helps leach out fugitive yellow)		Difficult to dye dark shades Fades toward tan with age	The native madder, harder to dye with than other madders. Its colors prized and ranked high during Nara, but the dye was no longer used during Edo. Medicinal name: *saikon*. Used to treat jaundice, rheumatism, bleeding
Mordant with rice vinegar and alum	Red (*aka* or *hi iro*); light red (*ake*)		
Soak and pound roots in warm water, preferably during cold weather			The redder, stronger dye of this madder made it more popular than *Nihon akane* from Muromachi on. Paid as tax in kind. Used sometimes in indigo vat for alizarin content. Root extract used to treat jaundice, rheumatism, bleeding
Mordant with alum	madder red (*akane iro*)		
Squeeze in water to leach out yellow,	yellow (*ki iro*)	Light-sensitive	Imported from China ca. 5th century and domesticated.
then squeeze in alkali bath to obtain red. Neutralize bath with vinegar. No other mordant	1 bath: pink (*ikkon-zome*); many baths: scarlet (*kurenai* or *beni*)	Heat-sensitive; fades to tan with age	Continual popularity peaked in Momoyama and early Edo. *Beni mochi* process invented before 1700. Pigment from sedimented dye (*beni sashi*) used as textile paint and cosmetic.
Top-dyed on indigo	lavender (*futa ai*)		Pesticide.
Squeezed in alkali without first extracting yellow dye	salmon pink (*hanezu*)		Medicinal name: *kōka*. Used to treat high blood pressure, dysmenorrhea, fever
Boil chips in water		Slightly light-sensitive; fades toward brown	Imported since Nara as dye and drug.

Mordants:
  alum
  iron
  top-dyed on yellow
  top-dyed on indigo
	crimson (*suō iro*)
	purple (*murasaki*)
	red (*aka*)
	fake purple (*nise murasaki*)
			Popular red during Edo.
			Medicinal name: *soboku*.
			Used internally to treat stomach ailments, topically for bruises, orchitis

Release dye from cotton in a light alkali solution. Neutralize bath with acid	deep red (*enji iro*)	Colorfast	Imported during Nara and Edo in stored form (*enji wata*). Affinity to cotton; popular on *yūzen* and *sara-sa* (stencil-printed cottons)
Boil dried material or cakes in water		Colorfast	Imported since Nara for use as drug. Takes well on cotton; use as dyestuff expanded during Edo.

Mordants:
  alum
  copper
  iron
	burnt umber (*kaba iro*)
	dark Venetian red (*hiwada*)
	dark brown (*koge-cha*)
			Medicinal name: *asen*. Used as tonic, stimulant, antithelminthic

	Dye Source	Plant Information

TAN, BROWN, BLACK from tannin

Jap.: *ume*
Bot.: *Prunus Mume Sieb. et Zucc.*
Eng.: plum

Deciduous tree grown throughout Japan. Inner bark and woody tissue, containing tannin, harvested just before flowering in early spring. Chopped and dried for storage

Jap.: *cha*
Bot.: *Thea sinensis L.*
Eng.: tea

Evergreen shrub grown throughout Japan. Leaves, containing tannin, dried and smoked

Jap.: *yashabushi*
Bot.: *Alnus firma Sieb. et. Zucc.*
Eng.: alder

Deciduous tree growing throughout Japan. Cones, wood, and bark dried and stored for dyeing

Jap.: *gobaishi*
Bot.: *Melaphis chinensis*
Eng.: gallnuts

Swellings caused by parasites in trees containing tannin. Best when freshly picked in fall, but can be dried and stored

Jap.: *chōji*
Bot.: *Eugenia aromatica Kuntze*
Eng.: clove

Tree growing in S.E. Asia. Seeds, containing flavanoid and possibly tannin, dried for storage

Jap.: *yamamomo* or *shibuki*
Bot.: *Myrica rubra Sieb. et. Zucc.*
Eng.: arbutus myrica

Evergreen tree growing south and west of Nagoya. Bark, containing flavanoid/ tannin, is dried and stored

Extraction Method and Mordants	Colors	Characteristics	Comments

Boil in water
 	
Mordants:
  alum
  ash lye
  iron
	
	flesh color (*hada iro*)
	reddish tan
	brownish gray (*ume nezumi*)
		Light-fast	Imported from China during Nara, then domesticated.
			Vinegar of fruits used as agent in dyeing (*ume-zu*,
			First used as dye during Muromachi.
			Medicinal name: *umeboshi*, *umeshu*; used to treat fever, stomach ailments

1. Boil in water
 	
  Mordants:
    ash lye
    alum
    iron
	
	beige (*usu-cha*)
	beige (*usu-cha*)
	beige-gray (*nezumi-cha*)
		Light-fast	First used as dye during Muromachi.
			Became generic name for browns.
			Senji-cha was variety commonly used during Edo.

2. Boil in lye bath
 	
  Mordants:
    alum
    iron
	
	terra-cotta (*aka-cha*)
	violet-gray (*fuji-nezumi*)
		Light-fast	Medicinal name: *cha*. Used as diuretic, stimulant, intestinal astringent, coronary stimulant

Boil in water
 	
Mordants:
  ash lye
  ash + iron
  iron
    repeated dips
	
	golden yellow (*ki-cha*)
	brown (*cha iro*)
	sepia (*kuro-cha*)
	black (*kuro*)
		
		Black fades toward brown
		
		Can cause fiber deterioration
			Rich source of tannin.
			During Nara, cones rubbed into linen to dye commoners' clothing brown.
			Source of black during Nara.
			"Ya" in *yashabushi* means "night"

Boil in water
 	
Mordants:
  alum
  iron
    top-dyed with other tannin
    dyes and iron mordant
	
	brown (*cha*)
	light gray (*nezumi*)
	
	black (*kuro*)
		Light-fast
		
		Black can cause fiber deterioration
			Used to make *ohaguro* (tooth blackener).
			Tannin can be used as agent in dyeing cotton.
			Medicinal use unclear

Boil in water
 	
Mordants:
  alum
  ash lye
  ash + iron
	
	tan (*chōji iro*)
	pale terra-cotta (*chōji-cha*)
	dark terra-cotta (*koge chōji-cha*)
		Fades with age	Came into use during Heian.
			Favored for aroma it imparts to clothes.
			Medicinal name: *chōji*. Stimulant, anesthetic, antispasmodic.

Boil in water
 	
Mordants:
  alum
  ash lye
  iron
top-dyed on indigo
mixed with other tannins
Weak solutions used to finish indigo dyeing
	
	gold (*kin-cha*)
	gold (*kin-cha*)
	olive to gray (*yamamomo iro*)
	black (*kuro*)
	brown (*cha iro*)
			Used since Nara.
			Popular as over-dye during Edo.
			Takes well on cotton.
			Medicinal name: *yōbaihi*

207

| | | **Dye Source** | **Plant Information** |

YELLOW

Jap.: *kariyasu*
Bot.: *Miscanthus tinctorius Hackel*
Eng.: miscanthus

A tall grass growing on mountain slopes.
Ibukiyama, Shiga Pref., esp. well-known source.
Stems and leaves, containing flavanoid, harvested in autumn just before tassels open

Jap.: *kihada*
Bot.: *Philodendron amurense Rupr.*
Eng.: philodendron

Deciduous tree growing throughout Japan.
Inner bark and woody tissue, containing berberine, chopped and dried for storage

Jap.: *kuchinashi*
Bot.: *Gardenia jasminoides Ellis f. grandiflora Makino*
Eng.: gardenia

Low evergreen shrub growing in south-central Honshū, Shikoku, Kyūshū.
Seed pod, containing crocin (carotenoid), harvested in late fall

PURPLE

Jap.: *murasaki*
Bot.: *Lithospermum erythrorhizon Sieb. et. Zucc.*
Eng.: gromwell

Also made by top-dyeing indigo and *beni* or *suō*

Perennial. 30–60 cm.
Grows in mountains and fields, principally Musashino (Tokyo area) before Edo and Nambu (no. Honshū) during Edo.
Roots harvested in fall, dried and stored for several months before use.
Contains *shikonin*, a naphthaquinone derivative.
Roots of 3- or 4-year-old plants give best dye

Extraction Method and Mordants	Colors	Characteristics	Comments
Boil in water		Colorfast	Popular since Nara as top-dye, esp. with indigo to make greens
Mordants:			
alum	mustard color (*karashi iro*)		
iron	moss green (*uguisu iro*)		
top-dyed on indigo			
with alum	grass green (*moegi*)		
Boil in water			Probably the oldest Japanese dye. Blends well with other dyes.
No mordant	lemon yellow (*kihada*)		
			Used to dye important papers and fabrics for pesticidal effect.
Mordant:			
iron	light olive (*hiwa iro*)	Iron can cause fiber deterioration.	Used internally for stomach ailments, typhoid fever, hepatitis; topically for skin disorders, conjunctivitis
repeated dips	olive (*miru iro*)		
top-dyed on indigo	grass green (*moegi*)		
top-dyed on *suō*	madder red (*akane iro*)		
Weak solution top-dyed on indigo removes purplish tinge			
Boil in water		Light-sensitive	Used since Nara.
			Top-dyes well with reds but not blues.
No mordant necessary	warm yellow (*kuchinashi, yamabuki iro*, "kerria rose color")		Medicinal name: *sanshishi*.
			Used to treat fevers, inflammations, bleeding, jaundice
top-dyed with *suō*	madder red (*akane iro*)		

Extraction Method and Mordants	Colors	Characteristics	Comments
1. Soak and pound roots in 60° C. water, preferably in winter. Premordant cloth for several months in ash lye containing alum. Deepen color by repeated dippings	Purple (*murasaki*); light purple (*waka murasaki* or *usu murasaki*); dark purple (*kōki murasaki*)	Light-sensitive; fade toward grays Color deepens when stored away from light for up to 1 year	Native to Japan. High rank-color during Nara and Heian, permitted to commoners in mid-Muromachi, restricted again in early Edo. Especially popular during Genroku (1688-1704).
2. Boil roots in water and mordant with ash lye	Lilac-gray (*keshi murasaki*)		Paid as tax in kind during Muromachi and Edo. Bath has distinctive (unpleasant) odor. Sedimented pigment used as textile paint. Medicinal name: *shikon*. Used topically for burns, frostbite, skin ailments

This chart summarizes information about some of the more common dyes traditionally used in Japan for dyeing silk.
Dyeplant drawings reprinted from Makino Tomitarō, *Genshoku Makino shinnippon shokubutsukan (Makino's new illustrated flora of Japan)* (Tokyo Hokuryūkan, 1961), except for *enji* from Yamazaki Seiju, *Kusaki-zome: iro to shuhō (Vegetable dyeing: colors and methods)* (Bijutsu Shuppansha, 1974), *katekyū* and *choji* from *Senryō shokubutsufu (Dyeplant album)*, ed. Goto Shōichi and Yamakawa Takahira, (Hakuōsha, 1937, 1972), *suō* from Watanabe Kiyohiko, *Zusetsu nettai shokubutsu shusei (Illustrated collection of tropical plants)* (Hirokawa Shoten, 1969).

FOOTNOTES

PREFACE

1. This quotation and the two immediately following come (in order of appearance) from the following sources: Lady Murasaki, *The Tale of Genji* [Genji monogatari], trans. Arthur Waley (New York: Modern Library Edition, 1960), p. 338; *The Ten Foot Square Hut* and *Tales of the Heike*, trans. A. L. Sadler (Rutland, Vt. and Tokyo: Tuttle, 1972), p. 154; and Donald Keene, ed., *Anthology of Japanese Literature* (New York: Grove Press, 1955), p. 337.
2. Keene, *Anthology of Japanese Literature*, p. 252.
3. Of the obi, four are brocaded in gold; the remainder are decorated with embroidery and/or dyed designs. The items classified as "bags" include thirty wallets for holding tissues or paper money (*kami ire*), seven bookmarks (*shiori*) decorated with drawings, seven embroidered women's purses (*hakoseko*), two tobacco pouches (*tabako ire*), and a small velvet bag carried in the sleeve pocket (*tamoto otoshi*). Among the toilet articles are several cosmetic boxes and brushes; the remainder are decorative combs (*kushi*) and hair ornaments (*kanzashi* and *kōgai*) made of various materials including ivory, tortoise shell, lacquer, boxwood, silver, and silver plate.

A CREATIVE CONNOISSEUR

1. Account taken from Helen B. Minnich in collaboration with Nomura Shōjirō, *Japanese Costume and the Makers of Its Elegant Tradition* (Rutland, Vt. and Tokyo: Tuttle, 1963), pp. 320–21.
2. Photographs of geisha modelling period costumes at a similar occasion may be found in Ema Tsutomu, *A Historical Sketch of Japanese Customs and Costumes* (Tokyo: Kokusai Bunka Shinkōkai, 1936), pp. 23–41.
3. The Metropolitan Museum of Art, *Japanese Art*, by Miyeko Murase (New York: The Metropolitan Museum of Art, 1975), pp. 163–64.
4. Jean Mailey, "Four Hundred Winters . . . Four Hundred Springs . . . ," *The Metropolitan Museum of Art Bulletin* 18 (December 1959): 116.
5. Pauline Simmons, "Artist Designers of the Tokugawa Period," *The Metropolitan Museum of Art Bulletin* 14 (February 1956): 136.
6. Simmons, "Artist Designers of the Tokugawa Period," p. 136.

KOSODE: TECHNIQUES AND DESIGNS
CHAPTER 1

1. See Nomura Shōjirō, *Yūzen kenkyū* (Kyoto: Unsōdō 1920).
2. Hinonishi Sukenori, ed., *Fukushoku*, Nihon no bijutsu, no. 26 (Tokyo: Shibundō, 1968), p. 29.
3. Painted by Takashina Takakane, donated to the Kasuga Shrine in Nara in 1309, and now in the Imperial Household Agency. See Kamiya Eiko, ed., *Kosode*, Nihon no bijutsu, no. 67 (Tokyo: Shibundō, 1971), fig. 11 (p. 23).
4. Kamiya, *Kosode*, pp. 23–35.

5. Kamiya, *Kosode*, pp. 25, 28.
6. The division of the Edo period into early, middle, and late is based on that employed by Gotō Shōichi in *Nihon senshoku bunken sōran* (Kyoto: Senshoku to Seikatsusha, 1980), although I have followed the more conventional practice of including the Keichō era (1596–1615) within the Momoyama period. The divisions are:

early Edo	Genna–Jōkyo eras	1615–88
mid-Edo	Genroku–An'ei eras	1688–1781
late Edo	Tenmei–Keiō	1781–1868

7. Itō Toshiko, *Tsujigahana: the Flower of Japanese Textile Art*, trans. Monica Bethe (Tokyo: Kodansha International, 1981), pl. 98, fig. 25, p. 86.
8. Kamiya, *Kosode*, pls. 4, 7, 13, 15 and figs. 40, 45. See also Itō, *Tsujigahana*, pl. 105 and fig. 26.
9. This is the width Kamiya gives for plain-weave silk in *Kosode*, p. 32; most but not all of the *kosode* she examined are of plain-weave silk. The width of the *kosode* back is a good indicator of the woven width of the fabric (the latter is not given in Kamiya's table, to which must be added 4–5 cm. for seam allowance.
10. Hashimoto Sumiko, "Edo shoki no ishō moyō ni tsuite: Sōōji byōbu ni kakareta jinbutsu chakuyō ishō ni yoru tenkai-zu sakusei to sono jidaiteki kōsatsu", *Tokyo Kokuritsu Hakubutsukan kiyō* 14 (March 1979): 47–92.

CHAPTER 2

1. Nunome Junrō (shitagao), "Kinu seihin", in *Tateiwa iseki*, ed. Fukuoka-ken Iizuka-shi Tateiwa Iseki Chōsa Iinkai (Tokyo: Kawade Shobō, 1977), p. 310.
2. Yamanobe Tomoyuki, ed. *Some*, Nihon no bijutsu, no. 7 (Tokyo: Shibundō, 1966), p. 39.
3. Nishimura Hyōbu, ed., *Orimono*, Nihon no bijutsu, no. 12 (Tokyo: Shibundō, 1967), pp. 47–48.
4. Nishimura, *Orimono*, p. 54.
5. Nishimura, *Orimono*, p. 57.
6. George Sansom, *A History of Japan 1334–1615* (Stanford: Stanford University Press, 1961), pp. 190–91.
7. Other exotic fabrics imported from China and elsewhere in Asia, such as velvet, taffeta, woolens, and striped and printed cottons, do not appear in the Nomura Collection, and indeed the first three play no role in the development of the *kosode*.
8. Tsunoyama Yukihiro, *Nihon senshoku hattatsushi* (Tokyo: Tabata Shoten, 1968), pp. 119–20.
9. Nishimura, *Orimono*, p. 66.
10. George Sansom, *A History of Japan: 1615–1867* (Stanford: Stanford University Press, 1963), pp. 5, 36.
11. Nishimura, *Orimono*, pp. 83–88.

CHAPTER 3

1. Irene Emery, *The Primary Structure of Fabrics* (Washington, D.C.: The Textile Museum, 1966), p. 74.
2. Emery, *Primary Structure of Fabrics*, p. 76. See also Dorothy K. Burnham, *Warp and Weft: a Dictionary of*

Textile Terms (New York: Scribner's, 1981), p. 139, "Tabby".

3. Since there is no exact English equivalent, I shall use the term *nerinuki* in this text.

4. *Asa* may refer specifically to hemp or, more broadly, to ramie, linen, and other bast fibers as well.

5. Emery, *Primary Structure of Fabrics*, p. 75.

CHAPTER 4

1. See Appendix 5, "Dyes and Colors".

2. An extensive study of *shibori* has been published recently; although the primary point of view is the contemporary dyer's, both the section on the history of *shibori* and the more extensive section describing the many different types and the techniques used to produce them are relevant to a discussion of the Nomura Collection. See Wada Yoshiko, Mary Kellogg Rice, and Jane Barton, *Shibori: the Inventive Art of Japanese Shaped Resist Dyeing* (Tokyo: Kodansha International, 1983).

3. See Helen Benton Minnich, in collaboration with Shōjirō Nomura, *Japanese Costume and the Makers of its Elegant Tradition* (Rutland, Vt.: Tuttle, 1963), p. 358; Noma Seiroku, *Japanese Costume and Textile Arts*, trans. Armins Nikovskis, The Heibonsha Survey of Japanese Art, no. 16 (Tokyo: Weatherhill/Heibonsha, 1974), p. 144 ff.; Victor and Takako Hauge, *Folk Traditions in Japanese Art* (Tokyo: Kodansha International, 1978), pp. 27, 158, 159; Royal Academy of Arts, *The Great Japan Exhibition: Art of the Edo Period 1600–1868*, edited by William Watson (London: Royal Academy of Arts, 1981), pp. 318, 320 ff; and Itō Toshiko, *Tsujigahana: the Flower of Japanese Textile Art*, trans. Monica Bethe (Tokyo: Kodansha International, 1981), p. 28 ff.

4. Wada et al., *Shibori*, p 115 ff.

5. Marie Jeanne Adams, "Tiedyeing, an art on the island of Sumba", *Handweaver and Craftsman* 22: 9–11; Judith R. Arness, "Tiedyeing in India: Weavers in Barpali Revive Traditional Craft", *Handweaver and Craftsman* 14: 6–8.

6. Itō, *Tsujigahana*, p. 28.

7. For photographs of good examples of stencilled *kanoko*, see Minnich, *Japanese Costume*, pls. 86–88 and p. 226.

8. Kamiya Eiko, ed., *Kosode*, Nihon no bijutsu, no. 67 (Tokyo: Shibundō, 1971), p. 68.

9. Yamanobe Tomoyuki, ed., *Some*, Nihon no bijutsu, no. 7 (Tokyo: Shibundō, 1966), pp. 82–89 and pls. 13, 76.

10. Yamanobe, *Some*, p. 82; Kamiya, *Kosode*, p. 44.

11. Stitch resist, or *nuishime shibori*, corresponds to the Javanese word *tritik*. The Javanese terms *plangi* and *tritik* are applied by a number of fiber artists, the former to bound-resist and the latter to stitch-resist techniques and textiles, whether made by contemporary Western artists or by peoples of various traditional cultures. See Jack Lenor Larsen, with Alfred Bühler and Bronwen and Garrett Solyom, *The Dyer's Art: Ikat, Batik, Plangi* (New York: Van Nostrand Reinhold, 1976), p. 15, and Lydia Van Gelder, *Ikat* (New York: Watson-Guptill, 1980). *Plangi* and *tritik* are also used by historians of Indonesian textiles specifically to describe bound-resist and stitch-resist techniques and textiles of that region. See Mattiebelle Gittinger, *Splendid Symbols: Textiles and Traditions in Indonesia* (Washington, D.C.: The Textile Museum,

1979), and Mary H. Kahlenberg, *Textile Traditions of Indonesia* (Los Angeles: Los Angeles County Museum of Art, 1977). The words are not, however, in general use by textile historians writing about other cultures, including Japan. I therefore prefer to use English terms or, failing an adequate English equivalent, Japanese terms.

12. Wada et al., *Shibori*, p. 94 ff.

13. Cf. Itō, *Tsujigahana*, p. 28 ff. For a discussion of *shibori* techniques, see Wada et al., *Shibori*, p. 54 ff.

14. Some at the Shōsō-in in Nara, others from the Hōryū-ji Treasure House and now at the Tokyo National Museum.

15. Yamanobe, *Some*, pp. 24–25, 29–31.

16. Itō, *Tsujigahana*, pls. 96, 97.

17. Itō, *Tsujigahana*, p. 128 ff.

18. Kamiya, *Kosode*, fig. 55.

19. Good examples of early Momoyama embroidery appear in The Metropolitan Museum of Art, *Momoyama: Japanese Art in the Age of Grandeur*, by Julia Meech-Pekarik et al. (New York: The Metropolitan Museum of Art, 1975), nos. 50–53. For reproductions in which the qualities of the embroidery are clearly visible, see *Senshoku no bi* 9 (Early Spring 1981), pls. 14–22, and 19 (Early Autumn 1982), pls. 36–53.

20. For embroidery terminology and clear illustrations of various stitches, see *McCall's Needlework Treasury* (New York: Random House-McCall's, 1964), pp. 22–23.

21. For a lengthy but not exhaustive discussion of these problems, see Itō, *Tsujigahana*, especially pp. 187–93.

22. Okudaira Hideo, *Narrative Picture Scrolls*, trans. Elizabeth ten Grotenhuis, Arts of Japan, no. 5 (Tokyo and New York: Weatherhill, 1973), pls. 14–21, 33.

23. Kitamura Tetsurō, "Senshoku ni okeru Edo shoki —Keichō nuihaku-kō", *Museum* 271 (October 1973): 4–13.

24. Itō, *Tsujigahana*, pls. 79, 80; see also Yamane Yūzō, *Momoyama Genre Painting*, trans. John M. Shields (Tokyo: Weatherhill/Heibonsha, 1973), pls. 12, 41, 42. *Maple Viewing at Takao* is in the Tokyo National Museum.

25. Itō, *Tsujigahana*, pp. 19, 189–90.

26. Complete text, from the Tenri Library edition, in Ishida Hisatoyo, ed., *Shokunin tsukushi-e*, Nihon no bijutsu, no. 132 (Tokyo: Shibundō, 1977), pp. 97–102.

27. See chap. 1, n. 4. Itō, *Tsujigahana*, pp. 20–21. These sources are quoted by Kirihata Ken, "Tsujigahana-zome", *Senshoku no bi* 1 (Early Autumn 1979): 55–56.

28. A number of hypotheses concerning the derivation of the word *tsujigahana* have been suggested by Japanese scholars, but none is fully convincing. Tsunoyama Yukihiro presents a theory (first put forth in the Meiji period) that relates *tsujigahana* to the Kitsuji area of Nara, which was famous from very early times for its fine ramie cloth, known as Nara *sarashi*. *Shibori*-dyed ramie from Kitsuji may have been known as Kitsuji *ga hana* (flowers of Kitsuji), eventually shortened to *tsujigahana*. *Katabira* were often made of Nara *sarashi*, but there is no documentary evidence relating Kitsuji with the production of *shibori* or *tsujigahana*. See Tsunoyama Yukihiro, *Nihon senshoku hattatsushi* (Tokyo: Tabata Shoten, 1968), p. 137.

Itō discusses several explanations of the subject. A

treatise on the rules of haiku composition published in 1651, probably after the production of *tsujigahana* had ceased, states that the term is a shortened form of *tsutsuji ga hana*, (azalea flowers), and came into use because *tsujigahana katabira*, like azaleas, are red (Itō, *Tsujigahana*, pp. 189–93.) But later writers, including Itō, reject this idea. Itō points out that in the seventeenth century a dyed *katabira* was referred to as *tsuji* or *sometsuji* but does not pursue this clue further. She prefers the suggestion of a late Edo period writer, Ryūtei Tanehiko (1783–1842), who interpreted the character for *tsuji* literally, to mean "crossroads". The shape of the *tsuji* (by extension "crisscrosses"), combined with flowers (*hana*), resulted in *tsujigahana*. The examples she cites in support of Ryūtei's hypothesis, however, display the jagged diagonal lattice known as pine-bark lozenge (*matsukawa-bishi*) and never, to my knowledge, called *tsuji*.

Kirihata ("Tsujigahana-zome", pp. 56–57) pursues the association of *tsuji* or *sometsuji* with dyed *katabira* in early Edo period sources. He assumes that *tsuji* was then a shortened form of *tsumuji*, meaning "cowlick" or "snail-shell curl of hair". Because of the resemblance between snail-shell curls and the bound knots of *shibori*, *tsuji* may have been used as the name for *shibori* dyeing. If this was in fact the case (though we cannot be sure it was), flower- (*hana*) patterned *shibori* might naturally have been called *tsujigahana*. Since the lower classes frequently employed *shibori* to decorate their *katabira*, these dyed *katabira* themselves came to be called *tsuji*, he reasons. Thus, Kirihata claims, the *tsujigahana* dyeing mentioned in early sources in connection with *katabira*, and what we today call *tsujigahana* are the same, namely, flower patterns created by means of *shibori*. No *tsujigahana katabira* have come down to us, he concludes, because the clothing of the common people was not preserved. This line of reasoning ignores the fact, pointed out by Itō, that all but the first of the early references to *tsujigahana* associate it with the military aristocracy.

29. See Itō, *Tsujigahana*, pls. 2–20, 46–50, 53–55, 105, 110.
30. Kamiya, *Kosode*, pp. 90–91.
31. For an explanation of contemporary methods of stencil dyeing in Japan, see Nakano Eisha and Barbara B. Stephan, *Japanese Stencil Dyeing: Paste Resist Techniques* (New York and Tokyo: Weatherhill, 1982).
32. Kirihata Ken, "Kinsei no senshoku kakusho—yūzen-zome ikō", in *Nihon no senshoku*, vol. 4: *Kosode II*, ed. Kirihata Ken (Tokyo: Chūōkōronsha, 1980), pp. 247–48.
33. Kitamura Tetsurō, ed., *Yūzen-zome*, Nihon no bijutsu, no. 106 (Tokyo: Shibundō, 1975), p. 20.
34. Kitamura, *Yūzen-zome*, pp. 49–53, figs. 89–93.
35. By Yūjinsai (Heki Tokueimon) Kiyochika, partially reprinted as "Yūzen hiinagata", in *Kosode monyō hiinagata bon shūsei*, vol. 1, pt. 7, ed. Ueno Saeko (Tokyo: Gakushūkenkyūsha, 1974). See also Kitamura, *Yūzen-zome*, p. 42, and Kirihata's discussion of the same in "Yūzen-zome no utsukushisa—sono tokuchō to Yūzensai no koto", *Senshoku no bi* 3 (Early Spring 1980): 54, and "Kinsei no senshoku", pp. 219–20; text of 1688 book quoted p. 247.
36. Kirihata, "Kinsei no senshoku", p. 220.
37. See Minnich, *Japanese Costume*, pl. 140; for a full-color illustration, see *Senshoku no bi* 3 (Early Spring

1980), pl. 11.
38. Kitamura believes that most of the "coloring" described in early sources on *yūzen* dyeing probably refers to dyes rather than pigments (*Yūzen-zome*, pp. 43–47).
39. Yoshioka Tsuneo, *Tennen senryō no kenkyū* (Kyoto: Mitsumura Suiko Shoin, 1974), pp. 89–94.
40. Kitamura, *Yūzen-zome*, pp. 25–35; Kirihata, "Kinsei no senshoku", pp. 229–36.
41. Kirihata, "Kinsei no senshoku", pp. 230–31.
42. See above, n. 35.
43. Yamanobe, *Some*, pl. 12.
44. Both Yamanobe and Kamiya refrain from stating this as fact, and I have concluded that firm evidence is lacking. See Yamanobe, *Some*, p. 97, and Kamiya, *Kosode*, p. 90.

CHAPTER 5

1. The period is sometimes referred to as Azuchi-Momoyama; Azuchi is the name of Nobunaga's castle and Momoyama the site of Hideyoshi's castle, both near Kyoto. Historians disagree about the beginning and end dates of the period; some would have it begin in 1568, the date of Nobunaga's entry into Kyoto, and it is variously stated to end in 1600, 1603, or 1615, all significant dates in the history of Japan's political reunification.
2. See chap. 1, n. 4.
3. For illustrations of typical *dan-gawari* and *kata-suso* garments, see The Metropolitan Museum of Art, *Momoyama: Japanese Art in the Age of Grandeur*, by Julia Meech-Pekarik et al. (New York: The Metropolitan Museum of Art, 1975), nos. 50–52.
4. Kirihata Ken, "Momoyama jidai no senshoku: Seiyōjin no kiroku o chūshin ni", in *Momoyama jidai no kōgei*, ed. Kyoto National Museum (Kyoto: Shikōsha, 1977), pp. 211–17.
5. See Itō Toshiko, *Tsujigahana: the Flower of Japanese Textile Arts*, trans. Monica Bethe (Tokyo: Kodansha International, 1981), pls. 5, 48, 49, 53, 73, 79, 80, 85, 89.
6. Kirihata Ken, "Nihon no shishū", *Senshoku no bi* 9 (Early Spring 1981): 70.
7. Kitamura Tetsurō, "Senshoku ni okeru Edo shoki—Keichō nuihaku-kō", *Museum* (Tokyo) 271 (October 1973): 5.
8. For explanations and illustrations of the types of Nō robe that had evolved by the Edo period, see Tokugawa Yoshinobu with Ōkochi Sadao, *The Tokugawa Collection: Nō Robes and Masks*, trans. Louise A. Cort and Monica Bethe (New York: Japan Society, 1977). See also Kitamura Tetsurō, ed., *Nō shōzoku*, Nihon no bijutsu, no. 46 (Tokyo: Shibundō, 1970), pp. 18, 21 ff.
9. Noma Seiroku, *Japanese Costume and Textile Arts*, trans. Armins Nikovskis, The Heibonsha Survey of Japanese Art, no. 16 (Tokyo: Weatherhill/Heibonsha, 1974), figs. 91, 97.
10. Itō, *Tsujigahana*, pp. 129–30 and pls. 96, 97.
11. Itō lists four categories, implying that there are no examples of *shibori* with foil that do not also include painting, but several of the pieces that she cites seem to be of this type. See Itō, *Tsujigahana*, p. 5 and pls. 96, 97, 104, 106.
12. See chap. 3, n. 26.
13. Kirihata Ken, "Tsujigahana-zome", *Senshoku no bi* 1 (Early Autumn 1979): 58–60. Kirihata credits Kita-

mura Tetsurō with the outlines of this chronology. It is based, however, on a very small sample—eight garments of known provenance, several of which can be dated only to within ten or twenty years. In considering a group of materials dating from 1566 to 1610, a mere forty-four years, that is insufficiently precise. Furthermore, it is clear from dated contemporary portraits that a given type of *tsujigahana* did not fall into disuse as soon as a new mode appeared. Itō shows three dated portraits and three fragments of one *kosode*, dated from 1587 to as late as 1610, in which the pattern is reserved in white against a dyed ground and sometimes supplemented with color or ink painting (see Itō, *Tsujigahana*, pls. 25, 71, 72, 85, 89 and fig. 34). The latest of these portraits depicts a deep red fabric similar in design to the *kosode* in Colorplate 1, left, while the other examples are all of the same type as the flower-patterned section of the other garment on the same screen.

14. Sometimes these paintings include small, vivid touches of red pigment on lips or flowers.

15. Part of this scroll is in the New York Public Library. Akiyama Ken et al., *Genji monogatari*, Nihon no koten, no. 7 (Tokyo: Shūeisha, 1978), figs. 115–18; Shirahata Yoshi, ed., *Monogatari emaki*, Nihon no bijutsu, no. 49 (Tokyo: Shibundō, 1966), pp. 29–30 and figs. 11, 12, 88–100.

16. Itō, *Tsujigahana*, pls. 74–76, 78, 81–88, 90–92.

17. Mizoguchi Saburo, *Design Motifs*, trans. Louise A. Cort, Arts of Japan, no. 1 (Tokyo: Weatherhill/Shibundō, 1973), fig. 95.

18. One cosmetic box in the Nezu Art Museum, Tokyo, has raised spots on the camellia leaves representing dewdrops. See *Nezu Bijutsukan meihin mokuroku* (Tokyo: Nezu Art Museum, 1968), no. 513; Mizoguchi, *Design Motifs*, fig. 90; *Kachō no bi* (Kyoto: Kyoto National Museum, 1982), nos. 110, 111. Stylized flowers carved in shallow relief, especially camellias, originally came from Ming China. A cinnabar lacquer tray carved in a design of camellias in the Nezu Art Museum is dated to the Yong Le era (1403–24) (*Nezu Bijutsukan*, no. 464).

19. *Nezu Bijutsukan*, no. 3.

20. Itō, *Tsujigahana*, pl. 98.

21. In her discussion of *tsujigahana* and *hakubyō-e* Itō mistakenly identifies a poem paper bearing a painting of cypresses by Hon'ami Kōetsu as a *hakubyō* painting, which it does not resemble. She is also mistaken in her conclusion that ink shading, snow-laden bamboo, and dewdrops are typical of *tsujigahana* but *not* typical of *hakubyō* painting (*Tsujigahana*, p. 79).

22. See *Momoyama: Japanese Art in the Age of Grandeur*, nos. 4–6, 13, 14, 16–18.

23. Yamanobe Tomoyuki, ed., *Some*, Nihon no bijutsu, no. 7 (Tokyo: Shibundō, 1966), fig. 32.

24. Other sections of the same *kosode* have been preserved in other private collections. See description of Colorplate 2, below.

CHAPTER 6

1. Among the clothing that belonged to Uesugi Kenshin (1530–78), now preserved at Uesugi Shrine, are two white figured-satin *kosode* and a shirt, made of *chirimen* crepe, that was worn under armor; these are the oldest known examples of figured satin and *chirimen* of known provenance in Japan, but they were probably woven in China. See Kamiya Eiko, ed., *Kosode*, Nihon no bijutsu, no. 67 (Tokyo: Shibundō, 1971), pp. 65–66.

2. See Itō Toshiko, *Tsujigahana: the Flower of Japanese Textile Art*, trans. Monica Bethe (Tokyo: Kodansha International, 1981), pls. 124–28, 133–45, 152, 153.

3. Itō, *Tsujigahana*, p. 156 and pls. 111, 145.

4. I am indebted to Yamanobe Tomoyuki, ed., *Some*, Nihon no bijutsu, no. 7 (Tokyo: Shibundō, 1966), pp. 65–75, and to Kawakami Shigeki, "Edo jidai zenki no kosode—Keichō kosode kara Kanbun kosode e", *Bunkazai* 228 (September 1982): 27–34, for their discussions of the characteristics and development of the Keichō style, which helped to clarify and formalize my observations of Keichō *kosode* in the Nomura and other collections. Kitamura Tetsurō, in his article "Senshoku ni okeru Edo shoki—Keichōnuihaku-kō", *Museum* (Tokyo) 271 (October 1973): 4–13, contrasts Keichō design and technique with those of the earlier Momoyama period. He asserts that since the Keichō *kosode* is more expressive of an aesthetic associated with the Edo period, the Keichō era should be considered part of the Edo rather than of the Momoyama period. Yamanobe also implies this in his discussion of Keichō *kosode* (*Some*, pp. 65–75 and captions for figs. 55, 67, 69, 70) but does not discuss it explicitly. See also The Metropolitan Museum of Art, *Momoyama: Japanese Art in the Age of Grandeur*, by Julia Meech-Pekarik et al. (New York: The Metropolitan Museum of Art, 1975), pp. 10–12.

5. Kirihata Ken, "Genna, Kan'ei-mei kosode-gire uchishiki (Shinju-an-zō) ni tsuite—Edo jidai zenki no senshoku shiryō", *Museum* (Tokyo) 376: 22–26. Kawakami Shigeki, "Keichō kosode no keifu—sono seiritsu to tenkai", *Museum* (Tokyo) 383: 13.

6. Kirihata, "Genna, Kan'ei-mei kosode-gire uchishiki", pp. 22–26.

7. Kirihata Ken, "Kinsei senshoku ni okeru bungei ishō", in *Kōgei ni miru koten bungaku ishō*, edited by Kyoto National Museum (Kyoto: Shikōsha, 1980), pp. 307–10.

8. Fujiwara no Okikaze (fl. ca. 910), *Kokinwakashū*, Bk. 6, no. 326.

9. Anonymous, *Kokinwakashū*, Bk. 20, no. 1093.

10. Ozawa Masao, ed., *Kokinwakashū*, Nihon koten bungaku zenshū, no. 7 (Tokyo: Shōgakukan, 1971), p. 162, n. 326, section 4.

11. Abe Akio et al., ed., *Genji monogatari*, Nihon koten bungaku zenshū, no. 12 (Tokyo: Shōgakukan, 1971–76), vol. 1: "Suetsumuhana", p. 369; vol. 6: "Ukifune", p. 168.

12. This interpretation of the theme depicted in the Nomura *kosode* is supported by Kirihata's findings. Of the three examples cited by him of literary allusion in Momoyama textiles, one, a late Keichō style *kosode* in the Tōyama Kinenkan, represents the same theme as the Nomura *kosode*. Kirihata's interpretation, however, does not take into account (although he mentions it) the presence of the character *shigeshi* (flourishing, luxuriant). The illustration of the *kosode* in "Kinsei senshoku ni okeru bungei ishō" is not sufficiently clear to permit further analysis.

13. Japanese scholars stress the new opposition of background and pattern in the design of dyed (as opposed to woven or embroidered) textiles as a key element in the evolution of early Edo style. See Yamanobe, *Some*, pp. 71–75, and Kawakami, "Edo jidai zenki no kosode", *Bunkazai* 228 (September 1982): 28–30.

CHAPTER 7

1. George Sansom, *A Short Cultural History of Japan* (New York: Appleton-Century Crofts, 1962), pp. 441, 467.

2. Bito Masahide, "Society and Economy in the Edo Period", trans. William Watson, in *The Great Japan Exhibition: Art of the Edo Period 1600–1868*, ed. William Watson (London: Royal Academy of Arts, 1981), pp. 24–26. See also Donald Keene, *World Within Walls: Japanese Literature of the Pre-Modern Era 1600–1867* (New York: Grove Press; 1976), pp. 4–5.

3. William Watson, "Art in Momoyama and Edo", in Royal Academy of Arts, *The Great Japan Exhibition: Art of the Edo Period 1600–1868*, edited by William Watson (London: Royal Academy of Arts, 1981), p. 28.

4. Also known by the title *Shinsen on-hiinakata* [New selection of patterns]. For a complete bibliography of the design books (*hiinagata bon*) published prior to 1704, see Mihashi Saeko, "Moyō hiinagata bon shūsei: Genroku made", in *Tenri Daigaku gakuhō* 39 (December 1962): 304–23. For later periods and for analyses of colors, motifs, and decorative techniques, see entries in Bibliography under Mihashi Saeko and Ueno Saeko.

5. Nagasaki Iwao, "Senshoku shiryō to shite no kosode moyō hiinagata bon: kosode moyō no kankei o chūshin ni", *Museum* (Tokyo) 373 (April 1982): 20, 25–26.

6. Nagasaki, "Senshoku shiryō", pp. 23–26, 29 and no. 14. See also Mihashi, "Moyō hiinagata bon", p. 304.

7. Kyoto National Museum, ed., *Kōgei ni miru koten bungaku ishō* (Kyoto: Shikōsha, 1980), fig. 120 and pp. 210, 271; Royal Academy of Arts, *Great Japan Exhibition*, no. 5, pp. 42–43. See also Edward Seidensticker, trans., *The Tale of Genji* (New York: Knopf, 1976), pp. 775–1090.

8. Kawakami Shigeki, "Edo jidai zenki no kosode —Keichō kosode kara Kanbun kosode e", *Bunkazai* 228 (September 1982), fig. 7 (p. 31).

9. Helen Benton Minnich in collaboration with Nomura Shōjirō, *Japanese Costume and the Makers of Its Elegant Tradition* (Rutland, Vt. and Tokyo: Tuttle, 1963), pp. 202–3.

10. Kawakami, "Edo jidai zenki no kosode," pp. 29–34.

11. Royal Academy of Arts, *Great Japan Exhibition*, p. 142.

12. Yamane Yūzō, *Konishi-ke kyūzō Kōrin kankei shiryō to sono kenkyū 1 (shiryō hen)* (Tokyo: Chūōkōron Bijutsu Shuppan, 1983), entries 36, 38–42; see also Kurihara Yoshiko, "Kariganeya chūmon-chō ni arawareta Edo jidai shoki no ishō moyō", *Shiron* 7 (November 1959): 448–62. The photographic reproductions in this publication are of such poor quality that any serious study of the order books must be made from the originals, which are in the collection of the Osaka Municipal Museum of Art and the Watanabe Collection, also in Osaka.

13. Kamiya Eiko, ed., *Kosode*, Nihon no bijutsu, no. 67 (Tokyo: Shibundō, 1971), pp. 66–69, fig. 109, sections 1–4.

14. Kitamura Tetsurō, ed., *Yūzen-zome*, Nihon no bijutsu, no. 106 (Tokyo: Shibundō, 1975), p. 18.

15. Kirihata Ken, "Kinsei no senshoku oboegaki—yūzen-zome ikō", in *Nihon no senshoku*, vol. 4: *Kosode II*, ed. Kirihata Ken (Tokyo: Chūōkōronsha, 1979), pp. 218–19.

16. Conversation with Imanaga Seiji, Curator of Textiles, Tokyo National Museum.

17. Kirihata, "Kinsei no senshoku", p. 234. I am indebted to Kirihata's study for my discussion of eighteenth- and nineteenth-century design (see "Kinsei no senshoku", p. 229 ff.).

18. Nishimura Hyōbu, Jean Mailey, and Joseph S. Hayes, Jr., *Tagasode: Whose Sleeves . . .* (New York: Japan Society, 1976), nos. 38, 16.

COLOR: DYES AND PIGMENTS
CHAPTER 8

1. Maeda Ujō, *Nihon kodai no saishiki to some* (Tokyo: Kawade Shobōshinsha, 1975), pp. 9, 17.

2. Ebata Jun, *Shikimei no yurai* (Tokyo: Tokyo Shoseki Kabushiki Kaisha, 1982), p. 20.

3. For a more complete chart of *go-gyō* interrelationships, see Wm. Theodore de Bary, Wing-Tsit Chan, and Burton Watson, *Sources of Chinese Tradition*, vol. 1 (New York: Columbia University Press, 1964), p. 199. Japanese charts are included in Nagasaki Seiki, *Iro no Nihonshi*, (Tokyo: Tankōsha, 1977), p. 107; Maeda Yukichika, *Nihon shikisai bunkashi* (Tokyo: Iwanami Shoten, 1960), pp. 203–4; and Ebata, *Shikimei no yurai*, pp. 28–32.

4. The Chinese disliked purple because the character for "intermediate" (*jun*) could also be read as "illegitimate throne", construed to be a bad omen.

5. Maeda Yukichika, *Nihon shikisai bunkashi*, p. 205, warns that the concept of intermediate colors is somewhat different from the Western idea of secondary, mixed colors. The Western concept is based on mixing paints, but the Chinese is more theoretical and the colors do not correspond exactly to paintbox mixtures.

6. Maeda Yukichika, *Nihon shikisai bunkashi*, pp. 137–41, gives probably the most extensive chart of rank-colors and their changes over time. More accessible are the charts in Ebata, *Shikimei no yurai*, pp. 28–32. Though the rank-colors were originally known as cap colors (*kammuri iro*), it soon became customary for *all* courtiers and officials to wear only black hats, so that the cap colors were in fact seen only in the gowns and came to be called rank-colors (*kurai iro*). The white and black ranks each had two grades, though not two shades.

7. Maeda Ujō, *Nihon kodai no saishiki to some*, p. 22, quotes the secret oral tradition of prayers to the elements.

8. *Manyōshū*, Bk. 18, no. 4109:

Kurenai wa	Scarlet is a color
utsurou mono zo	Quick to fade.
tsurubami no	How can it compare
narenishi kinu ni	With those long-
nao shikame ya mo.	accustomed robes
	Dyed in the gray of
	acorn.

9. *Manyōshū*, Bk. 10, no. 1993.

10. *Manyōshū*, Bk. 14, no. 3500:

Murasakigusa wa	The roots of *murasaki*
ne o ka mo ouru	Grow endlessly long.
hito no ko no	Would I could sleep as
uraganashike o	long
ne o oenaku ni.	Beside that man's
	Beloved daughter.

11. For an extensive list of *kasane iro* (color combinations), see Maeda Yukichika, *Nihon shikisai bunkashi*, pp. 524–30, and Ebata, *Shikimei no yurai*, pp. 46–47.

Kojima Shigeru, ed., *Iro no saijiki: me de asobu Nihon no iro* (Tokyo and Osaka: Asahi Shinbunsha; Nagoya: Kitakyūshū, 1983), pp. 14, 32, 50, 68, contains colorplates showing the approved color combinations (*kasane iro*) for each season. These combinations are also given in many classical dictionaries.

12. *Omodaka* refers to a type of armor dyed in a specific pattern. Information on the colors comes from Yamazaki Seiju, *Kusaki-zome: iro to shuhō* (Tokyo: Bijutsu Shuppansha, 1974), and from Nagasaki, *Iro no Nihonshi*, p. 148. A detailed history of Japanese armor, with colorplates, can be found in Ozaki Motoharu, *Yoroi*, Nihon no bijutsu, no. 24 (Tokyo: Shibundō, 1968).

13. For a sense of the types of official restrictions and the extent to which they were effective, see Itō Toshiko, *Tsujigahana: the Flower of Japanese Textile Art*, trans. Monica Bethe (Tokyo: Kodansha International, 1981), pp. 19–24, and Wada Yoshiko et al., *Shibori: the Inventive Art of Japanese Shaped-Resist Dyeing* (Tokyo: Kodansha International, 1983), pp. 20–23.

14. Kirihata Ken, "Iro no bunkashi", in *Iro no saijiki*, ed. Kojima, p. 154.

15. Nagasaki, *Iro no Nihonshi*, pp. 174–75.

16. Nagasaki, *Iro no Nihonshi*, p. 175.

17. Aubrey S. Halford and Giovanna M. Halford, *The Kabuki Handbook* (Tokyo: Tuttle, 1956), p. 322.

18. Nagasaki, *Iro no Nihonshi*, pp. 191–92.

19. Nagasaki, *Iro no Nihonshi*, p. 183.

CHAPTER 9

1. Nagasaki Seiki, *Iro no Nihonshi* (Tokyo: Tankōsha, 1977), p. 40.

2. *Kojiki*, Bk. 3, chap. 129, on Yūryaku Tennō. Akawiko's tears soak the sleeves of her red-dyed garment (*nizuri*, "rubbed with *nitsuchi*").

3. *Manyōshū*, Bk. 17, no. 3291 begins "Kakitsubata kinu ni suritsuke . . . " ("A gown rub-dyed with iris . . . "). Dayflower (spiderwort) has at least thirty-six different Japanese names. The impermanence of this blue dye was turned to advantage in *yūzen* dyeing, where it was used to outline designs and then washed away when the designs were completed. See Nakano Eisha and Barbara B. Stephan, *Japanese Stencil Dyeing: Paste-Resist Techniques* (New York and Tokyo: Weatherhill, 1982), p. 114.

4. *Kojiki*, Bk. 3, chap. 113. Blue robes with red cords may have been de rigueur for attendants.

5. Nagasaki, *Iro no Nihonshi*, p. 41.

6. Yamazaki Seiju, *Kusaki-zome: iro to shuhō* (Tokyo: Bijutsu Shuppansha, 1974), p. 114, suggests that *kihada*, being the simplest dye, is probably the oldest. The *Daihannya-kyō* [Greater Sutra of the Perfection of Wisdom] at Yakushi-ji is dyed pale yellow with *kihada* (see Yoshioka Tsuneo, *Nihon no iro* [Kyoto: Shikōsha, 1979], p. 34).

7. Maeda Ujō, *Nihon kodai no saishiki to some* (Tokyo: Kawade Shobōshinsha, 1975), p. 87. Nagasaki mentions only ash lye and iron (p. 69), and the tenth-century code *Engi shiki* mentions only ash lye.

8. *Manyōshū*, Bk. 12, no. 3101.

9. Note that *akane iro* always indicates the color *madder* red specifically; *aka* is the generic term for red of any hue and also a homonym with "bright" or "light".

10. Dye scholars tend to agree on this definition of *kōseikin*. See Nagasaki, *Iro no Nihonshi*, p. 70, and Nakae Katsumi, "Kusaki-zome no rekishi", in *Nihon*

no senshoku, vol. 3: *Kusaki-zome: Nihon no fūdo ga sodateta tezukuri no iro* (Tokyo: Tairyūsha, 1975), p. 193.

11. Donald L. Philippi, *Kojiki* (Tokyo: University of Tokyo Press, 1968), p. 466.

12. Both Yoshioka Tsuneo, *Tennen senryō no kenkyū* (Kyoto: Mitsumura Suiko Shoin, 1974), p. 12, and Yamazaki, *Kusaki-zome*, p. 118, have similar lists. Miura Saburō, "Nihon no murasaki: shikon no bunkashi", *Senshoku to seikatsu* 11: 18, mentions three periods when the Japanese imported significant amounts of *murasaki* from China—the sixth century, the fifteenth and sixteenth centuries, and modern times. The imports include at least four different species of plants (*Macrotamia euchorma Pauls.*; *Lithospermum officinale L.*, var. *erythrorhizon Maxim.*; *Onosma panieulatum Bur. et Fr.*; and *Arnebia guttata Rce.*). Only *Lithospermum erythrorhizon Sieb. et Zucc.*, related to the second, is grown in Japan and is probably native.

13. Proposed dates for the introduction of *benibana* vary considerably. Yamazaki puts it in prehistoric times (*Kusaki-zome*, p. 125), Suzuki Yoshio in the fourth or fifth century ("Benibana no saibai: hanshu kara hana tsumi made", in *Nihon no senshoku*, vol. 18: *Benibana-zome: hana no inochi o someta nuno* (Tokyo: Tairyūsha, 1978). Maeda Ujō, *Nihon kodai no saishiki to some*, p. 32, proposes a seventh-century date.

14. Maeda Ujō, *Nihon kodai no saishiki to some*, pp. 173–85, reprints both books with commentary. Yamazaki, *Kusaki-zome*, pp. 130–33, reprints Bk. 14 with slight commentary. The *Engi shiki* lists types of cloth made by various techniques; these lists also provide important information on the designs and methods used. Tax lists in the *Engi shiki* contain valuable clues to the distribution of dyes and techniques in the provinces.

CHAPTER 10

1. Another name for six-leaved madder is *seiyō akane* (Western madder, *Rubia tinctorum L.*). Essentially the same plant, grown along the Mediterranean coast, has been known for centuries in the West as madder. A similar madder grown in India and Southeast Asia differs from the Japanese madder primarily in bearing red rather than black fruit. It is known as *Indo akane* (*Rubia cordifolia Linn.*). Both these varieties grow in Japan and have been used since the early Muromachi period.

2. Both Yoshioka Tsuneo and Yamazaki Seiju agree that virtually no Edo period garments were dyed with *Nihon akane*, probably because the large quantity of yellow in the roots made it difficult to produce pure red with this dye. Taking his cue from the *Engi shiki*, which lists white rice as one ingredient for making dye out of *Nihon akane*, Yoshioka found that if the washed roots were let stand in a bed of white rice, the rice starch would absorb much of the yellow. The red could then be extracted with a weak solution of acetic acid (Yoshioka Tsuneo, *Nihon no iro* [Kyoto: Shikōsha, 1979], p. 44). Yoshioka also comments that in the Edo period book written in imitation of the *Engi shiki*, *akane* is mentioned only as being difficult to dye with. Miyazaki Antei's agricultural anthology, *Nōgyō zensho*, merely lists *Nihon akane* without commentary.

3. Yamazaki Seiju, *Kusaki-zome: iro to shuhō* (Tokyo:

215

Bijutsu Shuppansha, 1974), p. 145.

4. Yoshioka, *Nihon no iro*, p. 40.

5. Yoshioka Tsuneo, *Tennen senryō no kenkyū* (Kyoto: Mitsumura Suiko Shoin, 1974), pp. 158–59.

6. This quote comes from a group of proverbs collected by Miura Saburō and published under the heading "Edokko no sensu ni mirareru Edo murasaki" in "Nihon no murasaki", *Senshoku to seikatsu* 11: 41–44.

7. Despite some Edo period sources that state the opposite, Nagasaki Seiki and others feel that Kyoto *murasaki* must have been bluer (*Iro no Nihonshi* [Tokyo: Tankōsha, 1977], pp. 81, 82).

8. Yamazaki, *Kusaki-zome*, p. 140.

9. Yamazaki, *Kusaki-zome*, p. 140.

10. Maeda Ujō, *Nihon kodai no saishiki to some* (Tokyo: Kawade Shobōshinsha, 1975), p. 21. In conversation Maeda has suggested that this is the basis of Keichō black.

11. Yamazaki, *Kusaki-zome*, p. 145.

12. Yamazaki, *Kusaki-zome*, p. 145. Presumably Yamanobe Tomoyuki, *Some*, Nihon no bijutsu, no. 7 (Tokyo: Shibundō, 1966), p. 70, refers to the same process when he describes these robes as being *sumi*-dyed. As *sumi* is a pigment, not a dye, it would most likely have been applied with a brush to avoid blotching. The cloth would, of course, have been vat-dyed in indigo and the *sumi* brushed over the *shibori*-delineated areas. To me it seems improbable that the double layer of coloring would not be visible on close inspection, but I have not had opportunity to make such an inspection.

13. Upper-class women during Nara and Heian blackened their teeth, and the custom was still affected by courtesans in the Edo period. (Conversation with Maeda Ujō.)

14. A description of the contents of the *Zasshoshū* appears in Gotō Shōichi, *Nihon senshoku bunken sōran* (Kyoto: Senshoku to Seikatsusha, 1980), p. 53.

15. Nakae Katsumi, "Kusaki-zome no rekishi", in *Nihon no senshoku*, vol. 3: *Kusaki-zome: Nihon no fūdo ga sodateta tezukuri no iro* (Tokyo: Tairyūsha, 1975).

16. Yamazaki, *Kūsaki-zome*, p. 140.

CHAPTER 11

1. The *Engi shiki* mentions *akane* as a common tax item from many areas. See Yamazaki Seiju, *Kusaki-zome: iro to shuhō* (Tokyo: Bijutsu Shuppansha, 1974), p. 138.

2. Shimogamo Shrine, attached to the Imperial Household, still orders its garments from dyers who produce Heian court colors using traditional dye plants and traditional methods. The number of such places has greatly diminished, and their art, as Shimogamo priest Araki Naoto laments, is threatened by the modern practices around them. (From conversations with Araki.)

3. *Jinrin kinmōsui* [Illustrated instructions on social relations]. Woodblock-printed illustrations of artisans at work, with short explanations of their activities above the pictures. First published in 1690, it was reprinted by Watanabe Shoten, Tokyo, 1969. On page 232 of this edition we find mention of a dye house in Kyoto specializing in "Edo *murasaki*".

4. Yamazaki, *Kusaki-zome*, pp. 144–45, bases his list of dyestuffs on a variety of dye manuals from various dye houses in several cities. Although one dye house might produce over a hundred colors, browns and grays predominate, and the dyestuffs are limited to such

plants as *yamamomo* (*Myrica rubra*, whose blue-black, he warns, fades to brown), *suō* (sappanwood), *kariyasu* (*miscanthus*), and indigo.

5. Kitamura Tetsurō, *Nihon fukushoku shi* (Tokyo: Iseikatsu Kenkyūkai, 1973, 1979), p. 70.

6. Not all *mon* were paste-resisted. Many, including most of the larger, therefore earlier, ones on extant *tsuji-hana* pieces were done with *shibori*. See Itō Toshiko, *Tsujigahana: the Flower of Japanese Textile Art*, trans. Monica Bethe (Tokyo: Kodansha International, 1981), p. 195.

7. Yamazaki, *Kusaki-zome*, p. 137.

8. Nakano Eisha and Barbara B. Stephan, *Japanese Stencil Dyeing: Paste-Resist Techniques* (New York and Tokyo: Weatherhill, 1982), pp. 92–93.

9. The process and materials described by Yoshioka Tsuneo, *Tennen senryō no kenkyū* (Kyoto: Mitsumura Suiko Shoin, 1974), pp. 182–85, do not differ greatly in broad outline from the discussion in Anne W. Thomas, *Colors from the Earth: the Artist's Guide to Collecting, Preparing, and Using Them* (Ontario: Van Nostrand, Reinhold, 1980).

CHAPTER 12

1. Though it is possible to dye greenish hues by using iron mordant with plants that dye yellow, like *kariyasu* or *yamamomo*, none of these is pure green.

2. Yamazaki Akira, the father of Yamazaki Seiju, pioneered this work of preservation.

3. See chap. 9, n. 12.

4. *Kokinwakashū*, Bk. 17, no. 867; and *Sarashina Diary*, translated by Ivan Morris under the title *As I Crossed A Bridge of Dreams* (New York: Harper and Row: Harper Colophon Books, 1971).

5. These include the *hisakaki* (*Eurya japonica*) and the *nishi kohori*, or *sawafutagi*. See Katakura Nobumitsu and Satō Tadatarō, "Nambu no shikon-zome", *Senshoku to seikatsu* 11: 53–60.

6. Wada Yoshiko et al., *Shibori: the Inventive Art of Japanese Shaped-Resist Dyeing* (Tokyo: Kodansha International, 1983), pp. 78–79, summarizes the article mentioned in n. 5 above.

7. Yamazaki Seiju, "Murasaki gusa-zome", *Senshoku to seikatsu* 11: 63.

8. *Manyōshū*, Bk. 1, no. 21. This is not the standard interpretation of this poem, which usually likens the poet's beloved to the beauty of *murasaki* purple, as in Ian Levy's translation: "If I despised you/Who are as beautiful as the violet from the *murasaki* grass,/Would I long for you/Though you are another's wife?" (*Man'yōshū* [Princeton: Princeton University Press, 1981], p. 49).

9. The heat sensitivity of *murasaki* often figures symbolically in Heian literature. Most notably, the heroine of the *Tale of Genji*, Murasaki by name, must exercise great control over her increasing ardor for Prince Genji.

10. Finishing with vinegar is mentioned in the Edo dyer's secret recipes for *murasaki* and *akane iro*, published in *Senshoku to seikatsu* 11: 101.

11. Yamazaki Seiju discusses methods of stabilizing with methyl alcohol in "Murasaki gusa-zome", pp. 65, 68–70.

12. For a history of *benibana*, see Suzuki Yoshio, "Benibana no saibai: hanshu kara hana tsumimade", in *Nihon no senshoku*, vol. 18: *Benibana-zome: hana no inochi o someta nuno* (Tokyo: Tairyūsha, 1978), pp. 165–66.

Also Yoshioka Tsuneo, *Tennen senryō no kenkyū* (Kyoto: Mitsumura Suiko Shoin, 1974), pp. 89–94, and Yamazaki Seiju, "Beni-zome: sono rekishi to shuhō", *Senshoku to seikatsu* 2: 40–41. A good history of the production of *benibana*, by Imada Shinichi, appears in the same volume: "Mogami benibana no rekishi: sono seisan to ryūtsū", pp. 31–36.

13. *Benibana-zome* includes a number of descriptions of *benibana* planting, harvesting, and processing: these are based on accounts by contemporary local farmers and on Edo and Meiji period paintings and descriptions. Abe Kōun, "Mogami san benibana are kore", and Suzuki Takao, "Beni rōkechi made no nijūnen: hontō no iro o motomete fushi nidai", both in *Senshoku to seikatsu*, vol. 2, are similarly based on illustrations and literary sources.

Dating the beginnings of these plantations in Yamagata Prefecture seems difficult. The *Engi shiki*, referring to the Heian period, mentions tax payments of *benibana* from twenty-four provinces in central and eastern Japan but not from the area along the Japan Sea to the north. Imada, "Mogami benibana no rekishi", suggests that the plantations in northeastern Japan grew up after *benibana* was permitted to commoners and prospered due to good water transportation to Kyoto. (An official edict in 1471 allowed commoners to wear both *benibana*-dyed and *murasaki*-dyed silk; Edo period restrictions partially reversed this.) By the Edo period the Mogami River area provided forty to fifty percent of the country's *benibana*.

14. Yamazaki Seiju, *Kusaki-zome: iro to shuhō* (Tokyo: Bijutsu Shuppansha, 1974), p. 140, suggests that the yellow-ground garment belonging to Uesugi Kenshin (1530–78) and now in the Uesugi Shrine was dyed with *benibana* yellow. Leaching out the yellow in running water is described in Maeda Ujō, *Nihon kodai no saishiki to some* (Tokyo: Kawade Shobōshinsha, 1975), pp. 159–60. Squeezing out the yellow is described by Yamazaki and by Yoshioka, *Tennen senryō no kenkyū*.

15. Because *beni* will not adhere to even slightly greasy fabric, wool is difficult to dye unless extremely well scoured. Cotton often receives an additional application of *gojiru*, as does all cloth for brush dyeing.

16. *Manyōshū*, Bk. 11, no. 2623:

Kurenai no   A gown dipped
yashio no koromo   Eight times in scarlet—
asa na sa na   Day after day,
nare wa suredomo   Even as you become
iya mezurashi mo.   familiar,
                  Your freshness
                  beckons.

17. Endō Yasuo, chapter in *Benibana-zome: hana no inochi o someta nuno*, *Nihon no senshoku*, vol. 18 (Tokyo: Tairyūsha, 1978), p. 186, mentions the amounts. Yoshioka Tsuneo, *Nihon no iro* (Kyoto: Shikōsha, 1979), p. 16, quotes the proverb.

18. Detailed descriptions of the process and its arduousness are given by farmers and recorded in *Benibana-zome*. An illustrated one-page description, "Beni ichiran" [Beni in one glance], is found in *Oshiegusa*, a Meiji period publication containing explanations by specialists. It is reproduced on the back cover of *Senshoku to seikatsu*, vol. 2, and in Gotō Shōichi, *Nihon senshoku bunken sōran* (Kyoto: Senshoku to Seikatsusha, 1980), p. 34. Other illustrations appear

in the articles by Abe and Suzuki in *Senshoku to seikatsu*, vol. 2.

19. Imada, "Mogami benibana no rekishi", pp. 35–36.

20. "Beni-zome at the house of Iwai of Shinmachi Nijō agaru (Kyoto)" is reproduced in *Senshoku to seikatsu* 2: 53.

21. A description of this process appears in Yamazaki Seiju, *Kusaki-zome: kata-zome no kihon* (Tokyo: Bijutsu Shuppansha, 1978), pp. 52–54. It is unclear how much of the method is traditional and how much is his own invention, but various Edo period examples of *kata-zome* and *yūzen-zome* with *beni* suggest that a similar method was used then. The Edo period writings about *beni* dyeing, collected by Gotō Shōichi and published in *Senshoku to seikatsu* 2: 46–48, describe the storage of *beni* on bast-fiber cloth but not its use for *hiki-zome*.

22. Yoshioka Tsuneo, "Tennen senryō nyūmon—sono ichi—'Benibana'", *Senshoku no bi* 1: 115–18, describes this process. A description of *beni zara* used as a cosmetic is given by Nogami Rokurō, "Beni tsurezure", *Senshoku to seikatsu* 2: 37–39.

23. Tanaka Nao's personal experience of treatment with *kōka* is recounted in *Senshoku to seikatsu* 2: 80–81. Although *kōka* is best known as a preventative of high blood pressure, it can apparently also be used to discover weaknesses in the system by painting it on the body and watching for areas that do not dry easily.

24. Yoshioka Tsuneo, "Kyō no beni itajime-zome", *Senshoku to seikatsu* 2: 43–45, describes his hypothetical reconstruction of the *itajime* process. Old boards (carved very much like woodblocks except for the extra holes and ducts) and clamp systems still exist and can be investigated at the Kyoto Textile Research Center (Kyoto Senshoku Shikenjo) at Karasuma Kamidachūri.

25. For a discussion of dyeing with fresh leaves, see Yamazaki Seiju, *Kusaki-zome: iro to shuhō*, pp. 50–51. For a discussion of its applications to *hiki-zome* techniques, see Yamazaki Seiju, "Ai-zome: ito-zome, tsubo-zome, hiki-zome, namaha-zome", *Senshoku to seikatsu* 10: 90–92. Yoshioka discusses *namaha-zome* in *Tennen senryō no kenkyū*, pp. 51–53.

26. Maeda Ujō, *Nihon kodai no saishiki to some*, p. 163.

27. Maeda Ujō, "Kodai no ai", *Senshoku to seikatsu* 10: 74. See also Yoshioka, *Tennen senryō no kenkyū*, p. 54.

28. Scholars differ greatly on the dates of origin of the *sukumo* method and of the heated vats. Maeda Ujō, "Kodai no ai", infers from the mention of dried leaves in the *Engi shiki* that *sukumo* was then in use. He relates the invention of the *sukumo* process to the increased demand for indigo after blue was taken off the list of rank-colors in the mid-Heian period and permitted to commoners. Others place the invention of *sukumo* late in the Heian period or even after.

29. This method is described by Louise Cort in *Indigo Notes* (Tokyo: Bunseidō Press, 1978), and in *Aruku miru kiku* 117: 18–21. A variant method, in which the dried leaves are stuffed into straw sacks, is outlined in Wada et al., *Shibori*, p. 279, and is illustrated in a woodblock print in *Dai Nippon bussan zue* (Tokyo: Kineidō, 1881). Photographs of planting, harvesting, making *sukumo*, etc., appear in *Aruku miru kiku*, vol. 117, and in *Senshoku to seikatsu*, vol. 10. Adaptations of the Japanese methods to American circumstances are described by Dorothy Miller,

Indigo from Seed to Dye, ed. Mary Cranston-Bennet (Aptos, Ca.: Indigo Press, 1981).

30. A very good description of the chemistry of this process appears in Frederick H. Gerber, *Indigo and the Antiquity of Dyeing* (Ormond Beach, Fla.: By the Author, 1977), pp. 25–29. For the function of reducing agents, see p. 37.

31. The dates proposed for this invention range widely. The old method was probably continued in use long after the heated-pit method was invented. Maeda Ujō, "Kodai no ai", p. 75, suggests that *shōai-zome* began during Kamakura, in response to the growing demand for dark indigo from commoners and samurai alike. Yamazaki dates heated vats from the Muromachi period, Yoshioka from late Muromachi. Gotō Shōichi argues that they must have come later, since Muromachi depictions of dyers at work show exposed indigo vats but similar paintings of the Edo period show vats sunk in the ground.

32. There are as many opinions as dyers concerning the fluctuations of pH necessary to produce a good vat, but a sample chart of temperature and pH levels day by day appears in Yoshioka, *Tennen senryō no kenkyū*, pp. 60–62.

33. Yamazaki, *Kusaki-zome: iro to shuhō*, p. 139.

34. Cort, *Indigo Notes*, p. 9. A given quantity of *sukumo* could be reduced to about forty percent of its former bulk when made into *ai dama*.

35. A number of Edo and Meiji period illustrations depict the making of *ai dama*. The *Dai Nippon bussan zue* shows both *sukumo* and *ai dama* being made. Meiji period photographs of the pounding crews appear in Miki Bunko, *Zusetsu Awa ai* (Tokushi: Miki Sangyō Kabushiki Gaisha, 1976). *Senshoku to seikatsu*, vol. 10, includes illustrations of Tokushima indigo collected by Gotō Shōichi (pp. 4–14), and photographs of work in progress (pp. 17–20).

36. Endō Yasuo, "Shomin seikatsu o irodotta ai-zome", in *Shōai-zome: sawayaka na Nihon no iro, Nihon no senshoku*, vol. 16 (Tokyo: Tairyūsha, 1977), p. 137.

37. Miki Bunko, *Zusetsu Awa ai*, pp. 39–40.

38. Miki Bunko, *Zusetsu Awa ai*, pp. 15 and 17, illustrates the tools and their use.

39. Sawada Tokunosuke, "Yakubutsu to shite no ai no hanashi", *Senshoku to seikatsu* 29: 62–63, discusses various medical uses and pesticidal properties of indigo as recorded in old Chinese sources.

40. Nagasaki Seiki, *Iro no Nihonshi* (Tokyo: Tankōsha, 1977), p. 54. Indigo pigment darkened with *sumi* was used to color paper during the Nara period.

41. Yoshioka, *Tennen senryō no kenkyū*, p. 186.

42. Yoshioka, *Tennen senryō no kenkyū*, p. 186. According to Gerber, *Indigo and the Antiquity of Dyeing*, p. 27, Indian indigo was made quite differently from *sukumo*: indican was extracted, allowed to oxidize into indigo, and sundried till hard for shipping or storage.

43. An example is the *Ōsaka shichū kaimono tebikigusa*, published in 1785 and mentioned in Gotō, *Nihon senshoku bunken sōran*, p. 108.

GLOSSARY

AKIKUSA: "Autumn flowers and grasses" motif that includes Chinese bellflowers, chrysanthemums, wild pinks, bush clover, *ominaeshi*, pampas grass, and boneset.

ASA: specifically, hemp (also called *taima*; *Cannabis sativa* L.) More broadly, includes other bast fibers and the fabrics made from them, such as ramie and banana fiber.

"AUTUMN FLOWERS AND GRASSES": See AKIKUSA.

BAST FIBER: Fiber from the layer of various plant stems between outer bark and inner core. *See also* ASA, CHŌMA, TAIMA.

"BLUE WAVE": See SEIGAIHA.

BOKASHI: Shading or blending of color or ink, typical of *yūzen* dyeing and *tsujigahana*.

BŌSHI SHIBORI: Literally "capped *shibori*". The area to be reserved is stitched off (*nuishime shibori*), then wrapped, or "capped", in bamboo sheath. Used to reserve large areas.

BRUSH DYEING: See HIKI-ZOME.

BYŌBU: Folding screen, usually of two, four, or six panels.

CAPPED SHIBORI: See BŌSHI SHIBORI.

"CART WHEELS IN WAVES": See KATA WA GURUMA.

CHAYA-TSUJI: Summer *kosode* (*katabira*) made of ramie and decorated by the *chaya-zome* technique, sometimes supplemented with embroidery. *See also* CHAYA-ZOME.

CHAYA-ZOME: A type of dyeing employing resist paste to reserve the background in white while the delicate design is vat dyed in two or more shades of indigo. Usually applied to ramie summer *kosode* (*katabira*) worn by women of the highest echelons of the military elite. *See also* CHAYA-TSUJI.

CHIJIMI: General term for crepe, a plain-weave fabric with crimped surface produced by tightly twisted weft and/or warp yarns. Usually made of silk, cotton, or ramie.

CHIRIMEN: A heavily textured silk crepe with characteristic puckered, ribbed surface. Favored for *yūzen* dyeing. Produced by plain weave with untwisted warps and highly twisted wefts whose twist direction alternates with every two weft shots.

CHŌMA: Ramie or China grass (also called *karamushi*; *Boehmeria nivea Gaud.*). Bast fiber used for *katabira* and for clothing of the lower classes, particularly until the late Edo period.

CREPE: See CHIRIMEN, CHIJIMI.

CREST: See MON.

CURTAIN SCREEN: See KICHŌ.

DAN-GAWARI: A type of *kosode* design popular in the late Muromachi period, consisting of horizontal bands or checkerboard blocks of different colors or patterns.

DIP DYEING: See TSUKE-ZOME.

DŌBUKU, DŌFUKU: Man's outer garment, worn by samurai from late Muromachi through early Edo periods.

EMAKI, EMAKIMONO: Painted handscrolls.

EMBROIDERY: See NUI.

FIGURED SATIN: See RINZU.

FIGURED TWILL: See MON AYA.

FLORAL MEDALLIONS: See HANABISHI.

FOLDING SCREENS: See BYŌBU.

FURISODE: A variation of the *kosode* with long, fluttering sleeves, now worn by children and young unmarried women on special holidays.

GOJIRU: Soybean liquid used to help bond dyes and pigments to fabrics.

HAKAMA: Full, pleated trousers or divided skirt worn by men and women of the court and military elite.

HAKUBYŌ-E: A type of painting characterized by a fine, even black ink line on white ground; characteristic of certain painted handscrolls of the Kamakura through Edo periods. Similar painting found on *tsujigahana* fabrics.

HANABISHI: "Floral medallions" used as decorative motif.

HEMP: See TAIMA, ASA.

HIINAGATA BON, HIINAKATA: Catalogues of designs for women's *kosode*, published during the Edo period.

HIKI-ZOME: Application of dye, especially background color, by brush, as opposed to immersion dyeing (*tsuke-zome*).

HIRA-ORI: Plain weave. One of the three basic weave structures (along with twill and satin). (See Fig. 2-1.)

HITOE: Unlined *kosode* of silk, hemp, ramie, or cotton, generally for summer wear.

HITTA SHIBORI: See KANOKO SHIBORI.

IKŌ: Garment racks made of lacquered wood on which *kosode* and other robes were hung before being folded and put in boxes for storage.

IRO-SASHI, IRO-ZASHI: Application of color (especially pigment) to design area with small brush, especially in *yūzen* and some types of stencil dyeing (cf. *hiki-zome*, which refers to brushed application of background color).

JI-NASHI: Literally "without background". A *kosode* so densely covered with embroidery, metallic leaf, and other decoration that the background cloth is virtually invisible. Term is applied to *nuihaku kosode* of the Momoyama period and to *kosode* decorated in the Keichō style with *shibori*, embroidery, and metallic leaf.

JUBAN: Garment worn by both sexes under the *kosode*.

JŪNI HITOE: Literally "twelve single layers" of unlined robes, worn as formal attire by women of the imperial court. Actually ranged from fewer than five to as many as fifteen layers.

KAKI-E: Freehand-painted pictorial designs, usually in black ink. *See also* HAKUBYŌ-E.

KANBUN KOSODE: *Kosode* decorated in the Kanbun style, so called because it was typical of Kanbun era (1661–73) *kosode* design.

KANOKO SHIBORI: "Fawn spot" *shibori*. Parallel rows or scattered clusters of spots, each centered with a smaller dot of the background color, produced by tightly wrapping and tying each spot to be reserved before dyeing. Other varieties called *hitta*, *hitta shibori*, or *hitta kanoko. See also* SŌ KANOKO, KATA-KANOKO.

KARAKUSA: "Vine-scroll" motif, often combined with a flower (e.g., *kiku-karakusa*, "chrysanthemums and vine scrolls"; or *botan-karakusa*, "peonies and vine scrolls").

KARAMUSHI: *See* CHŌMA.

KASUMI: "Mist" motif, a diaper pattern of short, parallel horizontal lines.

KASURI: Ikat; a method of creating a reserved pattern by tie-dyeing yarn before weaving.

KATA WA GURUMA: Decorative motif of cart wheels partially submerged in waves.

KATABIRA: Unlined summer *kosode*, commonly made of ramie or hemp, but until the late Muromachi period made of silk as well.

KATA-KANOKO: Stencilled *kanoko*. A two-dimensional imitation of *kanoko shibori* in which resist paste is applied through a stencil before dyeing, creating a pattern resembling *kanoko shibori*. The "eye" in the center of each dot is painted in freehand. *See also* UCHI-DASHI KANOKO.

KATAMI-GAWARI: A type of *kosode* composition, common in the late Muromachi and the Momoyama periods, in which right and left sides are of different colors or patterns.

KATA-SUSO: A type of *kosode* composition, seen from the Kamakura through the Momoyama periods, in which only the shoulder and hem areas are decorated.

KEICHŌ KOSODE: *Kosode* decorated in the Keichō style, so called because it developed during the Keichō era (1596–1615). These *kosode* do not necessarily date to Keichō era.

KESA: Buddhist priest's stole or robe.

KICHŌ: Curtain screen, consisting of panels of silk hung from a frame.

KIKKŌ: "Tortoise-shell" motif, a diaper pattern of linked hexagons.

KIKU-SUI: "Chrysanthemums and flowing water"; common motif symbolizing longevity.

KIMONO: Term of ancient origin, meaning literally "the thing worn". Nowadays refers to the modern descendant of the *kosode*.

KOSHIMAKI: Literally "waist wrap". A heavily embroidered *kosode*, usually of black, red, or brown plain-weave or satin-weave silk. Worn slipped off the shoulders and held only at the waist by a separate sash. Worn over KATABIRA as formal summer dress by women of the military elite.

KOSODE: The principal outer garment for all classes since the Muromachi period, ancestral to the modern kimono, and similar in cut and proportion. Both sexes wore the *kosode*, but men usually wore other garments over it. The word *kosode* (small sleeves) refers to the relatively small wrist opening, not to the width or length of the sleeve itself. So called to distinguish it from the *ōsode* (large sleeves), the garments worn at the imperial court since Heian times, in which the wrist opening equals the length of the sleeve. *See also* HITOE, FURISODE, KATABIRA, KOSHIMAKI, UCHI-KAKE.

MATSUKAWA-BISHI: "Pine-bark lozenge" motif of overlapping triangles.

METALLIC LEAF: *See* SURIHAKU.

MON: Family crest, often dyed or embroidered on back and sleeves of *kosode*.

MON AYA, MON AYA-ORI: Figured twill. Woven pattern produced by contrasting warp-faced and weft-faced twill structures. Numerous structures are possible; one of the most common in Momoyama and Edo period textiles is 3/1 warp-faced twill ground with 1/3 weft-faced twill figure (see Fig. 2-3).

MORDANT: A chemical substance (usually a metallic salt) used in combination with a dye to produce and/or fix a color.

"MOUNTAIN PATH": *See* YAMAMICHI.

"MYRIAD TREASURES": *See* TAKARA ZUKUSHI.

NERINUKI: Plain-weave silk with unglossed reeled warps and glossed (reeled degummed) wefts. Favored for *tsujigahana kosode*.

NOSHI: Streamers, originally of dried abalone and later of paper, signifying longevity or continuity and used to decorate gifts.

NUIHAKU: Combination of embroidery (*nui*) and metallic leaf (*surihaku*) popular for *kosode* decoration in the Momoyama and Edo periods. Also, a category of Nō costume so decorated.

NUISHIME SHIBORI: Stitch-resist *shibori*. The area to be reserved is outlined with fine stitches which are pulled tight, as in shirring, and knotted. The cloth within the shirring line is then closely wound with thread. Dye cannot penetrate the thread-wound area or the deepest folds of the shirring, but it does seep into the outer folds where the shirring is looser. This produces a reserved pattern bordered by white dots along the stitching line, from which radiate lines of pale color where the dye has partially penetrated. The stitching-off is also a preliminary step in other *shibori* processes such as BŌSHI SHIBORI, TSUMAMI-ZOME, and OKE-ZOME.

OBI: Sash or belt worn with the traditional Japanese costume.

OKE-ZOME: Tub resist, or tub dyeing. A variant of *nuishime shibori* used to reserve large areas. The stitched-off areas are sealed inside a tub before the whole cloth is immersed in the dye bath.

OKUMI: Front overlap of the *kosode*.

"ORCHIDS and CHRYSANTHEMUMS": *See* RAN-GIKU.

OSHIROI: Face powder containing lead; often used to touch up accidentally dyed *kanoko* spots.

PIGMENT: Relatively insoluble coloring agent that does not penetrate textile fibers but adheres to their surface.

PINCH DYEING: *See* TSUMAMI-ZOME.

PLAIN WEAVE: *See* HIRA-ORI.

RAMIE: *See* CHŌMA, ASA.

RANGIKU: Design motif of orchids and chrysanthemums.

RINZU, RINZU-ORI: Figured satin, or damask; a woven pattern produced by contrasting warp-faced and weft-faced satin structures. The most common figured satin used in Edo period *kosode* is 4/1 warp-faced satin figured with 1/4 weft-faced satin (see Fig. 2-7).

"SANDY BEACH": *See* SUHAMA.

SATIN: *See* SHUSU.

SAYA, SAYA-ORI: Plain-weave ground with twill-weave figure (usually 3/1 warp-faced twill). (see Fig. 2-4).

SAYAGATA: A key-fret pattern composed of linked swastikas, common in woven figured satins of the Edo period (see Fig. 2-8).

SEIGAIHA: "Blue wave" motif of overlapping waves, resembling fish scales.

"SEVEN TREASURES": *See* SHIPPŌ.

SHIBORI: A method of resist dyeing, and the fabrics produced thereby, in which the pattern is reserved by compressing or squeezing part of the cloth and securing it against dye penetration before dipping the cloth in the dye bath. The resulting pattern is characterized by blurred outlines and a puckered surface. *See also* BŌSHI SHIBORI, KANOKO SHIBORI, NUISHIME SHIBORI, OKE-ZOME, TSUMAMI-ZOME.

SHIPPŌ, SHIPPŌ TSUNAGI: "Seven treasures" motif of interlocking circles, representing the seven treasures of Buddhism: gold, silver, lapis lazuli, coral, mother-of-pearl, carnelian, and crystal or amber.

SHIRO-AGARI, SHIRO-AGE: A style of *yūzen* dyeing in which the pattern is entirely reserved in white by means of resist paste, then supplemented with touches of bright embroidery.

SHŌAI-ZOME: Method of dyeing with indigo, using *sukumo* and heated vats.

SHUSU, SHUSU-ORI: Satin. One of the three basic weave structures (along with plain weave and twill). Satin *kosode* of the Edo period are usually 4/1 warp-faced satin (five-harness satin) or 7/1 warp-faced satin (eight-harness satin) (see Fig. 2-5).

"SNOW DISK": *See* YUKIWA.

SŌ KANOKO: Allover *kanoko shibori*, in which the entire surface of the cloth is covered by parallel diagonal rows of tiny reserved circles.

SODE: Sleeve.

SOMEWAKE: Literally "divide by dyeing". A type of *kosode* design in which a parti-colored background is created by *shibori* techniques, then further decorated with embroidery, metallic leaf, etc.

SOYBEAN LIQUID: *See* GOJIRU.

STENCILLED KANOKO: *See* KATA-KANOKO.

STITCH RESIST: *See* NUISHIME SHIBORI.

SUHAMA: "Sandy beach" motif, characterized by an undulating outline often combined with pine trees and cranes or other birds, plants, and shells of the shore. Sometimes referred to as a "sandbar" or "tide-pool" motif.

SURIHAKU: Literally "rubbed metallic leaf". Metallic (gold or silver) leaf pattern on cloth, often applied by spreading an adhesive through a stencil and pressing the leaf onto the glue. *See also* NUIHAKU.

TAGASODE: Literally "Whose sleeves?" A phrase used in classical poetry to suggest the presence of a beloved woman by reference to her garments. *Tagasode byōbu* are screen paintings depicting robes hung on lacquer racks (*ikō*).

TAIMA: Hemp (*asa: Cannabis sativa L.*). Bast fiber indigenous to Japan. Woven for clothing of the lower classes.

TAKARA ZUKUSHI: "Myriad treasures" motif, a collection of auspicious symbols connoting prosperity and long life.

TEGAKI-YŪZEN: In *yūzen* dyeing, the application of brushed color to small design elements outlined with resist paste applied through a funnel over freehand drawing in *aobana* juice.

TSUJIGAHANA: A combination of decorative techniques, also the fabrics and designs thus produced, which flourished from the late Muromachi through the Momoyama periods. Always included *shibori*, often supplemented by freehand painting (*kaki-e*), gold or silver leaf (*surihaku*), and embroidery (*nui*).

TSUKE-ZOME: Literally "dip dyeing" or "immersion dyeing". The most fundamental dyeing technique, in which cloth is immersed in a dye bath. Called vat dyeing when dyeing with indigo.

TSUMAMI-ZOME: Pinch dyeing. A type of *shibori* in which the ground area is stitched off and the pattern areas are dipped by hand into the dye vat. Produces dyed pattern on reserved ground.

TUB RESIST: *See* OKE-ZOME.

UCHIDASHI KANOKO: A repoussé technique for giving a three-dimensional effect to stencilled *kanoko* by pressing out the center of each dot with a blunt stick.

UCHIKAKE: A formal outer garment for cool weather, worn unbelted over the *kosode*.

UCHISHIKI: Altar cloth (Buddhist).

WATASHI NUI: A type of float-stitch embroidery common in the late Muromachi and the Momoyama periods, in which the long floats of embroidery floss catch the base cloth only along the perimeter of each embroidered shape.

YAMAMICHI: "Mountain path" motif; a vertical zigzag.

YUKIWA: "Snow disk", or "snowflake" motif, stylized as a crenellated roundel.

YŪZEN ZOME: Literally "*yūzen* dyeing". A combination of techniques employing resist paste to separate different-colored pattern areas, to create fine white lines, and to protect pattern areas from the background color, which is characteristically applied by brush (*hiki-zome*).

BIBLIOGRAPHY

BOOKS IN ENGLISH

*Burnham, Dorothy K. *Warp and Weft: a Dictionary of Textile Terms*. New York: Scribner's, 1981.

Cooper, Michael, trans. and ed. *They Came to Japan: an Anthology of European Reports on Japan, 1543–1640*. Berkeley, Los Angeles, and London: University of California Press, 1981.

Cort, Louise Allison. *Indigo Notes*. Tokyo: Bunseidō, 1978.

Doi, Tsugiyoshi. *Momoyama Decorative Painting*. Translated by Edna B. Crawford. The Heibonsha Survey of Japanese Art, no. 14. New York and Tokyo: Weatherhill/Heibonsha, 1977.

Dower, John W. *The Elements of Japanese Design: a Handbook of Family Crests, Heraldry and Symbolism*. New York and Tokyo: Walker/Weatherhill, 1971.

*Emery, Irene. *The Primary Structure of Fabrics*. Washington, D.C.: The Textile Museum, 1966.

Gerber, Frederick H. *Indigo and the Antiquity of Dyeing*. Ormond Beach, Fla.: By the Author, 1977.

Gittinger, Mattiebelle. *Splendid Symbols: Textiles and Traditions in Indonesia*. Washington, D.C.: The Textile Museum, 1979.

Grilli, Elise. *The Art of the Japanese Screen*. New York and Tokyo: Weatherhill/Bijutsu Shuppansha, 1970.

Hauge, Victor, and Hauge, Takako. *Folk Traditions in Japanese Art*. Tokyo: Kodansha International, 1978.

Honolulu Academy of Arts. *Exquisite Visions: Rimpa Paintings from Japan*. By Shimbo Tōru. Honolulu: Honolulu Academy of Arts, 1980.

Ihara Saikaku. *The Life of an Amorous Man*. Translated by Kengi Hamada. Rutland, Vt. and Tokyo: Tuttle, 1964.

*Itō Toshiko. *Tsujigahana: the Flower of Japanese Textile Art*. Translated by Monica Bethe. Tokyo: Kodansha International, 1981.

Japan House Gallery. *Autumn Grasses and Water: Motifs in Japanese Art*. Translated and adapted by Karen L. Brock and Sato Hiroaki. New York: Japan Society, 1983.

————. *Tagasode: Whose Sleeves . . . (Kimono from the Kanebo Collection)*. By Nishimura Hyōbu, Jean Mailey, and Joseph S. Hayes, Jr. New York: Japan Society, 1976.

————. *The Tokugawa Collection: Nō Robes and Masks*. By Tokugawa Yoshinobu, with Ōkochi Sadao. Translated and adapted by Louise Allison Cort and Monica Bethe. New York: Japan Society, 1977.

Japan Textile Color Design Center, comp. *Textile Designs of Japan*. Rev. ed. 3 vols. Tokyo: Kodansha International, 1980.

Keene, Donald. *World Within Walls: Japanese Literature of the Pre-Modern Era 1600–1867*. New York: Grove Press, 1976.

Larsen, Jack Lenor; with Bühler, Alfred; Solyom, Bronwen; and Solyom, Garrett. *The Dyer's Art: Ikat, Batik, Plangi*. New York: Van Nostrand Reinhold, 1976.

Los Angeles County Museum of Art. *Textile Traditions of Indonesia*. By Mary H. Kahlenberg. Los Angeles: Los Angeles County Museum of Art, 1977.

McCall's Needlework Treasury. New York: Random House-McCall's, 1964.

The Metropolitan Museum of Art. *Momoyama: Japanese Art in the Age of Grandeur*. By Julia Meech-Pekarik et al. New York: The Metropolitan Museum of Art, 1975.

*Miller, Dorothy. *Indigo from Seed to Dye*. Edited by Mary Cranston-Bennett. Aptos, Cal.: Indigo Press, 1982.

Mills College Art Gallery. *Fukusa: The Shojiro Nomura Fukusa Collection*. By Mary V. Hays and Ralph E. Hays. Oakland, Cal.: Mills College Art Gallery, 1983.

Minnich, Helen Benton, in collaboration with Nomura Shōjirō. *Japanese Costume and the Makers of its Elegant Tradition*. Rutland, Vt. and Tokyo: Tuttle, 1963.

Mizoguchi Saburō. *Design Motifs*. Translated by Louise Allison Cort. Arts of Japan, no. 1. New York and Tokyo: Weatherhill/Shibundō, 1973.

Nakano Eisha, and Stephan, Barbara B. *Japanese Stencil Dyeing: Paste Resist Techniques*. New York and Tokyo: Weatherhill, 1982.

Noma Seiroku. *Japanese Costume and Textile Arts*. Translated by Armins Nikovskis. The Heibonsha Survey of Japanese Art, no. 16. New York and Tokyo: Weatherhill/Heibonsha, 1974.

Nomura Shōjirō. *Historical Sketch of Nishiki and Kinran Brocades*. Boston: N. Sawyer and Son, 1914.

Okada Jō, and Yamanobe Tomoyuki. *Textiles and Lacquer*. Pageant of Japanese Art, no. 5. Tokyo: Tōto Bunka, 1954.

Okudaira Hideo. *Narrative Picture Scrolls*. Translated by Elizabeth ten Grotenhuis. Arts of Japan, no. 5. Tokyo and New York: Weatherhill, 1973.

Rodrigues João. *This Island of Japon: João Rodrigues' Account of Sixteenth-Century Japan*. Translated and edited by Michael Cooper. Tokyo and New York: Kodansha International, 1973.

Royal Academy of Arts. *The Great Japan Exhibition: Art of the Edo Period 1600–1868*. Edited by William Watson. London: Royal Academy of Arts, 1981.

Sansom, George. *A History of Japan 1334–1615*. Stanford: Stanford University Press, 1961.

————. *A History of Japan 1615–1867*. Stanford: Stanford University Press, 1963.

————. *A Short Cultural History of Japan*. New York: Appleton-Century Crofts, 1962.

Seidensticker, Edward G., trans. *The Tale of Genji*. 2 vols. New York: Knopf, 1976.

Sheldon, Charles David. *The Rise of the Merchant Class in Tokugawa Japan, 1600–1868: an Introductory Survey*. Locust Valley, N.Y.: J.J. Augustin, 1958.

Treasures of the Shosoin. Tokyo: Asahi Shinbun Publishing Co., 1965.

Van Gelder, Lydia. *Ikat*. New York: Watson Guptill, 1980.

Varley, H. Paul. *Japanese Culture: a Short History*. New York and Washington, D.C.: Praeger, 1973.

*Wada Yoshiko; Rice, Mary Kellogg; and Barton, Jane.

Shibori: the Inventive Art of Japanese Shaped Resist Dyeing. Tokyo: Kodansha International, 1983.

Yamane Yūzō. *Momoyama Genre Painting*. Translated by John M. Shields. The Heibonsha Survey of Japanese Art, no. 17. New York and Tokyo: Weatherhill/Heibonsha, 1973.

JOURNAL ARTICLES AND ESSAYS IN ENGLISH

Adams, Marie. "Tiedyeing, an art on the island of Sumba". *Handweaver and Craftsman* 22 (1971): 9–11.

Arness, Judith R. "Tiedyeing in India: Weavers in Barpali Revive Traditional Craft". *Handweaver and Craftsman* 14 (Winter 1963): 6–8.

Mailey, Jean. "Four Hundred Winters... Four Hundred Springs...." *The Metropolitan Museum of Art Bulletin* 18 (December 1959): 113–26.

Simmons, Pauline. "Artist Designers of the Tokugawa Period". *The Metropolitan Museum of Art Bulletin* 14 (February 1956): 133–48.

Toyoda Takeshi, and Sugiyama Hiroshi, with V. Dixon Morris. "The Growth of Commerce and the Trades". In *Japan in the Muromachi Age*. Edited by John W. Hall and Toyoda Takeshi. Berkeley, Los Angeles, and London: University of California Press, 1977.

BOOKS IN JAPANESE

Abe Akio et al., ed. *Genji monogatari* [Tale of Genji]. Nihon koten bungaku zenshū, nos. 12–17. Tokyo: Shōgakukan, 1971–76.

Akiyama Ken et al., ed. *Genji monogatari* [Tale of Genji]. Nihon no koten, no. 7. Tokyo: Shūeisha, 1978.

Ebata Jun. *Shikimei no yurai* [Origins of color names]. Tokyo: Shoseki, 1982.

Endō Motoo. *Nihon shokunin-shi* [History of artisans in Japan]. Tokyo: Yūzankaku, 1967.

Endō Yasuo. *Benibana-zome: hana no inochi someta nuno* [Safflower dyeing]. *Nihon no senshoku*, vol. 18. Tokyo: Tairyūsha, 1978.

Fukusō Bunka Kyōkai, ed. *Fukusō daihyakka jiten: bekkan shiryōshū* [Encyclopedia of costume: sources]. Rev. ed. Tokyo: Bunka Shuppan Kyōkai, 1976.

*Gotō Shōichi. *Nihon senshoku bunken sōran* [Compendium of sources on Japanese dyeing]. Kyoto: Senshoku to Seikatsusha, 1980.

Hinonishi Sukenori, ed. *Fukushoku* [Costume]. Nihon no bijutsu, no. 26. Tokyo: Shibundō, 1968.

Imanaga Seiji, ed. *Kosode 1. Nihon no senshoku*, vol. 3. Edited by Yamanobe Tomoyuki. Tokyo: Chūōkōronsha, 1979.

Imanaga Seiji, and Kirihata Ken. *Nō, kyōgen, kabuki. Nihon no senshoku*, vol. 5. Tokyo: Chūōkōronsha, 1980.

Ishida Hisatoyo, ed. *Nihon shokunin tsukushi-e* [Paintings of Japanese artisans]. Nihon no bijutsu, no. 132. Tokyo: Shibundō, 1977.

Itō Toshiko. *Tsujigahana-zome* [*Tsujigahana* dyeing]. Tokyo: Kōdansha, 1972.

*Kamiya Eiko, ed. *Kosode*. Nihon no bijutsu, no. 67. Tokyo: Shibundō, 1971.

*_____ . *Kishū Tōshōgū no senshokuhin* [Textiles from the Kishū Tōshō Shrine]. Kyoto: Unsōdō, 1980.

Kawaguchi Hisao, and Shida Nobuyoshi, eds. *Wakan rōeishū Ryōjin hishō* [Collection of Japanese and Chinese poems for recitation, and Secret selections from the dust of Liang]. Nihon koten bungaku taikei, no. 73. Tokyo: Iwanami Shoten, 1965.

Kitamura Tetsurō. *Nihon fukushoku shi* [History of Japanese costume]. Tokyo: Iseikatsu Kenkyūkai, 1973.

_____ , ed. *Nō shōzoku* [Nō costume]. Nihon no bijutsu, no. 46. Tokyo: Shibundō, 1970.

*_____ , ed. *Yūzen-zome* [Yūzen dyeing]. Nihon no bijutsu, no. 106. Tokyo: Shibundō, 1975.

*Kojima Shigeru, ed. *Iro no saijiki: me de asobu Nihon no iro* [The book of seasonal colors in Japan]. Tokyo and Osaka: Asahi Shinbunsha; Nagoya: Kitakyūshū, 1983.

Kyoto National Museum. *Momoyama jidai no kōgei* [Decorative arts of the Momoyama period]. Kyoto: Shikōsha, 1977.

_____ . *Kachō no bi* [Flowers and birds]. Kyoto: Kyoto National Museum, 1982.

*Maeda Yukichika. *Nihon shikisai bunkashi* [A cultural history of Japanese colors]. Tokyo: Iwanami Shoten, 1960.

Makino Tomitarō. *Genshoku Makino shokubutsu daizukan* [Makino's illustrated flora in color]. Edited by Honda Masaji. Tokyo: Hokuryūkan, 1982.

*Matsushita Daisaburō, and Watanabe Fumio, eds. *Kokka taikan* [Concordance to the poetic anthologies of Japan]. 4 vols. Tokyo: Kadokawa Shoten, 1951–58.

*Nagasaki Seiki. *Iro no Nihonshi* [Colors and Japanese history]. Tokyo: Tankōsha, 1977.

Nezu Art Museum. *Nezu Bijutsukan meihin mokuroku* [Catalogue of famous works in the Nezu Art Museum]. Tokyo: The Nezu Art Museum, 1968.

*Nihon Orimono Shinbunsha, comp. *Senshoku jiten* [Dictionary of textiles]. Osaka: Nihon Orimono Shinbunsha, 1931. Reprinted as *Zōho senshoku jiten*. Kyoto: Kyoto Shoin, 1976.

Nishimura Hyōbu, ed. *Orimono* [Woven textiles]. Nihon no bijutsu, no. 12. Tokyo: Shibundō, 1967.

Nishitsunoi Masayoshi. *Nenjū gyōji jiten* [Dictionary of seasonal events]. Tokyo: Tōkyōdō, 1958.

Nomura Shōjirō, comp. *Tagasode hyakushū* [Whose Sleeves...? a series of one hundred]. Kyoto: Unsōdō, 1919.

_____ . *Yūzen kenkyū* [Study of *yūzen* dyeing]. Kyoto: Unsōdō, 1920.

_____ , comp. *Kosode to furisode* [Short-sleeved and long-sleeved robes]. Kyoto: Unsōdō, 1927.

_____ , comp. *Zoku tagasode hyakushū* [Whose sleeves...? another series of one hundred]. Kyoto: Unsōdō, 1930.

_____, comp. *Zoku kosode to furisode* [Another series of short-sleeved and long-sleeved robes]. Kyoto: Unsōdō, 1932.

_____, comp. *Gosho-doki to Edo-doki* [Robe designs of the imperial court in Kyoto and the shogunal court in Edo]. Kyoto: Unsōdō, 1932.

_____, comp. *Jidai kosode hiinagata byōbu* [Antique *kosode* screens]. Kyoto: Unsōdō, 1939.

_____, comp. *Jidai fukusa* [Antique gift covers]. 2 vols. Kyoto: Unsōdō, 1939.

Numada Yorisuke. *Nihon monshōgaku* [Study of Japanese crests]. Tokyo: Meiji Shoin, 1926. Reprint ed. Tokyo: Jinbutsu Ōraisha, 1968.

Okada Akira. *Wa-Ei-Doku taishō senshoku kakōgaku yōgo jiten* [Comparative dictionary of textile-manufacturing terms: Japanese-English-German]. Tokyo: Nihon Senshoku Kakōkenkyūkai Shuppanbu, 1966.

Ozawa Masao, ed. *Kokinwakashū* [Collection of ancient and modern poems]. Nihon koten bungaku zenshū, no. 7. Tokyo: Shōgakukan, 1971.

Senshoku no bi special issues:

    1 (Summer 1979): *Tsujigahana*

    3 (Early Spring 1980): *Yūzen-zome* [*Yūzen* dyeing]

    4 (Spring 1980): *Nō ishō* [Nō costume]

    9 (Early Spring 1981): *Nihon no shishū* [Japanese embroidery]

    10 (Spring 1981): *Sekai no shibori* [*Shibori* dyeing of the world]

    12 (Summer 1981): *Chayatsuji to natsu ishō* [*Chayatsuji* and summer clothing]

    15 (Early Spring 1982): *Furisode*

    19 (Early Autumn 1982): *Momoyama jidai no senshoku* [Textiles of the Momoyama period]

    21 (Early Spring 1983): *Edo no kosode* [*Kosode* of the Edo period]

    23 (Early Summer 1983): *Heian, Kamakura, Muromachi no senshoku* [*Textiles of the Heian, Kamakura, and Muromachi periods*].

Shirahata Yoshi, ed. *Monogatari emaki* [Narrative handscroll paintings]. Nihon no bijutsu, no. 49. Tokyo: Shibundō, 1966.

*Tokyo National Museum. *Nihon no senshoku* [Textiles of Japan]. Exh. cat. Tokyo: Tokyo National Museum, 1973.

_____. *Tōkyō Kokuritsu Hakubutsukan zuhan mokuroku—kosode fukushoku hen* [Illustrated catalogue of the Tokyo National Museum: *kosode* and other clothing]. Tokyo: Tokyo National Museum, 1983.

Tsunoyama Yukihiro. *Nihon senshoku hattatsushi* [History of textile development in Japan]. Tokyo: Tabata Shoten, 1968.

*Ueno Saeko, ed. *Kosode monyō hiinagata bon shūsei* [Collection of design books of *kosode* patterns]. 4 vols. Tokyo: Gakushū Kenkyūsha, 1974.

*Yamane Yūzō. *Konishi-ke kyūzō Kōrin kankei shiryō to sono kenkyū, I (shiryō hen)* [Research materials relating to Kōrin formerly in the collection of the Konishi family: documents]. Tokyo: Chūōkōron Bijutsu Shuppan, 1983.

*Yamanobe Tomoyuki, ed. *Some* [Dyed textiles]. Nihon no bijutsu, no. 7. Tokyo: Shibundō, 1966.

_____, supervising ed. *Nihon no senshoku*. 6 vols. Tokyo: Chūōkōronsha, 1979–81. Also listed under editors of individual volumes.

Yamanobe Tomoyuki; Kitamura Tetsurō; and Tabata Kihachi. *Kosode*. Tokyo: San'ichi Shobō, 1963.

*Yamanobe Tomoyuki, and Kamiya Eiko. *Uesugi-ke denrai ishō* [Textiles transmitted by the Uesugi family]. Nihon dentō ishō, vol. 1. Tokyo: Kōdansha, 1969.

*Yamazaki Seiju. *Kusaki-zome: iro to shuhō* [Vegetable dyeing: colors and methods]. Tokyo: Bijutsu Shuppan-sha, 1974.

_____. *Kusaki-zome: kata-zome no kihon* [Vegetable dyeing: basics of stencil dyeing]. Tokyo: Bijutsu Shuppansha, 1978.

*Yoshioka Tsuneo. *Tennen senryō no kenkyū* [A study of natural dyes]. Kyoto: Mitsumura Suiko Shoin, 1974.

*Yujinsai Kiyochika. *Gosho miyako imayō Yūzen hiinagata* [Contemporary *yūzen* designs of the capital]. Jōkyō 5 (1688). 4 vols. Partially reprinted as "*Yūzen hiinagata*" in *Kosode monyō hiinagata bon shūsei*, vol. 1, part 7. Edited by Ueno Saeko. Tokyo: Gakushū Kenkyūsha, 1974.

JOURNALS AND JOURNAL ARTICLES IN JAPANESE

Hashimoto Sumiko. "Edo shoki no ishō moyō ni tsuite: Sōōji byōbu ni kakareta jinbutsu chakuyō ishō ni yoru tenkai-zu sakusei to sono jidaiteki kōsatsu" [Clothing designs of the early Edo period: clothing worn by personages depicted in the Sōōji screens]. *Tōkyō Kokuritsu Hakubutsukan kiyō* 14 (March 1979): 47–92.

_____. "Tōkyō Kokuritsu Hakubutsukan hokan no moji-chirashi ishō kosode ni tsuite" [On *kosode* whose designs include written characters]. *Museum* (Tokyo) 349 (April 1980): 4–20, and 353 (August 1980): 27–34.

*Kamiya Eiko. "Momoyama, Edo zen chū ki no ubugi jūsanryō ni tsuite—kinsei irui chōsa hōkoku" [Survey of premodern clothing: thirteen infants' robes of Momoyama, early Edo, and mid-Edo]. *Bijutsu kenkyū* 267 (January 1970): 1–17; 272 (November 1970): 10–23; 280 (March 1972): 14–29.

*Kawakami Shigeki. "Edo jidai zenki no kosode—Keichō kosode kara Kanbun kosode e" [Early Edo *kosode*: from Keichō to Kanbun styles]. *Bunkazai* 228 (September 1982): 27–34.

_____. "Keichō kosode no keifu—sono seiritsu to tenkai" [A geneaology of Keichō era *kosode*: their formation and development]. *Museum* (Tokyo) 383 (February 1983): 4–15.

*Kirihata Ken. "Momoyama jidai no senshoku: Seiyōjin no kiroku o chūshin ni" [Textiles of the Momoyama period: Westerners' records]. In Kyoto National Museum, *Momoyama jidai no kōgei* [Decorative arts of the Momoyama period], pp. 211–24. Kyoto: Shikōsha, 1977.

_____. "Tsujigahana-zome" [*Tsujigahana* dyeing]. *Senshoku no bi* 1 (Early Autumn 1979): 53–60.

*_____ . "Kinsei no senshoku oboegaki—yūzen-zome ikō" [Notes on premodern textiles from *yūzen* dyeing onward]. In *Kosode II*, pp. 218–49. Edited by Kirihata Ken. *Nihon no senshoku*, vol. 4. General editor Yamanobe Tomoyuki. Tokyo: Chūōkōronsha, 1980.

_____ . "Yūzen-zome no utsukushisa—sono tokuchō to Yūzensai no koto" [Characteristics of *yūzen* dyeing and its relationship to Yūzensai]. *Senshoku no bi* 3 (Early Spring 1980): 53–60.

*_____ . "Kinsei senshoku ni okeru bungei ishō" [Designs with literary themes in premodern textiles]. In *Kōgei ni miru koten bungaku ishō* [Classical literary themes in the decorative arts], pp. 307–24. Edited by Kyoto National Museum. Kyoto: Shikosha, 1980.

_____ . "Nihon no shishū kanshō" [An appreciation of Japanese embroidery]. *Senshoku no bi* 9 (Early Spring 1981): 65–72.

_____ . "Furisode-kō sode-take no hensen o chūshin ni" [Changes in *furisode* sleeve length]. *Senshoku no bi* 15 (Early Spring 1982): 65–72.

*_____ . "Genna, Kan'ei mei kosode-gire uchishiki (Shinjū-an-zō) ni tsuite—Edo jidai zenki no senshoku shiryō" [Shinjū-an altar cloths made from *kosode* of the Genna and Kan'ei eras—textile documents of the early period]. *Museum* (Tokyo) 376 (July 1982): 18–26.

*Kitamura Tetsurō. "Senshoku ni okeru Edo shoki—Keichō nuihaku-kō" [Early Edo period textiles: Keichō *nuihaku*]. *Museum* (Tokyo) 271 (October 1973): 4–13.

*Kurihara Yoshiko. "*Kariganeya chūmon-chō* ni arawareta Edo jidai shoki no ishō moyō" [Early Edo period costume designs . . . in the order books of the Kariganeya]. *Shiron* 7 (November 1959): 448–62.

Mihashi Saeko. "Monyō hiinagata bon shūsei: Genroku made" [Collection of design books—through Genroku era]. *Tenri Daigaku gakuhō* 39 (December 1962): 304–23.

Nagasaki Iwao. "Senshoku shiryō to shite no kosode moyō hiinagata bon: kosode moyō no kankei o chūshin ni" [*Kosode* design books as documents for research in textiles]. *Museum* (Tokyo) 373 (April 1982): 20–29.

_____ . "Edo no kosode" [Edo period *kosode*]. *Senshoku no bi* 21 (Early Spring 1983): 81–88.

Nishimura Sotoji. "Omoide no hito, 6: Nomura Shōjirō" [Recollections of Nomura Shōjirō]. *Senshoku no bi* 6 (Summer 1980): 84–86.

TRANSLATIONS OF JOURNAL AND SERIES TITLES:

Bijutsu kenkyū [Research in art]
Bunkazai [Cultural properties]
Nihon koten bungaku zenshū [Collected works of classical Japanese literature]
Nihon no bijutsu [Arts of Japan]
Nihon no koten [Japanese classics]
Nihon no senshoku [Japanese textiles]. The reader should note that three separate publications bear this title: a six-volume set published by Chūōkōronsha, a multivolume series published by Tairyūsha, and an exhibition catalogue issued by Tokyo National Museum.
Senshoku no bi [Textile arts]
Shiron [Historical essays]
Tenri Daigaku gakuhō [Tenri University reports]
Tokyo Kokuritsu Hakubutsukan kiyō [*Records of the Tokyo National Museum*].

*Works of particular importance to the study of *kosode* of the Muromachi, Momoyama, and Edo periods.

INDEX

Numbers in italics refer to illustrations or diagrams on those pages.

Cpl. refers to Colorplates, which begin on page 82.

A

abalone strips (*noshi*), in design, *15, 17, 37,* 120; cpl. 21
Adachi Kenji, administrator, 21
Agency for Cultural Affairs, 21
ai, see indigo
akane iro, see madder red
Akiko, princess, 134, *194, 195*
akudate, dyeing process, 74, 203
Aldrich, Lucy T., Collection, 15
allover patterns, 39, 53, 54, 56; cpls. 1, 2, 5, 6, 8, 14, 36
  ji-nashi style, 41, 44, 47, *87, 90*; cpls. 4, 5, 6, 8, 12, 13
altar cloths (*uchishiki*), *14,* 26, 44, *194, 195*
Andō Hiroshige, artist, 57
  see also Ichiryūsai Hiroshige
architecture, 23, 39
asa (hemp), 29, 31, 35
Asakura Hanzō, *kosode* of, *199*
Ashikaga shogunate, 24, 28, 39
Asuka period, 23, 26, 63, 77
aya-ori, see twill weaves
Azuchi Castle, near Kyoto, 39

B

bamboo motif, 47
  with pine and plum (*shōchikubai*), 54, *124, 138*; cpls. 23, 30
ban (temple banners), *14,* 26, 41, 42
banana fiber, 29
Ban Dainagon ekotoba, handscroll, *34*
bassen dyeing, *170*
bast fibers, 28–29, 35
  chaya-zome technique, *see chaya-zome*
benibana, see safflower
beni mochi 72, 204
Benton, Helen, 20
bingata garments, 65
Biwa, Lake, 39, 72
black-background style, 47–49, 52–53; cpls. 2–4, 12–14, 21, 22
black colors and dyes, 66, 202–3, 206–7
block-resist (*itajime*), 72, 73
blue colors and dyes, 61, 65, 202–3
  see also indigo
blue wave (*seigaiha*) patterns, *92*; cpl. 7
Bo Juyi, Chinese poet, *130*
bokashi, shading process, 37; cpl. 36
bōshi (capped) *shibori*, 32, 41, 47, 48
brown colors and dyes, 61–62, 66, 202–3, 206–7
  red-browns, 204–5
brush dyeing, 30, 36, 67, 68

hiki-zome, 30, 36, 68, 69, 72
iro-sashi, 30, 36, 68
Buddhism, 27, 65
  introduction of, to Japan, 26, 63
  posthumous names in, *193*
Buddhist art priests' vestments (*kesa*), *14, 15,* 26, 44, *192*
Buddhist temples, donations of *kosode* to, 17, 19, 26, *144, 192*
bunjinga, see literati school of art
Bunka-Bunsei era, 51, 57, *160, 184*

C

capped (*bōshi*) *shibori*, 32, 41, 47, 48
cartwheel motifs, *128*; cpl. 25
characters, written, in design motifs, 51, 54, *130, 132, 138, 140, 144, 146, 148*; cpls. 26, 27, 30, 31, 33, 34
Chaya Sōri, dyer, 38
chaya-zome (or *chaya-tsuji*) process, 38, 55–56, 65, 76, *166*; cpls. 44, 45
chijimi, see crepe
China, 23
  cosmology, 59–60
  decorative techniques, 33, 34
  dyes and dyeing, 26, 63, 70, 71, 76, 203, 205
  fabrics, 25–29, 30, 43
  landscape paintings, 55, *136*
  literature, 48, *98, 108, 130, 132, 138,* 152
  motifs derived from, 40, 42, 46–48, 50, *124*
  See also Ming dynasty
chirimen crepe, 29, 43, 53, 55, 65, *147*
chōma, see ramie
chōnin (townsman) class, 27, 50, 55, 138, 140, 147, 174
chōyō celebration, *108, 116, 120*
Christian symbols, *178*
"chrysanthemum banquet" (*kiku no en*), *108*
chrysanthemums, symbolism of, 116, 120, 122
chrysanthemums and flowing water (*kiku-sui*) motif, 52–53, *108, 110, 116, 122, 126*; cpls. 15, 16, 19, 22, 24
chrysanthemums with key fret and orchids (*sayagata rangiku*), *197*
Codes of the Engi era (*Engi shiki*), 64, 67, 73
collections, Western, 15
color(s)
  basic, 64–66
  names and meanings, 60–61
  social rank and, 59, 61, 65
  symbolism of, 59–60
coloring substances, generally, 30
  See also dyes; pigments
compartmentalized design, 39–40
cosmology, 59–60
cotton, 28, 29, 57, 65
court (*yūsoku*) patterns, 33, *188*; cpl. 55
cranes, symbolism of, 47, *92, 98, 132*; cpls. 7, 8, 10–12, 27

crepe (*chijimi*), 29, 36
  chirimen, 29, 43, 53, 55, 65, *147*
cutch (*katekyū*) dye, 204–5

D

Daigo, emperor, 64
damasee weave (*saya-ori*), *129, 196*
damask weave structure, 29
dan-gawari, design composition, 40; cpls. 1, 4
decorative techniques, 30–38
Deshima, Japan, 65
design books (*hiinagata bon*), *18, 19, 36, 37,* 51–53, 61, 120
design motifs, generally, 37, 40, 47–49, 55–56, *160*
dewdrop motif, 42, *80*; cpl. 1
diaper pattern, 40, 52; cpls. 10, 16, 20
  tortoise-shell, 33, 47, *98*; cpls. 7, 12, 17
dip (immersion) dyeing (*tsuke-zome*), 30–33, 36, 67
  resist techniques, *see* resist dyeing
divided-background (*somewake*) style, 44–47, 66, *88*; cpls. 4–11, 37, 43
divided skirt (*hakama*), 24, 42–43
doro-zome (mud dyeing), 63
drumheads and waterfall motif, *142*; cpl. 32
Dutch settlers and traders, 50, 65
dyes and dyemaking, 30–33, 202–9
  early, 62–64
  houses, 67, 72
  plant sources, 59, 63, 65, 69–70, 73, 202, 204, 206, 208
  process, 30–33, 69–75, 203, 205, 207, 209

E

Edo, Japan, 16, 17, 49, 53, 61, 120
  dyeing industry, 67, 70
  scenes of, on *kosode*, *16, 55, 57, 190*; cpl. 56
Edo-doki robe designs, 17, 20
Edo period, 13, 19, 25, 26, 77
  colors and dyeing, 43, 59, 61–62, 64–67, 69–76, 203, 205, 207–9
  culture and customs, 17, 24, 100, 120, 147, 192
  decorative techniques, 30, 31, 34, 35–38, 112
  designs, *18, 42,* 44–57, *112, 118, 124, 130, 132, 136, 170, 188*
  extant *kosode*, 16, 23
  history, 39, 49–50, 53
  transition to, *see* Keichō era
  weaving industry, 27–30
  See also Genroku era; Kanbun era; Kan'ei era; Tenna era
Eight Views of Ōmi, landscape theme, 55
Eitoku, *see* Kanō Eitoku
Ema Tsutomu, professor, 16, 19
embroidery (*nui*), 29, 33–34, 40–41
  float-stitch (*watashi nui*), 34
  Genroku style, 54

Keichō style, 43–46
  with metallic leaf (nuihaku), 34, 40–41, 43, 46
  yūzen dyeing and, 36, 37
Engi shiki, see Codes of the Engi era
enji (lac), 65, 204–5

F

fan paintings, 37
fashion, emergence of, 51
fawn-dot shibori 19, 31, 32, 37, 41
  Keichō style, 44, 45, 48
  stencilled (kata-kanoko or suri-hitta), 19, 31–32, 55, 184
  sumptuary laws against, 36, 53
fermentation process in indigo dye making (akudate), 73–74, 203
float-stitch embroidery (watashi nui), 34
flower motifs, generally, 40
  in tsujigahana, 41–43
flowing water motif, 52, 56, 108, 116, 142; cpls. 15, 16, 22, 24, 32, 33, 44, 45
  with chrysanthemums, see chrysanthemums and flowing water
freehand painting (kaki-e), 30–31, 34, 37, 42
fuchi-dori technique, 112; cpl. 17
Fujiwara Motohira, kosode of, 25
Fujiwara no Okikaze, poet, 83
fuki (padded hem), 122
Fukuoka, Japan, 26
fukusa (gift covers), 17, 20
Fukushima, Japan, 29
furisode, garment, 21, 23, 25, 32, 57, 188; cpls. 44, 55

G

Genji hinakata, design book, 36
Genji stories, see Tale of Genji
Genroku era, 16, 53–56, 77
  colors and dyeing, 51, 138, 209
  design, 50, 53–56, 124, 128, 130, 148; cpls. 23–29, 32, 33
gift covers (fukusa), 17, 20
Gion mamori crests, 178; cpl. 50
gojiru (soybean liquid), 36, 62, 68, 69
gold, see metallic leaf; metallic thread
Go-Mizunoo, emperor, 53, 134, 194
Gosho-doki robe designs, 17, 20, 184
Gosho imayō yūzen hiinagata, design book, 36, 37
Gosho miyako imayō yūzen hiina-gata, design book, 37
Goshun, see Matsumura Goshun
grapevine motif, 39, 40, 42, 43, 82; cpls. 2, 3
gray colors and dyes, 66, 67, 207, 209
green colors and dyes, 65–66, 69, 202–3
guilds (za), textile, 27–28

H

hakama (divided skirt), 24, 42–43

Hakubyō Genji monogatari emaki, handscroll, 42
hakubyō style, 42, 55, 82
handscrolls, 24, 25, 34, 35, 39–40, 42
hanpu cloth, 33
haori jacket, 14
happi coat, 14, 15
Hasegawa Tōhaku, artist, 42, 80
Hashimoto Sumiko, scholar, 26
Heian period, 23–27, 50, 77
  color and dyeing, 59, 60, 64, 67–71, 73, 203, 207, 209
  customs, 59, 61
  decorative techniques, 33
  design, 39, 42, 48, 98, 128, 152, 184, 188
  weaving, 26–27
hem, padded (fuki), 122
hemp (asa, taima), 29, 31, 35
herbs, see plants
Hidetada, see Tokugawa Hidetada
Hideyori, see Kanō Hideyori
Hideyoshi, see Toyotomi Hideyoshi
hiinigata bon, see design books
hiinagata screens, 19–21
hiki-zome, see under brush dyeing
hira-ori, see plain weaves
Hiroshige, see Andō Hiroshige; Ichiryūsai Hiroshige
Historical Sketch of Nishiki and Kinran Brocades, An, book (No-mura), 14
hitta (kanoko) shibori, see fawn-dot shibori
Hōitsu, see Sakai Hōitsu
Hokkaidō, Japan, 63
Hon' ami Kōetsu, artist, 50
Hōrai, Mount, 98
human figures motif, emergence of, 55, 158; cpls. 40, 56

I

Ichikawa Danjūrō, actor, 62
Ichiryūsai Hiroshige, artist, 160
  style of, 16
Ieyasu, see Tokugawa Ieyasu
Ihara Saikaku, novelist, 10, 36, 37, 180
ikat (kasuri) dyeing, 31, 33
ikō (kosode racks), 18
immersion dyeing (tsuke-zome), see dip dyeing
Imperial Clothing Office, 27
Important Cultural Property, 15
India, dyes from, 63, 65, 71, 76
indigo (ai), 73–76, 202–3
  chaya-zome use, see chaya-zome process
  dyeing process, 68, 73–75, 203
  early use, 62, 63
  growing and marketing of, 69, 73, 75–76, 202
  pigmentized, 38, 68, 76, 168
  used with other dyes, 65, 66, 76, 202, 205, 208, 209
ink painting (suiboku-ga), 42–44, 50, 69

ink-wash shading, 42
Inokuma Asamaro, museum direc-tor, 16, 19
insect-bitten leaves motif, 42, 80; cpl.1
iro-sashi (iro-zashi), see under brush dyeing
Ishikawaya firm, Kyoto, 67
itajime, dyeing technique, 72, 73
Itō Shōha, artist, 17
Iwanaga Tei, Nomura's mother, 13
Iwate Prefecture, Japan, 25, 70

J

Japanese Costume and the Makers of Its Elegant Tradition, book (Min-nich, Nomura), 20
Japanese history, 13, 23, 24, 39, 49–50, 53
  chronology, 77
Japan Society, 21
Japanese Textiles (Nihon no sen-shoku), catalogue, 21
Jesuit missionaries, 40
ji-nashi kosode, 41, 44, 47, 87, 90; cpls. 4, 5, 6, 8, 12, 13
Jinrin kinmōsui, book, 67
juban, garment, 57, 190; cpl. 56
jūni hitoe, (twelve-layered dress), 23

K

Kabuki theater, 13, 61, 114
Kaga yūzen process, 38
Kaihō Yūshō, artist, 42, 50
kaki-e, see freehand painting
Kamakura, Japan, 24, 27
Kamakura-bori, lacquer style, 42
Kamakura period, 24, 25, 50, 77
  colors and dyes, 61, 65, 203
  design, 42, 48
kami, spirits, 59
Kamiya Eiko, textile historian, 19, 24, 25
Kanbun era, 18, 77
  aftermath, 55
  colors and dyeing, 61, 64, 66, 67
  design, 37, 43, 46, 47, 51–54, 56, 98, 104, 106, 110–26, 130, 140, 142, 147, 148; cpls. 14–24
  evolution of style, 51–53
  waning of style, 55
Kan' ei era, 26, 32, 44
Kanō Eitoku, artist, 39, 42, 50
Kanō Hideyori, artist, 35
kanoko shibori, see fawn-dot shibori
Kanō school of art, 50, 112
Kanō Yukinobu, artist, 180
kara-ori ("Chinese weaving"), 33
Kariganeya shop, kyoto, 53, 67
Kasuga Gongen reigenki emaki, handscroll, 24, 25, 35, 39–40
kasumi, see mist pattern
kasuri (ikat) dyeing, 31, 33
katabira (summer kosode), 28, 29, 35, 38, 47, 54–56; cpls. 33, 37, 44, 45
kata-kanoko, see under stencil dye-ing
Katakura family, 198

katami-gawari, design composition, 40

kata-suso style, 24, 40

katekyū (cutch) dye, 204–5

Katsura no onna, poem, 35

Kazuko, emperor's consort, 53

Keichō era, 33, 43–49, 53, 77
  colors and dyeing, 61, 64, 66, 67, 87, 92, 104, 106
  dating designs, 43–44
  design, 44–47, 51, 52, 55, 56, 88, 94, 100, 104, 106, cpls. 2–11
  weaves, 83, 84

Keishō-in, of *kosode*, 32

Kenshin, *see* Uesugi Kenshin

kesa (priests' vestments), 14, 15, 26, 44, 192

key-fret pattern (*sayagata*), 30
  with orchids and chrysanthemums (*sayagata rangiku*), 30, *197*

kichō (screen-sail) motif, 140; cpl. 31

kihada, see philodendron

ki iro, see yellow dyes

kikkō hanabishi, see tortoise-shell lozenge

Kiku jidō, play, 108

kiku no en (chrysantheum banquet), 108

kiku-sui, see chrysanthemums and flowing water

Kimura Yoshibei, *kosode* of, 164

kinran brocades, 14

kin sha (gold-figured gauze), 53

Kirihata ken, textile historian, 35–36, 37, 48, 61, 142, 148

Kiryū, Japan, 28

Kita no Mandokoro, shogun's wife, 33

Kobe, Japan, 15

Kōetsu, *see* Hon' ami Kōetsu

Kojiki, chronicle, 62, 63

Kokinwakashū, poetry anthology, 48, 83, 146

komon (small repeat designs), 68

Konoe, princess, 195

Konoe Shoshi, Regent, 194

Korean influences, 23, 26, 28, 63, 69

Kōrin, *see* Ogata Kōrin

Kōrin designs, 164

koshimaki, garment, 56, 176; cpl. 49

kosode
  artist-decorated, 19, 23, 57, 180; cpls. 51, 52
  cutting layouts, 200–201
  dating difficulties, 19–20, 43–44
  defined, 13, 23
  dimensions, 78, 198–201
  earliest extant, 24–25
  evolution of, 23–26
  men's and women's, similar, 26, 40
  parts, listed, 25
  shape, 24–25

kukushi dyeing, 31

Kunisuke, *see* Tsumori Kunisuke

Kurata Bunsaku, art historian, 21

Kusumi Morikage, artist, 180

kyōkechi dyeing, 73

Kyoto, Japan, 13–17, 20, 21, 26, 37
  history, 24, 27, 33, 39, 40, 50, 53, 61
  Sanjūsangendō statues, 192
  scenes of, on *kosode*, 16, 55, 158, 160; cpls. 40–42
  as textile center, 27, 28, 38, 43, 67, 70, 72, 75

Kyoto no sakigake, consumer's guide, 72

L

lac (*enji*), red dye, 65, 204–5

lacquer artwork, 42

landscape motifs, 55–56, 136; cpl. 51

Ledoux, Louis V., 15
  and family, 21

Life of an Amourous Man, The, novel (Ihara Saikaku), 180

lining inscriptions, 19, 192–95

literary themes, 46, 48, 128, 130, 132, 140, 142, 144, 146, 148

literati (*nanga*) style, 50, 57, 180; cpl. 51

lozenge patterns, 40, 82, 98, 112; cpls. 2, 10, 12, 17

M

madder red (*akane iro*), 36, 63, 64, 68, 69, 204–205, 209

Mailey, Jean, 21

Manji era, 18, 32

Mansai hiinagata, design book, 51

Manyōshū, poetry anthology, 60, 62, 63, 70, 71

Maple Viewing at Takao, painting (Kanō Hideyori), 35, 41, 80

Maruyama Ōkyo, artist, 50, 180

Maruyama school of art, 50

Matsudaira clan, 193

Matsuhime monogatari emaki, handscroll, 42

Matsumura Goshun, artist, 19, 31, 57, 180; cpl. 51

Matsuzaka store, Nagoya, 16

Mayberry, Bella, 15, 17

medicinal herbs, 59, 203, 205, 207, 209

Meiji period, 13–15, 34, 77, 178

Meireiki era, 53

metallic leaf (*surihaku*), 33, 34, 37, 41, 49
  with embroidery (*nuihaku*), 34, 40–41, 43, 64
  Keichō style, 43, 44

metallic thread, 34, 40, 45

Michinoku, Japan, 48

Ming dynasty, China, 33, 34, 45
  trade with, 27, 30, 40

Ministry of Central Affairs, 27

Ministry of the Treasury, 27

Minnich, Helen Benton, 20

Mirror for Women (Onnakagami), catalogue, 18

mist (*kasumi*) pattern, 41, 46, 47, 48, 88, 96, 102, 104, 106; cpls. 4–6, 9, 10, 12–14

Mitsukuni, *see* Tokugawa Mitsukuni

Miyako, *see* Kyoto

Miyazaki Yūzensai, artist, 37, 38

Mogami River, 71, 72

Momoyama period, 23, 25, 26, 39, 49, 53, 77
  colors and dyeing, 61, 64, 205
  decorative techniques, 18, 30–34, 36, 112
  design, 39–43, 44, 45–49, 50, 52, 55, 136
  weaves, 28, 47

mon aya, see under twill weaves

mordants, use in dyeing, 30, 36, 62–63, 70, 203, 205, 207, 209

Morikage, *see* Kusumi Morikage

motifs, generally, 37, 40, 47–49, 55–56, 160

Motohira, *see* Fujiwara Motohira

mountain and waves motif, 48

mountain path motif, 102; cpl. 12

Mt. Hōrai motif, 98

mud dyeing (*doro-zome*), 63

murasaki purple, 62, 65, 209
  dye, 63, 65, 67, 68, 69, 71, 209
  plant, 65, 69, 70, 208

Murasaki Shikibu, writer, 37–38

Muromachi period, 24–26, 49, 59, 77, 130
  colors and dyeing, 61, 64, 66–68, 71, 73–74, 203, 205, 207, 209
  decorative techniques, 34, 36
  design, 39–43, 44, 98
  weaving industry, 28

Musashino, Japan, 70

myriad treasures (*takara zukushi*) motif, 52, 102 & *n.*, 176; cpls. 21, 49

N

Nagasaki, Dutch settlement at, 50

Nagoya, Japan, 13, 16, 26

Nakamura Daizaburō, artist, 17

namaha-zome, dyeing process, 73

nanga, see literati school of art

Nara, Japan, 26, 27

Nara period, 23, 26, 28, 33, 42, 77
  colors and dyeing, 59, 60, 62, 63–67, 69, 71, 73, 203, 205, 207, 209

nerinuki guild, 27

nerinuki silks, 27–30, 43, 86

Nihon no senshoku (Japanese textiles), catalogue, 21

Niigata, Japan, 29

Nishijin district, Kyoto, 27, 28, 43

nishiki silk, 14, 33

nitsuchi, red pigment, 62

Nō, theater
  costumes, 15, 21, 34, 39, 41, 106
  plays, 51, 52, 108, 114, 130, 142

Nobunaga, *see* Oda Nobunaga

Nomura Akezu, 13

Nomura Kōjirō, 14

Nomura Masako, 20

Nomura Shizuo Morris, 20, 21

Nomura Shōjirō, *12*, 13–21, 41, 43
  family of, *17*
  store of, 14, *16*

Nomura Tei, 13, 14

noshi kosode, see abalone strips design

nuihaku, see under embroidery
nuishime, see stitch-resist *shibori*
nui, see embroidery

O

obi, 56, 150, 182
Odani ware, 76
Oda Nobunaga, ruler, 39
Ōeyama ekotoba, painting, 25
Ogata Kōrin, artist, 50, 53, 56, 182*n.*
oke-zome (tub-resist dyeing), 32–33
Okinawa, textile industry, 20, 29, 63, 65, 73
Okikaze, *see* Fujiwara no Okikaze
Ōkyo, *see Maruyama Ōkyo*
omodaka armor, 61
On-gachō, book, 53
On-hiinakata, design book, 51
Ōnin War, 24, 27, 28
  aftermath, 39, 40
Onna-kagami (Mirror for women), catalogue, 18
Oribe no tsukasa (Weaving Office), 26–27, 67
Osaka, Japan, 27, 49, 50, 61, 75
Osaka Castle, 39
oshiroi (white face powder), 31, 118
ōsode, garments, 23
Ōtsu, Japan, 72

P

painting, as decorative technique, 30–31
  on *tsujigahana,* 41–43
  See also brush dyeing; freehand painting, paste-resist dyeing, 31, 35–38, 68
  See also chaya-zome; yūzen dyeing
philodendron *(kihada),* as dye source, 62, 66, 208, 209
pigments, 30, 59, 62, 72, 76
  in *yūzen* dyeing, 37, 68–69
pinch dyeing *(tsumami-zome),* 33
pine, symbolism of, 42, 43, 47, 92, 98, 132, 140, 146; cpls. 2, 3, 7, 13, 27, 31, 34
pine-bamboo-plum motif *(shōchiku-bai),* 54, 124, 138; cpls. 23, 30
Pine Mountain of Sue, scenic spot, 48
pine-sheltered shore motif, 47; cpl. 37
pine-wistaria motif, 56–57, 184; cpls. 5–7, 10, 53
plain weaves *(hira-ori),* 28–29, 34, 86, *196*
  silk *(nerinuki),* 27–30, 43, 86
plants
  as dye sources, 59, 63, 65, 69–70, 73, 202, 204, 206, 208
  medicinal, 59, 203, 205, 207, 209
plum trees with bamboo and pine *(shōchikubai),* 54, 124, 138; cpls. 23, 30
Priest, Alan, 21
priests' stole *(kesa),* 14, 15, 26, 44, 192
purple colors, symbolism of, 43, 59–61, 65
  See also murasaki

R

ra (figured gauze), 27
rakuchū-rakugai, Kyoto scenes, 16, 158
rakuichi, free markets, 28
rakuza, free guilds, 28
ramie *(chōma, karamushi)* 28–29, 35, 38
red colors and dyes, 34–37, 40, 62, 64–65, 204–5
  See also madder red; safflower; sappanwood
resist dyeing, 19, 31–33
  with stencil, 31, 68
  See also paste-resist dyeing; *shibori*
Rikyū, *see* Sen no Rikyū
rimpa design, 50, 56, 174, 180 & *n*; cpls. 43, 46, 48
rinzu-ori, see under satin weaves
Rockefeller, John D., Jr., 15
Ryerson, Mrs. Martin A., 15

S

safflower dye *(beni),* 37, 40, 60–62, 64
  dyemaking process, 65, 71–73, 205
  pigmentized, 68
  plant source, 69, 71, 204
Saikaku, *see* Ihara Saikaku
St. Denis, Ruth, 14–15
Sakai, Japan, 27, 43, 65, 67
Sakai Hōitsu, artist, 17, 19, 31, 56, 57, 170, 182; cpl. 52
Sakata, Japan, 72
Sakura, Japan, 18, 21
sandy beach *(suhama)* motif, 39–40, 98; cpls. 10, 37
Sanjūsangendō statues, 192
sappanwood *(suō)* dye, 36, 64–65, 68, 204–5, 209
Sargent, Porter E., 14
satin weaves *(shusu-ori),* 29–30, *196*
  figured *(rinzu-ori),* 29–30, 34, 43, 44, *197*
sayagata patterns, *see* key fret
saya-ori, (damasee weave), 29, 30, *196*
screen-sail *(kichō)* motif, 140; cpl. 31
Segawa Kikunojō, actor, 62
seigaiha, blue wave patterns, 92; cpl. 7
Sekigahara, battle of, 49
sengoku jidai, "era of the country at war", 39
Sen no Rikyū, tea master, 66
shibori, decorative technique, 29, 31–33
  capped *(bōshi),* 32, 41, 47, 48
  kanoko, see fawn-dot *shibori*
  Keichō style, 43–47
  with metallic leaf, 40
  pinch dyeing *(tsumami-zome),* 33
  stitch-resist *(nuishime),* 32, 35, 41; cpl. 1
  in *tsujigahana,* 34–35, 41, 43, 44
  tub-resist *(oke-zome),* 32–33
  in *yūzen* dyeing, 37
Shigisan engi emaki, handscroll, 34

Shijō school of art, 180
Shikibu, *see* Murasaki Shikibu
Shikō, *see* Watanabe Shikō
Shikoku, Japan, 75
shinden style of architecture, 23
Shingen, *see* Takeda Shingen
Shinohara Kazutake, portrait of wife, 44
Shinsen on-hiinagata, design book, 52
Shinto religion and shrines, 16, 27, 178
Shinzoku Kokinwakashū, poetry anthology, 144
shiro-agari technique, 57, 184; cpl. 53
shōai-zome, indigo dyeing process, 74
shōchikubai, see pine-bamboo-plum motif
Shōjō, Nō play, 108
shoreline (or tide-pool) motif *(suhama),* 39–40, 98, 152; cpls. 10, 37
Shoshi, *see* Konoe Shoshi
shoulder-and-hem style *(kata-suso),* 24, 40
shusu-ori, see satin weaves
  silk, 26–30, 57
  nishiki style, 14, 33
  plain-weave *(nerinuki),* 27–30, 34, 43, 47, 86
silver, *see* metallic leaf; metallic thread
Simmons, Pauline, 21
sleeves *(sode),* 23, 25, 40
snow roundels *(yukiwa),* 45, 48, 124, 132; cpls. 10, 13, 23, 27
Sōtatsu, *see* Tawaraya Sōtatsu
Society for the Study of Japanese Customs and Costume, 19
sode (sleeves), 23, 25, 40
somewake, see divided-background style
Song Chinese art, 42
soybean liquid *(gojiru),* 36, 62, 68, 69
stencil dyeing, 31, 68
  kata-kanoko (suri-hitta), 19, 31–32, 55, 184
stitch-resist *(nuishime) shibori,* 32, 35, 41; cpl. 1
  capped *(bōshi),* 32, 41, 47, 48
  tub resist *(oke-zome),* 32–33
Study of Yūzen (Yūzen kenkyū), book (Nomura), 20
Sue no Matsuyama, scenic spot, 48
suhama, see shoreline motif
suiboku-ga, see ink painting
sukumo (composted indigo), 74
sumi (black ink), 30, 42, 69
summer *kosode, see katabira*
sumptuary laws, 36, 53, 57, 62, 64, 72
suō, see sappanwood
suri ai (rubbing with fresh indigo leaves), 62, 203
surihaku, see metallic leaf
suri-hitta (stencilled *kanoko),* 19, 31–32, 55, 184

suritsuke, dyeing technique, 62, 203

T

tade ai, Japanese indigo, 63, 73, 202–3
tagasode ("whose sleeves"?), 17–20
Taika Reform Edict of 646, 26
taima, see hemp
Taishō period, 13, 14, 16, 77
takara zukushi, see myriad treasures motif
Takeda Shingen, portrait of, 80
Tale of Genji, classical narrative, 37, 42, 48, 52, 128, 146, 184
Tama River, 67
tan dyes, 206–7
Tang dynasty, China, 23, 98
tarashikomi technique, 182; cpl. 52
Tawaraya Sōtatsu, artist, 50
tea ceremony, 39, 66
tegaki yūzen, dying process, 68
Teimei, empress, 16
"Temmon" *kosode*, 134
temple banners (*ban*), 14, 26, 41, 42
Tempō era, 57
Tenna era, 19, 53
Tenshō era, 43
textile industry, *see* dyes and dyeing; weaving
tide-pool (or shoreline) motif (*suhama*), 39·40, 98; cpls. 10, 37
"tie-dyeing", 31
Tōdai-ji Kenmotsu-chō, inventory, 192
Tōfukumon-in, emperor's consort, 53, 134
Tōhaku, *see* Hasegawa Tōhaku
Tōkaidō, highway, 55, 160; cpls. 41, 42
Tokugawa house, women of, 38, 166
Tokugawa Ieyasu, ruler, 32, 35, 39, 49, 61, 82, 86, 193
Tokugawa Mitsukuni, ruler, *kosode* of, 25
Tokugawa period, *see* Edo period
Tokugawa shogunate and rule, 62, 178, 193
Tokuko, shogun's wife, 53
Tokushima, Japan, 75, 76
Tokyo, 14, 15
 ancient, *see* Edo, Japan
toneri, textile producers, 27
tooth blackener (*ohaguro*), 66
tortoise, symbolism of, 47, 92, 98,

132; cpls. 7, 8, 27
tortoise-shell lozenges, 112; cpl. 17
 in diaper pattern (*kikkō mon*), 33, 47, 92, 98; cpls. 7, 10, 12, 17
Tōryū moyō hiinagata tsuru no koe, design book, 51
Toyotomi Hideyoshi, ruler, 33, 35, 39, 53, 61, 82, 86
 death of, 49
tsujigahana robes, 28, 33–35, 39, 41–44
 colors and dyeing, 25, 64, 66, 67, 69
tsuke-zome, see dip dyeing
tsumami-zome (pinch dyeing), 33
Tsumori Kunisuke, poet, 140
Tsunayoshi, *see* Tokugawa Tsunayoshi
Tsuruga, Japan, 72
Tsutumi no taki (The Waterfall of Drums), Nō play, 142
tub resist dyeing (*oke-zome*), 32–33
twill weaves (*aya-ori*), 29, 34, 43, 196
figured (*mon aya*), 29, 196

U

uchidashi technique, 32, 184
uchikake, garment, 33, 54, 56, 178, 182, 186; cpls. 28, 48, 50
uchishiki, see altar cloths
Uemura Shōen, artist, 17
Uesugi Kenshin, feudal lord, 25, 35
Uji River, 52; cpl. 17
ukiyo-e art, 14, 18, 19, 50, 57, 61, 160

W

Wakan rōeishū, poetry anthology, 130, 148
Wakayama, Japan, 42, 140
Waka no Ura, scenic spot, 140
Watanabe Shikō, artist, 136
watashi nui (float-stitch embroidery), 34
waterfall motifs, *see* flowing water
Waterfall of Drums, The (Tsutsumi no taki), Nō play, 142
Watson, William, 50
weaves, 28–30, 196–97
 See also plain weave; satin weaves; twill weaves
weaving industry, 26–30, 33, 40
Weaving Office (Oribe no tsukasa), 26–27, 67

Wei, Chinese kingdom, 26, 33, 63
Western influences, 13–15, 55
white face powder (*oshiroi*), 31, 118
wistaria-pine motif, 56–57, 184; cpls. 5–7, 10, 53
woven patterns, 28, 39, *197*

Y

yama ai (mountain indigo), 63, 73, 202–3
Yamagata Prefecture, 25, 71
Yamanobe Tomoyuki, scholar, 34
yamato-e handscrolls, 42, 50
Yamazaki Seiju, textile historian, 64–66, 71
yellow colors and dyes (*ki iro*), 66, 204–5, 207–9
Yodogimi, shogun's mistress, 53
Yojō hiinakata (Yosei hiinakata), design book, 37
Yoshikawa Kampo, collector, 19
Yoshino hills and river, 75, 136, 144
Yūjinsai Heki Tokueimon Kiyochika, artist, 37
Yukinobu, *see* Kanō Yukinobu
yukiwa, see snow roundels
Yūshō, *see* Kaihō Yūshō
yūsoku patterns 33, 188; cpl. 55
yūzen dyeing, 15, 16, 20, 23, 35–38, 53, 138
 characteristics, 55, 112, 150, 158, 162
 colors and dyes used, 64, 65, 203, 205
 dye houses, 67
 early, 29, 43, 51, 55–56, 61
 Kaga style, 38
 motifs, 55–56, 160
 problems of, 67–68
 techniques, 68–69, 203
Yūzen hiinagata, design book, 36, 37
Yūzen kenkyū (Study of Yūzen), book (Nomura), 20
Yūzensai, *see* Miyazaki Yūzensai
Yūzen Society, 15, 20

Z

za (guilds), 27–28
Zassoshū, miscellany, 66, 68
zinc dust, 36

Index prepared by Elinor Goettel.